The City of
WORCESTER
in the sixteenth century

The City of
WORCESTER
in the sixteenth century

Alan D. Dyer

Leicester University Press

1973

First published by Leicester University Press 1973
Distributed in North America by Humanities Press Inc., New York

Copyright © Leicester University Press 1973

Designed by Arthur Lockwood
Set in Linotype Granjon
Printed in Great Britain by
Western Printing Services Ltd
Bristol
ISBN 0 7185 1102 6

The publication of this book has been assisted
by a grant from the Twenty-Seven Foundation

Preface

This book is an amended and re-written version of my Ph.D. thesis of the same title which was submitted to the University of Birmingham in 1966. It is my pleasant duty here to acknowledge the great help I have received from many quarters in my work. To Bob Knecht of the University of Birmingham I owe the original suggestion to work in urban history, and continual help, encouragement and kindness since. I owe a considerable debt to the archivists and staff of a number of repositories, in particular those of the County Record Office at Worcester and the Town Clerk and his staff at the Guildhall. I am also especially grateful to the Dean of Worcester and the Librarian of the Cathedral Library and the staff of the Literary Search Room at Somerset House.

I also owe a large debt of gratitude to those who have made suggestions for the improvement of the original typescript, in particular Professor W. G. Hoskins and Professor J. Simmons of the University of Leicester. The staff of the Press at Leicester have been helpful and patient: it only remains for me to thank those many others who have assisted in the emergence of this book but who cannot be all mentioned by name. Needless to say, the errors and deficiencies which remain are my own responsibility.

Alan D. Dyer
University College of North Wales
June 1971

Contents

List of figures

List of tables

Introduction

One of the major features of the history of modern Britain is the growth of towns in size and influence, until they become in the nineteenth century the environment of the majority of the population. This process had a long history, but one of its most important and dynamic phases took place in the sixteenth century, for then began a process of growth which, despite changes in momentum, has never since been stopped.

To look at a town under the Tudors is to examine a self-contained community which looked upon strangers from beyond its walls as 'foreigners'; however it was unavoidably influenced by historical forces operating on a more national scale. This study of Worcester is a picture both of a separate urban society with its own distinct and individual history, and of a cross-section of many of the themes which touched the lives of Tudor Englishmen in general.

This book tries to investigate the life of an English city in the early modern period in as broad a way as its records allow. Its terms of reference are as wide as the subject demands: the surrounding countryside has not been forgotten, for at this time towns were intimately connected with their rural regions in many ways, and this inter-dependence must emerge in a study of an urban community. Neither has the chosen period, the sixteenth century, been strictly adhered to. This is an enquiry into topics, problems and subjects rather than a span of time, for local history cannot be forced into strict chronological limits. So although centred upon and principally concerned with the sixteenth century, we frequently refer to the medieval past and the seventeenth-century future. In particular we stray into the early seventeenth century, for many of the topics and trends treated at length here extend naturally into the next century and must be followed there.

Much urban history written in the past deals with constitutional matters – it is a study of local government rather than of the local community. This is only natural when the principal collection of records is usually that of the municipal corporation. A conscious effort has been made here to escape from this limitation, with its sometimes dry and legalistic overtones, and to use sources other than the city archives, leading especially to a much greater use than has been customary of the wills and associated documents of Worcester citizens.

Our basic theme is the functioning of the urban community in all its aspects, and this inevitably becomes an analysis of a static situation, for much of the city's medieval life continued long into the seventeenth and eighteenth centuries. But elements of change there were, and if any more distinct theme underlies this study it is that much of what changed in the Worcester of this period was above all else the result of one phenomenon, the growth of population.

For this reason the demography of the city and its region has been analysed in considerable detail, both because it is of vital importance to an understanding of what happened in Worcester, and because the general topic is still largely ignored by historians. If any justification for this is required, it will emerge in the way in which population expansion and the manifold problems it brought in its wake impinge upon so many of the major themes treated.

This study is also deeply concerned with economic matters. The really fundamental factor which made towns different from other communities was that their citizens earned their livings in a different way; in other respects townsmen closely resemble their country cousins. Therefore the urban economy is dealt with at length because it was the most important force which made towns distinct societies and Worcester distinct among them.

I

The setting

The past

As an urban community, Worcester had perhaps a thousand years of life behind it when the medieval period drew to a close: to understand its situation then, we must look back at its origins and previous development. Geographically, Worcestershire consists of the valleys of the Severn and Avon, with the edges of the higher land surrounding this basin forming its boundaries. This river system is the key to Worcester's origin. The vales of the Severn and its tributary the Avon, that is to say Worcestershire except its north-west corner, plus the southern half of Warwickshire and that part of Gloucestershire between the Severn and the Cotswolds, together probably formed the territory of a major Anglo-Saxon tribe, the Hwicce. This area was perpetuated by the pre-Reformation diocese of Worcester.[1] The city lay on the Severn, the major highway of this area: it was an important river-crossing and became an ecclesiastical centre when the bishop of the Hwicce established himself there by the later seventh century. The site had already been occupied, for it had been a Romano-British settlement of some significance; it lay near a ford, yet the eastern bank of the Severn on which it stands is raised above flood level. Upon the ford converged a number of natural communication routes, both along the valley and across it, from the Midlands towards Wales. This was the origin of Worcester's importance, a cathedral dominating the broad valley of the Severn.

By the early medieval period Worcester was still a town of second or even third rank – it paid substantially less in taxation than many other towns in the more prosperous south and east. Ecclesiastically its diocese was a very large one, stretching to Bristol in the south and to Warwick in the east, and its cathedral-priory was large and wealthy, but commercially there is no evidence that its development was very distinguished. It acquired a castle at the Norman Conquest and had a bridge by the eleventh century, rebuilt in stone in the four-teenth. Its first royal charter was obtained in 1189 when the citizens bought the right to render their taxes direct to the Crown and not via the county sheriff. This elementary piece of self-government was acquired later than some other towns, and such constitutional back-wardness was to be an abiding characteristic. The real foundation of its privileges and self-government was to be the charter of 1227 which created a merchant guild. Later monarchs confirmed and extended its liberties but the city's basic constitution seems to have changed little after the thirteenth century.[2]

Worcester was governed by two bailiffs who were joined by two pairs of aldermen and chamberlains to form the major civic officials; the merchant guild, as one would expect, seems to have been the basis of the town government. The later medieval period was one of constitutional stagnation. Worcester was not formally incorporated until 1555 and did not become a mayorality with county status until 1621, advances which many major cities were beginning to make in the later fourteenth and fifteenth centuries. But economically and commercially the later middle ages were of great importance for Worcester: in 1377 it was the twenty-fifth largest provincial town in terms of polltax-paying population, itself almost certainly a sig-nificant improvement on its early medieval position, but in the 1520s it had risen to sixteenth position in terms of taxable wealth.[3] In the sixteenth century Worcester was above all else a cloth-making town, and this rise in wealth and importance must reflect the growth of this industry, although the evidence for it, as with so much else in medieval Worcester, is a little thin.

So by the end of the Middle Ages Worcester was a city of increas-ing prosperity and significance, a major provincial town, although not of the first rank. Its government was deeply traditional, the result of slow medieval accretions. The broad outlines of its early modern position were all present – the predominance of the cloth industry, the roads, the river and bridge, the markets, cathedral, and government in the Guildhall. The medieval origins of many of the topics to be dealt with below will be explored in more detail when they arise, but there are two elements above all which perhaps need emphasizing. The first is that Worcester was backward in acquiring its fair share of independent self-government, and this element in its administrative life continued into the seventeenth century. Secondly, Worcester's economic position saw a very marked improvement during the later Middle Ages so that it entered the sixteenth century on the crest of a wave of wealth brought by the booming cloth industry. As we shall see, the early modern period changed the traditional medieval pattern of life in this urban community only very slowly, and even by the time of the Civil War there were few really fundamental changes evident in the city.

Topography

What was the physical appearance of Worcester in the sixteenth century? The map on page 16 (figure 1) reproduces the plan of the Tudor city. It is based primarily on the sketch-plan of the city given by Speed as part of his map of Worcestershire dated 1610, supplemented by the use of more accurately surveyed eighteenth-century plans.[4] Another view of the city, valuable because of its date, was probably drawn in the 1650s to show the city as it was fortified to face the siege of 1651.[5]

The plan of Worcester was primarily determined by the river. The built-up area lay along the raised eastern bank between the bridge and the cathedral. Its spine was formed by the main north–south road, the High Street and the Foregate, which runs along the summit of the bank. Most of the inhabited area lay within the walls, which formed a rough rectangle with the river supplying the western side, entered by six gates and the bridge. The cathedral and castle areas formed an enclave in the south-western corner of the city, exempt from its jurisdiction and covering the parish of St Michael-in-Bedwardine. Inside here lay the houses of a number of people following ordinary urban occupations, beside the residences of the cathedral dignitaries in what had been the priory courtyard, and the county gaol in the now derelict precincts of the castle.

North-west of the cathedral was the bishop's palace, very little used by the bishops, who preferred their rural retreat at Hartlebury,

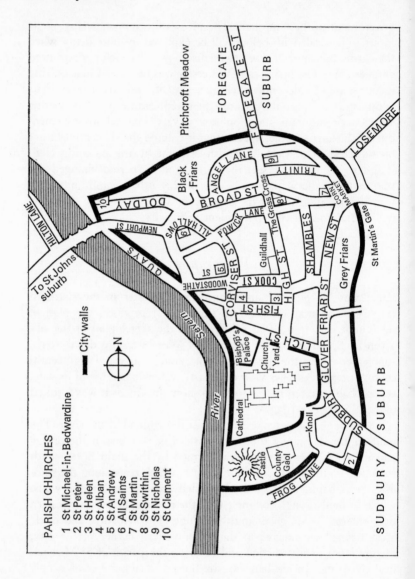

1 The Tudor city plan.

but employed for the reception of important visitors like the queen and her court who stayed here in 1575. The High Street and Broad Street were the principal streets of the town and in them lived many of the wealthier citizens. At their junction, the Grass Cross, was one of the city's market places; the Corn Market, a small square in the east of the city, was the only market place which was more than a roadway. Broad Street ran into Newport Street and so down to the bridge, a fourteenth-century structure still impressive enough for Leland to call it a "royal piece of work".[6] The quays for the use of boats lay downstream from the bridge on the city bank.

The city was divided into ten parishes, forming the basis for the wards into which it was split for administrative purposes. Beyond the walls lay the suburbs, already present quite early in the Middle Ages. The principal one was the Foregate which ran along the road to Droitwich and the north; building spread over the city boundary here by the early seventeenth century, to form the tithing of Whistones. Outside the eastern walls, at St Martin's Gate, lay a smaller suburb, and the London road, Sudbury, was also lined with houses for a short distance. The suburb of St Johns, on the far side of the river straddling the road to the west, seems to have grown up around a separate nucleus rather than as a piece of ribbon development; it was separate from the city economically and administratively and was essentially a country village which happened to lie near the town, and will not here be considered as part of the city.

Although Worcester seems to have had common fields early in its life, their only survival by the sixteenth century was Pitchcroft, a large area of river meadow between the Severn and the Droitwich road, already partly enclosed.[7] The meadows on the western bank of the river were almost exclusively owned by the cathedral-priory and were leased out to townsmen. Along Hilton Lane lay some fields which were worked by citizens, but the main agricultural area lay to the east of the walls. Sansome fields, Losemore fields and Port fields were names indicative of their common origins, but by the later Middle Ages they were almost completely enclosed and in individual ownership. The cultivated area around the city was small, for agriculture was only a very minor element in the city's economy compared with that of most other towns of its size; the citizens were mainly interested in Pitchcroft, as pasture for their horses and for the stock owned by butchers, supplemented by pasture fields at a greater distance, especially towards the east.

The topographical changes which took place in the sixteenth and early seventeenth centuries were mainly the result of the Reformation and of the growth in the city's population. The Reformation made little difference to the cathedral or its precinct, but it removed the two friaries, the Black Friars between Broad Street and the north wall, and the Grey Friars between Glover (Friar) Street and the eastern walls. The Grey Friars was in part converted into a town house, but the Black Friars was completely razed. Beyond the walls the Commandery, a hospital in Sudbury, became a private house, but the nunnery of Whistones and the hospital of St Oswald, both in the Foregate suburb, were demolished with the exception of small sections of their structures.

The other main physical change was one of growth. Speed's plan still shows considerable areas of open ground used as gardens or just left waste within the walls; this was in particular true of the site of the Black Friars by the northern wall. These garden areas were gradually built over during the late sixteenth and earlier seventeenth centuries. A general plan of filling in the gaps in the existing built-up area rather than of extending it seems to have been followed, with the exception of the suburb at St Martin's Gate which seems to have been a Tudor development. This general subject is dealt with in greater detail below. Certainly the amount of new building was not great – far less than the growth in population – and one of the characteristics of the period under review may well have been a general decline in the standard of housing, especially for the poorer classes, due to overcrowding.

The broad visual impact of the city on visitors seems to have been favourable: Leland repeatedly uses the word "fair", Camden was impressed by the "fair and neat houses", "the number also of churches" and the cathedral. Speed describes it as "most pleasantly seated, passing well frequented and very richly inhabited" while Celia Fiennes at the end of the seventeenth century remarked upon its broad streets with "very good and lofty" buldings, its wall, market place and Guildhall.[8]

Worcester's continuing prosperity has led to the destruction of many of its earlier buildings, a process which began with the 'improvements' of the eighteenth century, such as the new Guildhall and bridge, and has continued ever since, so that of the Tudor and early Stuart buildings which once existed, the only significant surviving collection is in Friar Street.

2

Population movements

The study of population in the early modern period is even more important than for other times; recent scholarship has begun to acknowledge the fundamental significance of the rise in population which took place in the sixteenth and earlier seventeenth centuries. The effects of this rise were felt, directly or obliquely, in the drastic price inflation of the period and more generally in many aspects of the economic, social and political life of the country. Surprisingly enough, we remain remarkably ignorant of where and why population increased after the demographic disasters of the later Middle Ages, and of the extent of this increase. The object of this chapter is to investigate these problems in Worcester in as much detail as possible.

Traditional sources of information for the student of population have been rather inadequate, but now that the parish register has been recognized as the invaluable source of fresh data that it is, a more satisfactory analysis of the basic characteristics of communities becomes possible. Parish registers were first introduced in the autumn of 1538, and all christenings, weddings and burials should have been recorded in them. Parish registers may be treated at two different levels to yield different kinds of information: the total annual numbers of christenings and burials tell us whether the population is increasing or decreasing, and at what speed, while by breaking down the entries into family groups we may recover the demographic characteristics of individuals and their families. This latter approach makes it possible to hazard some provisional statistics on a variety of issues – like child mortality for example – which not only throw light on population movements but are also valuable commentaries on the lives and experiences of the bulk of the people of the time.

Parish registers are reasonably accurate documents, but there are practical problems in using them to help in the history of a city like Worcester, for like all towns it received immigrants in fair numbers from the countryside, thus distorting the picture given by the city registers by supplying people who die in the city but were not born there; this slightly depresses the surplus of christenings over burials which exists in an age of rising population. Two more points need to be made about this particular study; firstly it carries on beyond the formal limits of this book's title until 1640, since the wave of population increase seems to be slackening then and so supplies a more natural terminus, and secondly the countryside around Worcester receives considerable attention because immigration from this area was always a major factor in the city's own population and more importantly because towns were the environment of the minority in our period and their experience always needs to be set in perspective by comparing it with that of the rural majority.

The parish registers of the city of Worcester are fortunately well preserved, with six out of the ten parishes possessing a substantial coverage of our period.[1] What do they tell us of the history of the city's population during the century 1540–1640? They firstly supply a series of annual totals of burials and christenings; the variations from year to year are so great that a series of five-yearly moving averages has been used to make trends more intelligible (see figures 2 and 3). These figures show firstly that there was a substantial population increase over the period, punctuated at more or less regular intervals by a sudden increase in the number of burials and a short period when the population actually fell. We may perhaps distinguish two broad periods in the demographic history shown in visual form in the graphs.

The first is in existence when our records begin in 1538, and continues until the early 1570s. It is marked by a downward trend in the number of christenings, very slow at first but quite marked in the 1560s. The corresponding burials show an irregular period marked by seriously high mortality in several years, culminating in a major epidemic in 1558, followed by a decrease in burials very

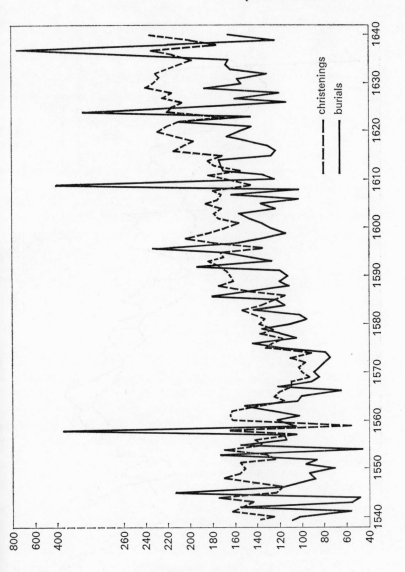

2 *Worcester (six parishes): annual totals of christenings and burials, 1540–1639.*

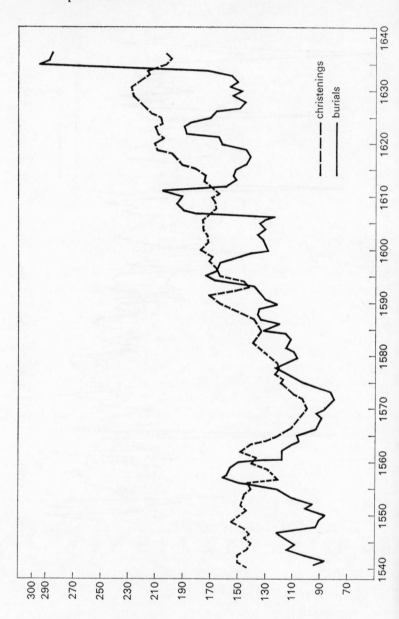

3 *Worcester (six parishes): five-yearly averages of annual totals of christenings and burials, 1541–1636.*

similar to that in christenings. Leaving aside the epidemics, burials show a downward trend, ending in a sharp decline in the 1560s. Both these trends halt in the early 1570s, virtually at the same time.

The second period shows both series pursuing a predominantly upward course, punctuated by years of high mortality, but still in a fairly regular manner, the only major exceptions being a certain stagnation in baptisms between 1600 and 1616, and perhaps a slowing down in burials in the second and third decades of the seventeenth century. During this second period the general level of christenings rises from about 100 per annum to over 200, and that of burials by about the same amount, so that both series roughly double. These trends form a background to the most important conclusion to be drawn from such statistics, which is the relationship between the burial and baptismal series, showing the nature of population growth or decline. In this case the christenings are clearly and predominantly in excess of burials, showing that both periods were marked by comparatively uninterrupted population growth.

Although these figures tell us when growth was going on, they do not allow us to measure and compare different periods of growth. This may be done by converting these figures to a series which shows the number of christenings per cent of burials. A series of this kind allows comparison to be made between communities, regardless of their size (see figure 4). This graph again shows the familiar division into two distinct periods, the transition taking place around 1560. The first period is one of great growth, but at a declining rate, terminating in a temporary period of declining population in the 1550s. The second period shows a quite rapid recovery leading to a fairly substantial rate of growth which increases fairly steadily until in the 1630s it reaches a level which, if well below that achieved in the period before 1560, still approaches a level of 50 per cent growth per generation.

This trend is really the result of a series of cyclical movements, each taking between seven and 15 years, and each showing a growth rate which rises to a peak and then falls to a trough in which the population temporarily falls; this cycle is repeated about seven times during the second demographic period. This sensitive means of analysing population change reveals then a high growth rate before the late 1550s, followed by a major demographic crisis which resolves into a long period of fairly well-sustained growth continuing up to the 1630s, with the rate of increase quickening as time went on.

We have measured the rate of population growth and have shown when it took place, but what does all this mean in terms of the actual numbers of people who lived out their lives in these six Worcester parishes? If we add each year's surplus of christenings over burials (or subtract when burials are greater) to the aggregate of the previous years, we arrive at a series of figures showing the actual variations in the total population which were superimposed on whatever the population was in 1539. This shows an increase of 2,000 people up to 1639 (see figure 5). This method is subject to a high margin of error, for the cumulative arithmetic ensures that early errors continue throughout, and also any under-recording of burials during epidemics (when emergency conditions overwhelmed paperwork) will remain in all the later figures. With this proviso, the graph does show how this increase was achieved and the division into two periods around the 1550s, but the main conclusion seems to be that the pattern is one of ever-increasing violence. Each period of growth

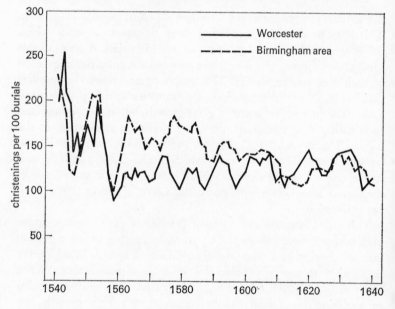

4 *Worcester and the Birmingham area: rate of growth expressed as five-yearly moving average of christenings per cent of burials, 1541–1640.*

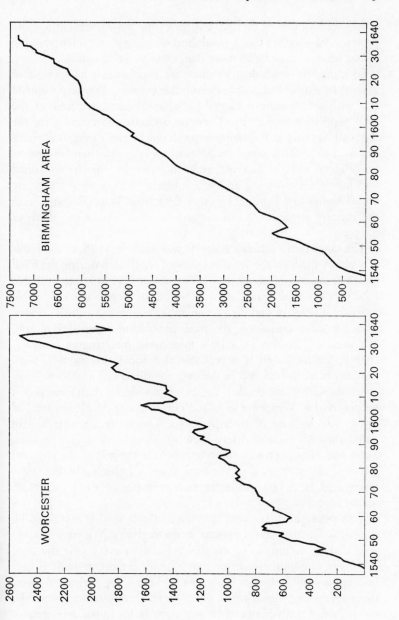

5 *Worcester and the Birmingham area: total aggregate population increase, 1539–1639.*

is followed by one of decline, but each time the movement is more pronounced – rather like a pendulum which with each lengthening swing becomes more and more dangerously out of control.

So it may be concluded that these six parishes saw an increase of at least two thousand people during this century. We may compare this with the increase indicated by what estimates we have of the total population of the city. The most accurate enumeration for the sixteenth century is the estimate produced by the diocesan authorities in 1563.[2] This seems to be reasonably comprehensive and to make an effort to be accurate, and concludes that the city contained 937 families. Presuming an average household size of 4.5, a figure which seems well justified by other data from Worcester and from the country in general, this suggests a total population of about 4,250.

The other fairly accurate estimate was made in 1646, as the result of a survey made by the royalist forces of occupation during the Civil War's second siege of the city.[3] The object was to relate available food supplies to the population to be fed, so there was considerable practical interest in making this an accurate figure. With due allowance for some omissions, the total population revealed is 8,300. We must reduce this by a little to account for refugees from the countryside (although it is probable that some citizens who were parliamentarians had fled in the opposite direction) and so we may conclude with some modest degree of confidence that some 8,000 people lived in Worcester in 1646. This is nearly double the total of 1563 – an increase of perhaps 3,750. The six parishes studied in detail through their registers show an increase of 1,300 between 1563 and 1639, perhaps 1,500 by 1646. If the rest of the city had followed this pattern, then the total increase indicated by the registers would be 2,150, while the two estimates of 1563 and 1646 would suggest 3,750.

This discrepancy between the two methods used is explained by the particular distortions present in the registers. We have already seen that by accumulating surplus population every year the total is subject to cumulative error, but a more important fault is that immigrants will be buried in the city without being christened there, thus depressing the figures given here. Immigration from the countryside has always been an important factor in the demography of towns, and in this period it must have been accentuated by rural over-population bringing great pressure on the available supply of land. So the discrepancy of 1,600 people may be principally attributed to the migration of people into the city, thus appearing in the surveys but not as christenings in the registers. Granted that immigration was similarly present between 1539 and 1563, and this seems very likely, the population of the city could not have avoided doubling in the century 1540–1640, with a greater growth still if we look back to 1500. The factor of 'natural increase' – the excess of births over deaths – may well have accounted for rather over half of this, with migration responsible for the remainder.

How does this figure of 4,000 rising to 8,000 compare with other towns? In about 1540, when Worcester's population must have been rather below 4,000, London had over 70,000, Norwich 13,000, Bristol 10,000 and Exeter and Salisbury over 8,000.[4] Worcester clearly could not rival these major provincial centres in terms of population, but it made a fair showing by comparison with the large class of towns below the first 15 or so in size, having populations of between 3,000 and 5,000. In terms of wealth it was the sixteenth richest provincial town in the 1520s, a more impressive position than its population total would suggest. On the other hand Worcester appears very large by comparison with the great majority of country towns with populations of 1,000 or 2,000 or even less. Probably Worcester was more of a growth area than many towns, but by 1600, when most provincial centres had populations of 8,000 to 12,000, the city still lay below the first rank of provincial towns.

Thus it has been established that the population of Worcester doubled approximately in the century in question, and the way in which this was achieved has been outlined. How does this picture compare with the countryside? To determine this a survey was carried out of a large rural region covering north-east Worcestershire, north-west Warwickshire and south-east Staffordshire. This area, comprising ten contiguous parishes covering about 80 square miles, was chosen because it presented a group of registers technically suitable, reasonably near to Worcester and geographically akin to the region around the city.[5]

The result of this survey of the demographic characteristics of this area are shown in graphs and statistics similar to those produced for Worcester itself (see figures 4 and 6). Christening and burial figures show trends broadly similar to those at Worcester, but what is strikingly different is the size of the margin between baptisms and burials. In this rural area, burials rarely exceed baptisms in any

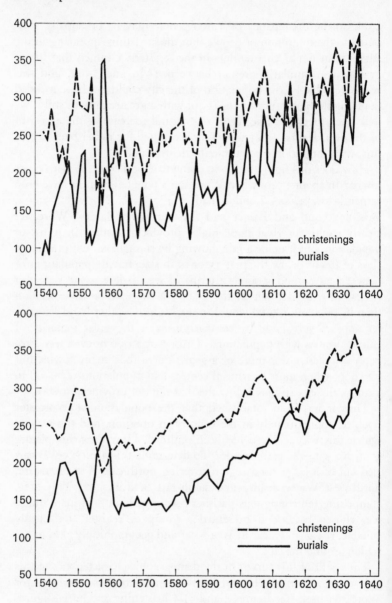

6 *Birmingham area: actual annual totals and five-yearly moving averages of annual totals of christenings and burials, 1540–1640.*

year, and the increase in burials is much more steady than at Worcester. So although the broad trends are quite similar, both, and especially burials, are less liable to violent fluctuation in the countryside. This is in fact what one would expect – the city was far more liable to epidemics. The much larger margin between burials and christenings is most clearly shown in the figures for the number of christenings when burials have been standardized.

Here there is a significant contrast with the city. The rate of growth, although showing the by now familiar crisis in the 1550s, moves generally in a downward direction (except for a slight recovery about 1620) while in Worcester the growth rate increases with fair consistency. Despite this contrasting trend, population in the countryside still increases at a much higher rate than in the city throughout the Elizabethan period, although in the early seventeenth century it falls to a level much nearer to that of the city.

We may conclude therefore that although rural population was growing twice as fast as the city's in the earlier part of our period, the rate of increase fell to the urban level in the earlier seventeenth century, in contrast with the upward movement seen at Worcester. The actual numerical, cumulative increase in population shows a similar story to Worcester, except that it is much more stable, and here again the striking smoothness of growth during most of the Elizabethan period is notable.

The last of these rural comparisons may be made with the south Worcestershire villages of Bushley and Bretforton, used below for comparative purposes in family reconstitution, but useful because they represent a contrast to the rural area we have just been examining in being open-field, arable villages, the other element in Worcester's region apart from the wooded, pastoral, enclosed north.[6] The graph showing christenings compared with standardized burials (figure 7) illustrates the essentials of their demographic history. These two similar villages are an object lesson in the problems of comparing different areas demographically, for although little more than ten miles apart, their population moved in quite different ways at times. What they have in common is a higher rate of growth (figure 8) than the northern area (at least double that of Worcester) and they also support, if somewhat dubiously, the idea of a steadily declining rate of growth in the countryside.

Of the conclusions to be drawn from comparing Worcester's growing population with what was happening in the surrounding

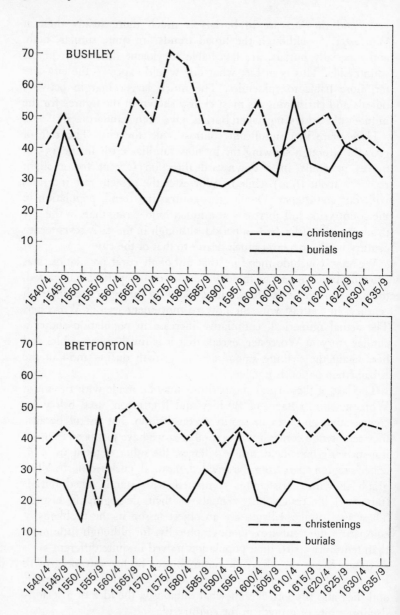

7 *Bushley and Bretforton: five-yearly totals of christenings and burials, 1540–1639.*

countryside, the salient feature is that it was growing much more slowly in the city. In the most fertile rural areas the growth rate was twice as large. The second feature is the radical difference in the way growth was going on, with the rate of increase getting ever larger in the city and ever smaller in the country. The burial figures make it abundantly clear that the countryside was much less subject to epidemics and other factors which led to years of high mortality. Unfortunately, because no accurate estimates exist, we cannot compare total populations before and after the population movement in the countryside as we can in the city, but growth cannot have been as great as the rates of increase derived from the parish registers would suggest, for emigration would account for some, and would

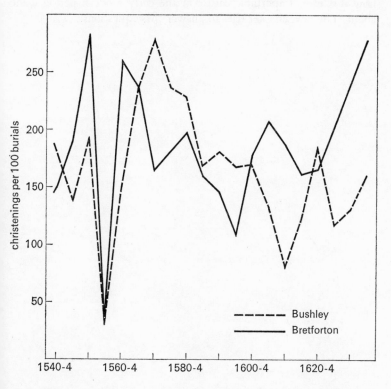

8 *Bushley and Bretforton: rate of growth expressed as five-yearly moving averages of christenings per cent of burials, 1539–1634*

also inflate the original figures by providing christenings whose eventual burial takes place elsewhere. But it remains clear that population pressure in the countryside around Worcester was very severe, and that there must have been considerable encouragement to leave the villages and move to the city.

Thus we have shown how in Worcester itself the population probably doubled between the mid-sixteenth century and the mid-seventeenth, over half of this due to the natural excess of births over deaths and the rest due to immigration. The rate of growth increased with fair consistency over the period, unlike the countryside where it was in decline, but was for long considerably higher than the urban rate. However it remains to try to distinguish the factors which determined this general situation, to explain why and how this most important feature of the early modern period came about. The next chapter tries to answer these questions.

3

Causes of population growth

The technique used to investigate in greater depth the demographic history of Worcester and its region is a simplified version of the French system of family reconstitution explained above. Registers were chosen which were as complete as possible, and also easily accessible. In Worcester the registers of the parishes of St Helen and St Michael were used, and those of Bushley and Bretforton in south Worcestershire for purposes of rural comparison.

The problem of investigating the reasons for the great growth in population outlined above can be split into two halves. An increase in population may be due to two factors, either acting together or one or the other in isolation: births may increase or deaths may decrease. This chapter will deal with these two factors separately, and firstly with the possibility that more people were born. The graph of christenings over the period (figure 2) shows that the numbers double during the century 1540–1640; this may be because there were twice as many people in the population available to have children, but that this is not entirely true is shown by variations in the size of families during this period.

The average number of children christened in each family (excluding childless families) in each decade from the 1540s to the 1630s shows that significant changes in the fertility of marriages did take place (table 1). Although difficult to interpret very certainly, this indicates that the average woman christened a generally decreasing number of children, from just under three in the period of high growth before the 1550s down to a little over two by the early seventeenth century. The 1570s and the 1610s are exceptions, with unusually fertile families present.

	WORCESTER	BUSHLEY	BRETFORTON
1540–9	2.9	2.8	2.7
1550–9	2.8	2.5	3.3
1560–9	2.3	3.4	4.6
1570–9	3.3	3.4	3.4
1580–9	2.0	3.0	2.7
1590–9	2.5	3.0	3.4
1600–9	2.3	3.5	3.3
1610–19	2.9	3.1	3.0
1620–9	1.8	2.9	3.6

Table 1   Average number of children per family

(Based on parish register analysis dated to decade in which first child was born.)

If these figures are compared with those for the rate of population growth, it will be seen that there seems to be a fairly clear connection between variations in family size and changes in the total population. During the later sixteenth century, decades of low fertility – like the 1560s and 1580s for instance – correspond with decades of reduced growth. But in the seventeenth century this correlation is much less obvious – the high growth rate of the 1620s is not accompanied by a larger number of births per family. What we see then is a general decrease in the size of the family, subject to some temporary disruption due to short-lived extraneous factors, while at the same time the rate of growth of the population is steadily increasing. In other words, the birth rate is dropping, which suggests that in the early and mid-sixteenth century it may have been unusually high and so one of the original causes of growth. However the acceleration of growth in the face of a falling birth rate shows that this is only one factor among several at work.

A most valuable insight into the effects of a raised level of fertility in the first half of the sixteenth century is provided by an analysis of the numbers of children revealed in the families of Worcester people whose wills have survived: there are 607 families here, spread over the years 1500 to 1620, excluding apparently childless couples (see table 2). An analysis of these figures shows that there was a very

	Number of wills concerned	Average number of children referred to
1500–9	9	1·9
1510–19	9	1·9
1520–9	20	2·3
1530–9	16	2·2
1540–9	66	2·8
1550–9	108	2·6
1560–9	47	3·0
1570–9	50	3·4
1580–9	41	3·2
1590–9	56	3·2
1600–9	76	3·2
1610–19	105	2·9

Table 2   Average number of children referred to in Worcester wills

significant rise in the number of children per family over the period 1520 to 1580. We must push back the dating by perhaps ten or 15 years to approach the period when the children were being born. With this modification, these figures suggest that the fertility of marriages was static until about 1510, when it began to increase: despite temporary falling off in the 1520s and 1540s, a peak was reached in the 1560s after which a prolonged decline set in. The level reached in the 1560s was 75 per cent above that prevailing at the start of the sixteenth century, while the period of slowing down was a gentle one, at least as far as the 1620s. These figures indicate that the parish registers only cover the later part of the sixteenth-century population explosion since it began in about 1510: interestingly, this is very close to the date when price inflation began, and tends to confirm the supposition that population growth and inflation were very closely connected phenomena; even circumstantial evidence like this rarely survives to support such a view.

Do the country villages agree with this thesis of a high level of fertility in the sixteenth century which is less significant in the seventeenth? Bretforton does in fact do so, with a family size at its maximum in the 1560s and dropping thereafter; the Bushley figures are at variance with both the others, at least in the early seventeenth century, but the village is demographically eccentric during this period in other ways too (see table 1).

Thus there seems a general concurrence that both country and town experience an early high rate of fertility which decreases during the rest of the period, changes in the size of families corresponding to variations in the growth rate in the sixteenth century but not in the seventeenth. An incidental point of interest is the larger size of country families at all times; at Bretforton often the average number of children is double the city figure: the larger number of children baptized must be a major factor behind the high rural growth rate.

Thus we have established that marriages began to be more fertile in Worcester in about 1510, and we may surmise that this led to a growth in population reaching its peak in the middle years of the century. Thereafter fertility declines slowly, and since population growth continues we must presume that fertility in itself was gradually superseded during the Elizabethan period as the major factor behind the population explosion. However the reasons which account for this raised fertility have yet to be probed. The main factors which would control this are the age at which people, and in particular women, married, and also the length of time during which wives were both alive and capable of bearing children.

The age at which women married at Worcester is difficult to calculate, especially as there are some deficiencies in the marriage registers, but the average during the later sixteenth century seems to have remained fairly consistent at about 23 years (see table 3). This may well have been a rather low figure compared with the fifteenth or later seventeenth centuries; it is not at present possible to be sure, but this evidence does not suggest that within our period there was very much variation. The age at which men married shows a distinctly upward trend, from the mid to the late twenties. This might tend to reduce the fertility of marriages a little by producing earlier widowhood, but the effect is far less than a similar change in the bride's age.

The statistics from the villages give a rather better coverage. In Bushley the age of brides was fairly stable at between 25 and 26, while Bretforton suggests about 25. The figures for men tend to fluctuate, but a drift towards later marriage does take place, in Bretforton for instance rising two or three years during the last three decades of the sixteenth century. But the vital factor, the age of women at marriage, seems to be without any very significant variation. However by employing mean averages instead of arithmetical ones, at Bretforton there does seem to be an upward movement in the marriage age of women of a year or two between

	Women			Men		
	WORCESTER		BRETFORTON		BUSHLEY	
		BUSHLEY		WORCESTER		BRETFORTON
1560–9	22	23	22	23	23	22½
1570–9	24	29	25	25	30	26½
1580–9	23	26	24½	29	27	27
1590–9	26	25	25	30	31	27
1600–9	23	25	25	28	23½	30
1610–19	–	25	25	–	30	29
1620–9	–	25	25	–	25	23
1630–9	21	–	27	–	31	–

Table 3   Average age at first marriage

Age	WORCESTER		BUSHLEY		BRETFORTON	
	1560–99	1600–39	1560–99	1600–39	1560–99	1600–39
16–17	1	–	–	1	1	2
18–19	4	–	1	3	6	2
20–1	5	–	3	–	10	3
22–3	7	–	3	4	8	7
24–5	3	–	4	4	5	5
26–7	4	–	4	4	2	2
28–9	4	–	4	3	2	3
30+	4	–	5	1	8	4
total	32	–	24	20	42	28

Table 4   Number of first marriages per age group (women)

the sixteenth and earlier seventeenth centuries. It is difficult to assess the significance of this, for the Worcester figures cannot be treated in this way, so it remains possible that the age of women at marriage during the sixteenth century was rather lower than it was to be later, but variations in the fertility of marriages within the period 1540–1640 cannot reasonably be attributed to any great extent to variations in the age at marriage. However it is worth noting that here, as in a number of other factors, there are distinct demographic differences between country and town: in this case women tend to marry about two years earlier in the city.

The main other measurable factor affecting the fertility of marriages is the length of time over which wives were able to bear children. The number of years which elapsed between marriage and the baptism of the last child of each wife was investigated (see table 5). In Worcester the figures show that the fertile period of marriages during the first decades after 1540 was quite long, and this improved until in the 1570s the last child was born on average 10½ years after marriage. By the early seventeenth century a substantial fall to only 5 years has occurred. In the countryside this period extended to about 16 years during the early Elizabethan period, but fell to about 6 years by the turn of the century. A similar trend is revealed when the age at which women have their last child is examined: this shows that a reduction from 36 to 30–1 or from 40 to 32 took place between about 1570 and about 1610–21.

| | Years from marriage to last child's christening | | |
	WORCESTER	BUSHLEY	BRETFORTON
1540–9	7	8	9
1550–9	9	5	16
1560–9	7	16	12
1570–9	10½	9	12
1580–9	6	12	8
1590–9	5½	5½	8
1600–9	5	6	6
1610–19	7	7	8
1620–9	–	6½	6

Table 5   Length of child-bearing period

These statistics, reflecting the length of the child-bearing period after marriage and showing a high level in the early Elizabethan period dropping drastically by the early seventeenth century, are perhaps the most significant explorable factor in explaining the raised fertility of sixteenth-century marriages. They do not, however, solve the problem completely. Women may have gone on to bear children for a longer space of time because their general standard of health was high, or because they lived longer and were less likely to die in childbirth, and so were alive for a longer period of marriage. Both of course are linked factors, for both reflect raised standards of health, hygiene, housing and nutrition. Thus the population increase is at least partly rooted in a broad improvement in the standard of living during a large part of the sixteenth century, but there seems room to suspect that this improvement was being eroded by the later years of Elizabeth's reign.

So the major factor in causing the population increase of the six-teenth century was an upswing in the birth rate as reflected in the fertility of marriages. This was partly due to more women having more children over a longer span of time and to a more advanced age, features only attributable to a broad improvement in the stan-dard of physical strength and health. But from the last decades of the sixteenth century onwards, marital fertility, and so presumably the birth rate, went down, while population went on rising.

The other major class of forces affecting population growth are those concerned with changes in mortality. We have already seen how variations in maternal mortality could affect the birth rate. Perhaps the most interesting and significant factor in all this is the incidence of child and infant mortality. The family reconstitution method provides the date of death of every child whose birth is also recorded (in ideal circumstances) so that it is possible to tell in any period what proportion of those baptized die within a relatively short period. Thus the child burial rate may be expressed as a percentage of the baptismal total.

Worcester shows a significant trend if we look at the total numbers of children of all ages between birth and maturity whose deaths are recorded (see figure 9). This figure shows a downward trend, from the 1560s, when of all those who are baptized some 45 per cent die before maturity, to between 30 and 35 per cent in the decade 1575–1584. They then increase again until a level of over 50 per cent is reached in the 1590s – implying that over half the children baptized

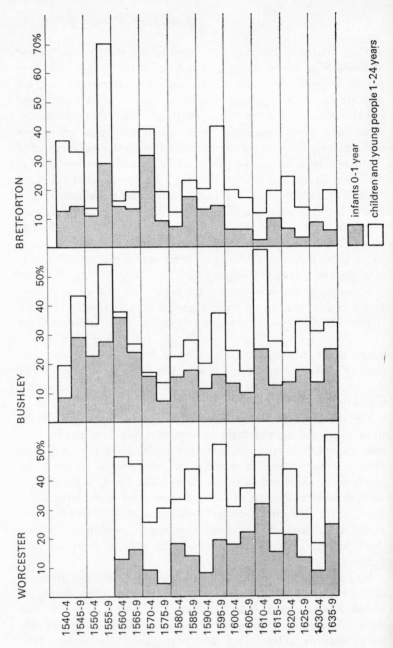

9   Worcester, Bushley and Bretforton: child mortality expressed
    as a percentage of christenings, 1540–1639.

then die before grown up. This shocking level is then reduced until in the early 1630s it drops below 20 per cent. The variations here are very considerable, but can only be understood in conjunction with the rural figures.

In Bushley the mortality rate is very high between 1540 and 1560, rising to over 50 per cent in the later 1550s. A sharp drop from this level then rises at the turn of the century and then stabilizes again at between 25 per cent and 35 per cent. In Bretforton the figures show a fairly low figure before the high mortality of the 1550s, then dropping to about 20 per cent, rising to over 40 per cent at the turn of the century and then falling to a general if erratic level of about 15–20 per cent in the early seventeenth century.

The broad pattern of Worcester child mortality then resembles that of the countryside, a low figure in the early Elizabethan period and the seventeenth century separated by a raised level at the turn of the century. There is no reason to believe that the Worcester figures for the missing period 1540–59 did not resemble those from Bushley, where for the rest of the period they are broadly similar, so that we may presume that the decade of the 1550s was the climax of a mounting child mortality rate, and when Worcester's own figures begin in the early 'sixties they represent the first stage in the reduction of this toll. The rural areas show at most times a markedly healthier situation; in the decade 1600–9 for instance, 30–35 per cent of Worcester's baptized children died, but only about 20 per cent in Bushley and Bretforton. This example represents the general pattern, with the city mortality rate between one-and-a-half and twice the rural one.

If we look more closely at these figures by splitting them into two groups of those under and those over 12 months old, some more significant trends are revealed (see figures 9 and 10). In the country-side the mortality rate for infants under twelve months old is high up to the mid-sixteenth century crisis, and only drops slowly there-after, but the level it achieves in the mid-Elizabethan period is maintained right up until 1640. At Worcester the corresponding rate increases steadily between 1560 and 1610–14, from a level of 5–15 per cent to a peak of over 30 per cent. Thereafter it reduces to 10 per cent in the early 1630s. The rate for children over one year of age behaves somewhat differently. In the villages it is well below the level of infant mortality in the early period, falls rapidly after the 1550s, but then gradually increases from a very low level until in

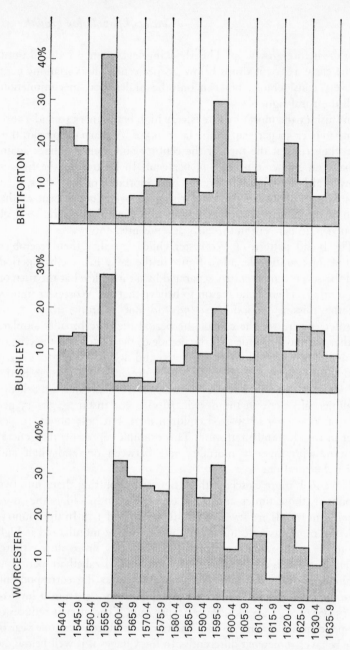

10 Worcester, Bushley and Bretforton: mortality at age 1–24,
    expressed as a percentage of christenings, 1540–1639.

the early seventeenth century it exceeds that of infant mortality. In Worcester by contrast the general trend is downward, from a level of 20–30 per cent in the sixteenth century to 5–15 per cent in the seventeenth.

What may be drawn from all this as an explanation of population growth? First of all, the child mortality figures show what an important factor this is, how considerable variations take place over relatively short periods. In particular the low level of child burials in the earlier Elizabethan period is significant, and the deterioration during the last two decades of the sixteenth century is paralleled by a fall in the population growth rate. The predominantly low level of child mortality in the seventeenth century is perhaps the most significant feature, for it may well explain why the population growth of Worcester continued after the fertility of marriages decreased. The issue has another interest. It would be difficult to find a more sensitive barometer of the general standard of living than the proportion of children dying before maturity. These figures are a reflection of the prevailing level of nutrition, health and housing, and indicate what trends were in action in these most important aspects of human welfare, quite apart from their great importance in determining the nature and level of population growth.

The proportion of the child population which failed to reach maturity, can, as has been seen, vary greatly, and can be a major determinant in deciding how many children are to be available to replace adult deaths. Unfortunately we cannot analyse adult mortality in the same way, because the total number of adults in the population cannot be determined with sufficient accuracy. But the period as a whole may represent a low level of adult mortality and a high expectation of life. This expectation of life may be measured through the statistics provided by family reconstitution, in this case by tracing the date of death of everyone born between 1539 and 1569. In Worcester men who reached the age of 20 could expect on average to live until they were 46, and women until 49. In the villages the equivalent figures are 54–5 for men and 49½–50 for women. The main significance of these figures is that they may suggest that this period was one when the expectation of life was relatively high, compared with the fifteenth or later seventeenth centuries, but in the absence of very much comparative data, it is difficult to be certain. Such evidence as exists suggests that adult males in the fifteenth century reached an average age of 48 or 49, and since these examples are drawn from the upper classes they should probably be compared with the figures from rural Worcestershire quoted above: if this is a fair comparison then the later sixteenth century does seem to represent a period of raised longevity in rural areas.[1] A glance at both the rural and urban expectations quoted above serves to make one clear point. Men living in the countryside could hope to live for eight or nine years longer than the city-dweller, ample testimony to the unhealthy conditions of urban life and its susceptibility to epidemic disease.

One most important last factor needs to be considered. This is the effect upon mortality (and so on population growth) of famine and epidemics. The graphs of burials in Worcester show the incidence of years of high mortality, but how significant were these disasters in determining the rate at which population increased? The annual totals of burials seem always liable to a high degree of fluctuation, but they do show that some years in Worcester were marked by exceptionally heavy mortality (see figure 2). In the first of our two demographic periods, that running up to the late 1550s, the year 1558 stands out with over 320 burials, while the years 1542, 1545, 1553, and 1555 are years of distinctly raised mortality in which burials outnumber baptisms. In the second period, the year 1609, with 400 burials, and especially 1637 with 780, stand out. There were years of heavy mortality in 1624 and 1597, and more people were buried than christened in 1563, 1567, 1577, 1580, 1587 and 1593. However in the 1560s this seems mainly due to decreased baptisms rather than high burials, so that over the whole period from 1540 to 1640, the principal years of high mortality seem to have been 1545, 1558, 1580, 1587, 1593, 1609, 1624 and 1637, with the years 1558, 1609 and 1637 considerably more serious than any of the others.

We may distinguish two periods when years of heavy mortality were common, separated by a lull: 1558 was the culmination of a series of crisis years, followed by a period of comparatively uninterrupted growth right up to the later 1580s. These latter years see the beginning of a pattern of periods of heavy mortality, occurring fairly regularly every 10 or 15 years. This basic outline may be compared with other documentary evidence of the existence of famine or epidemic in the city. The incidence of epidemics in the city in the first half of the sixteenth century is difficult to reconstruct because of lack of records, but there were certainly outbreaks in 1502 and 1528.[2]

The grave epidemic of 1558 aroused no comment in the existing records, but the minor plague attack of 1563–4 caused some disruption. Minor outbreaks of plague took place in 1577, when it was brought from Oxford by the assize judges, and in 1581.[3] The most serious epidemic for some time took place in 1593–4, and again in 1603, while further outbreaks attracting the attention of local government happened in 1609–10, 1612, 1625 and 1630, culminating in the disaster of 1637.[4]

It will be noted that not all these outbreaks, especially in the Elizabethan period, led to years of exceptional mortality, for a minor outbreak of plague could be contained without dramatic demographic consequences. Some practical preventive measures were possible, for the corporation was well aware of the connection between poor standards of hygiene and the spread of epidemic disease, and in 1579 it specifically ordered the removal of refuse from public spaces for just this reason.[5] Some towns were successful in keeping out epidemics by cutting off all contact with infected areas, a sort of voluntary communal quarantine, as Ludlow, Shrewsbury and Winchester did, but Worcester was curiously reluctant to do this, probably because it was too much of a communications centre by road and river to make it practically or economically feasible. However, the isolation of infected households was a sound measure, in aid of which those breaking the quarantine were threatened with most severe punishment in 1581.[6]

But if an epidemic could not be restricted in this way – and many were halted before they really started – there was little left to be done to prevent disaster. The key to the seriousness of epidemics is probably to be found in the natural resistance of the population to disease, and this in turn largely depended on nutrition. Only two documented famines took place, one in 1556–7 and the other in 1597: it will be noted that both are closely associated with years of heavy mortality through epidemic disease.[7]

These years of epidemic and high mortality may be compared with the situation in the rest of the country. Although different regions were hit in different years, and areas which were geographically close to each other were affected in widely different ways, the general pattern in the rest of the country seems to resemble very closely the situation in Worcester – an increasing crescendo in the middle of the sixteenth century followed by a minor crisis around 1600 and then a sporadic but increasingly grave series of attacks in the years leading up to the Civil War.[8] But Worcester is probably slightly atypical in being less subject to serious epidemics of plague than many major cities, for it suffered no really serious epidemic in the second half of the sixteenth century, when many places were hit at least once, and its worst epidemic, the plague of 1637, killed only 10 per cent of the population. This was of course a major disaster, and must have caused serious and long lasting damage in many ways, but compared with the proportion killed by plague in some other towns, it was an attack of only moderate severity.

The two most likely explanations for these years of high mortality are epidemic, famine, or a combination of the two. What accounts for the years of heavy mortality in Worcester? The main clue to the reasons for an increased death rate is the season at which it occurs, for in normal years the smallest proportion of burials takes place in November and the highest in March and April, with the rest of the year rising or falling between these two poles. This pattern seems associated more with food supply than with the weather, for November is the month when the full effects of the harvest are felt, and the late spring, when food is shortest, sees the most deaths.

This seasonal pattern of mortality must be kept in mind when examining the pattern of the years of abnormally high mortality. The most serious years, 1558, 1609 and 1637 were all marked by an extra-high death roll from mid-summer to mid-winter, the exact opposite pattern to one associated with harvest failure. On the other hand, heavy mortality in the spring and early summer would indicate the failure of the previous year's harvest, a pattern which is evident in 1587, 1593 and 1597. Most of the worst epidemics seem to have begun in the high summer and run through until mid-winter, and these were concentrated in the periods before 1560 and after 1590.

This is not to suggest that years of heavy mortality in these periods were unconnected with failures in the food supply, but death was caused by disease primarily and in its own right, although the debilitating effects of a prolonged series of poor harvests is still a major factor. In the Elizabethan period itself, when population growth was very heavy, the pattern of the milder and rarer years of heavy mortality seems to have been much more directly connected with harvest failure, but the minor ailments which caused the actual deaths in these years were short-lived and kept down by the generally good standards of nutrition.

What effect did these epidemic years have upon the population? Their impact seems to have been temporary in the main, with the exceptions of 1558, which removed the previous eight years' growth, 1609, which accounted for the previous six years', and 1637 which put the population back to the level of 1621, and whose long-term effects are lost beyond the bounds of this study. Single epidemics did not have a very serious limiting effect on population growth, and were not major obstacles to it, especially as they were often followed by a spurt in growth, due to early marriage following the deaths of parents and the inheritance of the financial means to marry. The effect of epidemics was most serious when they came bunched together, as occurred in the 1540s and 1550s, the area about the 1590s and to some extent throughout the first 40 years of the seventeenth century. The absence of epidemics could have a substantial impact in allowing population growth to go on unchecked, and this fact was a major influence behind the expansion of the Elizabethan period, and closely associated with it must be placed an absence of serious, consistent harvest failure.

Two general points which emerge from this particular topic must be made. Firstly, the pattern of the seasons had a very great effect on the city dweller of this period. Around the harvest moved the pattern of his life, the pattern of birth and death. The majority of the citizens of Worcester were completely dependent on the market for all their food, and because a poor harvest might simply reduce the surplus which the farmer sent to market without drastically removing his own sustenance, the city dweller might go hungry while the countryman still ate. Thus paradoxically enough, the townsman was in one way more dependent on the harvest, more caught up in the vagaries of the weather and other country matters than the countryman himself: certainly any gulf between the interests and pre-occupations of country and town lay far in the future.

The second point is that serious epidemics were a feature of almost everyday life with which townsmen had to learn to live. An epidemic was not only a nerve-racking experience, with sudden death occurring daily, it also caused the dislocation of many of the most basic aspects of everyday life. A poem written by one of the cathedral officials on the plague of 1637 describes the cessation of most forms of economic activity, the collapse of the market and the severance of most forms of contact between individuals.[9] Generally speaking, this intensive examination of the population of Worcester and its behaviour has revealed a number of broad conclusions which may, or may not, be of general application beyond Worcestershire, but certainly throw a good deal of light on some of the most fundamental trends taking place in Worcester itself. It has first of all suggested that the total population of the city approximately doubled in size between 1540 and 1640. This was mainly due to natural causes but also to a substantial amount of immigration. This growth took place at an ever-increasing rate as the century progressed, and although the rural growth rate was much higher than the city's, it was on the decline.The reasons for population growth probably changed in emphasis during the period, high fertility in the sixteenth century, present since its first decade, being replaced during the last quarter of that century by a low rate of mortality, especially among children.

The period of population growth here examined from about 1510 to about the middle of the seventeenth century seems to have had two distinct phases. The first, about which little is known, culminated in a great demographic crisis in the middle of the sixteenth century, perhaps due to the pressure of this first wave of growth upon food resources; the second period saw during the reign of Elizabeth fairly steady growth, without the 'normal' checks of famine and disease, and this led on to another extended demographic crisis, beginning in the 1590s and coming to some kind of crucial stage in the 1630s, a crisis marked by fresh harvest failures and devastating epidemics. But the demographic crises did not alter the basic fact that there took place very heavy, even revolutionary population growth. The impact of this growth on the lives of the citizens of Worcester is perhaps the most important single theme in this book.

4

The economy

The object of this part of the book is to examine the way in which the citizens of Worcester earned their livings. This chapter begins by looking at some of the broad, basic factors which controlled the particular structure of the city's economy. The first of these factors is a most important one, the inflation of prices and wages, for this phenomenon which began nationally in the early sixteenth century was one of the major formative influences operating at the time, placing such stresses and strains on the old order of things that change to meet this challenge was made almost inevitable. Unfornately the available documentary sources are too sparse to produce any complete indices of wages and prices, but it has been possible to assemble some idea of the general level of some particular wages and prices in the city, from which we can make a rough comparison with other regions in the extent and timing of the inflationary process in this particular area.[1]

The only group of commodities of which some price statistics can be assembled are building materials. These are probably not entirely typical, and must especially have been subject to changes in demand which reflected the amount of building work going on at the time. As with most of the Worcester material, loss of records prevents us from detecting the moment when prices began to rise in the early sixteenth century, but the general pattern follows the national one, with a sharp rise in the middle of the century followed by a period of relative stability in the 1560s and 1570s and then another rise.[2]

As an example we may take the price of bricks and tiles, which rose from 5*s*. per thousand in 1529 to 10*s*. in the early 1560s; this level was held until some time after 1580 when they rose again to something approaching 15*s*. by 1600. This was the steepest rise of all, for other commodities normally increased in price by about two-thirds of their level before the mid-sixteenth century – lime and nails were more typical.

The only region of Britain where price levels have been studied in detail is the south-east of England, so this is the only area with which we may compare Worcester. The price of tiles at Winchester moved in the same way as at Worcester but usually some ten years later; at Eton the situation was again broadly similar except that Worcester tiles rose in price in the 1590s but at Eton not until about 1610; at Westminster the movement of tile prices resembled that at Worcester fairly closely.[3] It is difficult to find any comparable commodity, but on this basis the prices of manufactured building materials not only moved in the same way as in the south and south-east but the levels reached at any one time were as high, so that Worcester prices resemble closely those in London, which were usually the highest in the country. Although the basis of comparison is a slender one, we may tentatively suggest that, at least in this class of goods, Worcester prices were as high as the most economically advanced parts of the country, and inflation was certainly as pronounced, and possibly more so, than in many parts of the south: this is an unexpected state of affairs for normally one would expect that the level of prices in any area would depend mainly on its distance from the capital.

As the local agent of Tudor government, the corporation of Worcester was responsible for implementing the national policy of trying to stabilize prices by legal and administrative action. This was normally done through the three annual 'law days' when the court leet met.[4] The items whose price was most often regulated were in fact candles – 42 separate orders fixing the price of candles were made between 1559 and 1591. This may well have reflected a seasonal difficulty in the supply of tallow, but must be mostly due to a chronic imbalance between supply and demand. Since the city was very well supplied with livestock, and so with animal fats, the reason may well partly lie in an increased use of artificial light. No other item ever approached this frequency of regulation, but prices of beer and ale were fixed over 20 times during the period referred to above. Bread was controlled only on four occasions. Building materials were the only other commodities whose prices were regulated, in 1552, 1555, 1560 and 1595.

The level of the maxima fixed on all these occasions seems to have been the price currently prevailing – it was an attempt to stabilize prices and prevent profiteering rather than to bring prices down. Apart from the case of candles the regular thrice-yearly setting of price maxima seems to have been a measure to be applied only in extreme cases, for after the early 1560s, when the rapid inflation of the previous half-century slackens off for a time, regulation becomes much more sporadic. The rarity of attempts to limit the price of bread is perhaps significant. The enforcement of price maxima was an attempt to keep down the prices of manufactured goods like beer, tiles and candles, rather than the prices of foodstuffs like bread which were mainly the result of a relationship between supply and demand quite beyond the control of local government.

The study of wage levels on a local scale is restricted in the same way as that of prices is, and in particular is almost entirely concerned with building workers. The pattern in Worcester resembles the national one, a rise in the middle years of the sixteenth century followed by a period of stability beginning in the 1560s. However, in Worcester there is evidence of a further upward movement of wages in the last two decades of the sixteenth century, in particular in the case of carpenters, who are better documented than most. This is an exception to the pattern found in the south of England where no clear rise in wages is discernible between the accession of Elizabeth and the 1630s. The general amount by which wages increased in the south was about 70 per cent between the early and late sixteenth century, and in this respect Worcester was quite typical. However, wage levels in Worcester were below those prevalent in the south and east. In the 1570s building workers in Worcester were being paid between 10 per cent and 20 per cent less than their co-workers in London, Oxford, Cambridge and other south-eastern towns.[5] In this respect the atypical upward movement of wages in Worcester at the end of the sixteenth century may be a partial correction of this imbalance.

Wages in Worcester were regulated by the corporation in the same way prices were. Two general assessments of wages are recorded, apparently arrived at in conjunction with the justices of the shire: they date from 1561 and 1563, that is, one from just before the Statute of Artificers (which prescribed the regular and systematic assessment of wages) and the other from just after it.[6] The 1561 assessment is a simple affair, merely dividing the whole artisan group into two, consisting of masters and servants. The 1563 assessment is far more complex, with nine categories of urban artisans, all however connected with the building trade. A comparison between the two assessments shows that the later one is far more realistic and raised the maximum levels considerably. Where before a master craftsman was allowed to receive 8*d*. per day in summer without his keep, this limit was raised to 10*d*.; his labourers and assistants had their rates raised from 6*d*. to 7*d*. Rural workers received some slight increase but many of them had their wages frozen at the 1561 level: the urban artisan enjoyed a substantially improved rate while his rural cousin was largely ignored. Perhaps the self-interest of the country gentry justices is the most important factor here, keeping down the wages which concerned them most.

If we compare the wage levels fixed in these two assessments with those in contemporary measures in other parts of the country some significant factors appear. The city seems to have belonged to a broad area embracing the southern half of England, but excluding the London region where wages were higher. Worcester wages were however above those in the north-east Midlands and very distinctly above the northern half of the country. Thus in terms of wage levels at least, and this may well reflect the general economic situation, Worcester lay within, but at the edge of, the Lowland zone of Britain in economic terms. It is difficult to say what effect the 1563 assessment had on the actual wages paid in Worcester. The general levels both before and after the assessment were a little above the appointed maxima: whether the stabilization of wage levels in the 1560s had any connection with the assessment is difficult to judge.

The corporation was quite aware of the need to control the wages of building workers. Through the court leet, as with prices, it attempted to fix tilers' wages in 1559 and continued to campaign against excessive wages in the industry in 1560 and 1562. It ordered the observance of the limits prescribed by the 1563 statute and was still trying to keep down building wages in 1568 and 1569.[7] After this there is silence, with no record of a resumed campaign when wages began again to go up in the last two decades of the century. That the corporation had mounted a determined offensive against rising wages is clear, but whether it abandoned it because such action was successful, unnecessary or useless is less certain. The reason for the concentration on building workers is mainly because they were the only wage-earners in the city capable of bargaining with their employers from a strong position, for they were engaged for short periods by many different employers, whilst most workers served a long-term contract with the same employer. However, part of the reason may have been the existence of a building boom in the city. In any case building workers are exceptional from many points of view and it is unfortunate that studies of both prices and wages have to rest upon a group of trades which is unusual in many ways.

It is clear from the foregoing that prices in Worcester followed the pattern of at least the southern half of the country in this period. Indeed, at least as far as one industrial product is concerned, prices in the city were as high as anywhere else in the south or east, while increases took place in advance of some areas much nearer to London. But wages remained rather below the level prevailing in the more economically advanced region near the capital, so it is probable that the general movement of prices and wages was more damaging to the poorer classes of Worcester than it was in many towns in other parts of the country, for although prices were as high as anywhere, wages were not. The factor which needs explanation here is perhaps not the higher prices so much as the lower wages. Possibly, population growth and migration from the countryside had together held down the level of wages by inflating the supply of labour. In any case, conditions for the wage-earner, bad everywhere in England in this period, were perhaps a little worse in Worcester, although the evidence upon which a firm conclusion can be built is rather slight.

One major element in the economic history of this period is the fuel crisis. An increasing shortage of natural fuel was evident in many areas of Britain before the later sixteenth century. This resulted from the combined effects of greater demand due to population growth and increased industrial consumption, coupled with a dwindling supply as woodland was cleared. Worcester seems to have found itself in a worse situation than many other towns, for its fuel shortage was chronic and on occasions quite serious. One of the main reasons for this shortage of fuel was the demand for wood to heat the furnaces of the Droitwich salt industry nearby. Leland observed that there was a considerable shortage of wood near the town and that the salters were forced to go far afield in search of fuel.[8] Much of Worcester's firewood came down the Severn from the Wyre forest around Bewdley, so that Droitwich could absorb the supply before it reached the city.

The problem of the scarcity of wood was already emerging by the end of the fifteenth century. An ordinance of 1496 complains of the "greatly enlarged" price of wood and forbids the buying of standing timber in bulk within a seven-mile radius, except for building purposes.[9] Shortage of wood can be demonstrated in a number of ways. The city was involved in disputes with barge owners from the Bewdley area because it was sufficiently desperate for fuel to force boats to unload their cargoes of wood when the owners wished to carry on downstream to Tewkesbury and Gloucester, where better prices presumably prevailed. The theft of firewood from hedgerows and gardens was first condemned in 1568, and the law was repeated in the following year with the very severe punishment of banishment from the city for offenders. This law was repeated again in 1575 when persons taking wood from "hedges, bridges, stiles, gates, or cropping of trees" were to be liable to banishment on the third offence.[10] This shortage probably hit the poor hardest, for in 1565 and 1574 the corporation was buying wood in bulk to give away to the poor, and fuel was occasionally bequeathed to the needy in contemporary wills.[11]

The methods used by the city to try to ameliorate the situation were various. Attempts were made to freeze the price of wood in 1570 and of both wood and coal in 1582, but these were probably times of exceptional scarcity, for it was most difficult to regulate effectively prices determined so simply by demand exceeding supply. Attempts were made to see that profiteering at least did not occur and two offenders, significantly both boat owners, were fined in 1554. Buying in bulk from those who brought it to the city in order to retail it again was forbidden in 1570 and 1580. These restrictions seem to be associated with the attempts at price control outlined above, so both 1570 and the early 1580s must have been periods when the problem was especially acute. The demands of industry were also restricted where possible, for in 1548 bakers, brewers and tile-makers (the principal fuel-consuming trades of the city) were forbidden to buy up wood by the boat load. A statute of 1559 prohibited the felling of timber for iron smelting within 14 miles of the Severn.[12]

These were all attempts to modify rather than to solve the basic problem, which was that the available supply of wood fuel had been outstripped by demand. The only available solution was to augment the fuel supply by introducing coal. It is probable that in 1570 coal was first brought downriver by boat from the coalfields of southern Shropshire and north-western Worcestershire.[13] The city corporation showed admirable enterprise in this respect, for in March 1565 it sent its two aldermen to inspect a coal pit at Pensax, in the parish of Lindridge in north-western Worcestershire, then owned by the cathedral. By December of that year it was decided to start trial working, and operation on a commercial basis had begun by the autumn of 1566, for the relevant city accounts show £12 received for coal sold at the pit, and that money had been spent on bringing the coal to the city storehouse by the quay in Worcester, and also on miner's tools and wages. In 1567 the pit was making a profit and still being run by the corporation, but in the following year the work of running the pit was contracted out to a Worcester man, and no revenue from it is recorded. In 1574 further work was carried out at the pit but after this no further record exists of it.[14]

The venture was clearly a commercial failure, probably because the distance from the mine to the Severn added heavy transport costs. But the most important fact is the enterprise of the corporation in developing and running a coal mine; no evidence has been found of another municipal authority doing so. Possibly it was more enterprising and civic-spirited than some, but certainly the fuel problem which faced the city was more serious than most towns had to overcome. The ultimate reason for the failure of the Pensax pit – and for the solution of the fuel crisis – was probably the development of other mines along the banks of the Severn which could produce and transport coal more easily.

The coal field in southern Shropshire was developed greatly in the Elizabethan period and the Broseley area became a particularly important fuel source; by the 1640s this group of mines supplied a very large part of the coal shipped downstream to Worcester and Gloucester, and was evidently a vital element in the economy of the whole Severn basin.[15] The date at which coal first began to be supplied to Worcester from this source is difficult to determine, especially as the word 'coals' can refer to charcoal in this period, but the earliest reference in probate records to the presence of 'sea coals' in a Worcester house is in 1567, so the Pensax pit may well have brought coal to the city for the first time. There are further references in

1575 and 1576, and by the 1580s coal is uncommonly but regularly found in houses.[16] It may well be that it was used mainly by the very poor, whose homes are rarely inventoried, for coal does not appear in the records as often as one would expect.

The price of this newly-introduced fuel was recorded as 4s. per ton in 1588 and 5s. in 1582, when wood was priced at 3s. 4d. per hundredweight, so that clearly coal was very much the cheaper fuel.[17] Despite this early start the use of coal does not seem to have become a regular part of the city's life until the 1590s. Coal hammers are mentioned in inventories of 1592 and 1602 and a firegrate for coal in 1605. Buildings for the storage of fuel which are specifically called coal-houses occur first in 1595 and 1604.[18] But by the Civil War the use of coal had become very general, and the cutting off of the supply of river-borne coal by hostile forces caused the city very considerable distress.[19]

Both wood and coal were brought down the Severn to Worcester by its boatmen, indeed fuel was one of their staple cargoes. A boatman's inventory of 1579 lists large debts owed to men from Broseley and Madeley, suggesting that he was buying coal from them, while a boatman was owed for coal he had carried to a Droitwich man in 1586.[20] The boatmen appear to have acted as retailers of fuel rather than just hauliers; it was a completely new undertaking for those adventurous enough to see their opportunity, and the distribution of coal must have grown into a quite lucrative minor trade: an innkeeper in 1590 owned a "little iron bound wain without the doors to carry coals."[21]

Thus the acute fuel shortage in Worcester, at its peak by the early 1570s and still present in the 1580s, was solved by the supply of coal by river, partly as a result of the conspicuous enterprise of the corporation, whose failure was quickly compensated by the development of the riverside mines of south Shropshire. As the supply of coal became regular, legislation to ensure a steady supply of cheap fuel disappears from the corporation records. Without the development of coal mines in the upper Severn valley at this time Worcester would almost certainly have been in serious difficulties by the early seventeenth century, difficulties which could have hampered its continuing economic growth.

5

Communications

All towns rely on communications, and all major ones must be placed on important land or water routes, for without the inflow of people and goods from the outside world the city could no longer fill its basic function as a centre for the exchange of goods and the supply of services. Worcester was well placed as a centre of communications. From contemporary maps and documentary references it is possible to reconstruct the major routes which crossed the area (see figure 11). A fourteenth-century map shows the city as the junction of four major land routes – one running to Bristol and the south, one to Shrewsbury and the north-west through Chester, and two to the north, dividing at Droitwich with one arm passing through Birmingham to Lichfield and the other to Coventry, Leicester and Grantham.[1] This places Worcester as an important point on roads linking the south-west with the north of England. In addition, the city was in frequent contact with London along an important road which ran across the Avon valley and into the Cotswolds through Broadway and Stow-on-the-Wold.

Worcester was also well situated as a focus of contact between England and Wales, a point which will emerge in a number of ways below. The routes over Worcester's bridge on the Severn to Hereford and also along the valley of the Teme to Ludlow were of great importance in communications between England and central Wales – probably the most important of all. Habington describes the bridge as "the passage over Severn to the west of England and south

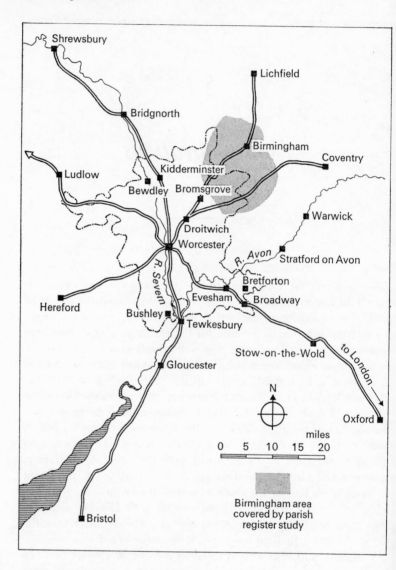

11   *Worcester in its region.*

of Wales" and the bridge over the Teme at Tenbury was described
in the early seventeenth century as on the road from most of Wales
to London.[2] Thus the Worcester crossing of the Severn was used by
many of the major routes from central Wales and its borders to
London and from southern Wales to the Midlands and north. Quite
apart from this importance as a river crossing point, as a gateway in
the border, Worcester lay on a major route running up the western
side of England from south to north, and was also well connected
with London.

It was on this network of major roads, and on its good local
network, that much of the city's economy depended. Along these
roads came wool from Shropshire and Herefordshire to be made into
cloth and sent to London. These were the routes which made
Worcester an important market and fair centre. Travellers on every
kind of mission passed through and were provided with hospitality
and goods. An ordinary country town could survive with little more
than a local road system: Worcester's position depended upon the
flow of goods and people along the major communication routes
which converged upon it.

All Worcester's people depended ultimately upon the basic fact
of the existence of these roads and the traffic upon them, but for
a few they provided a direct livelihood – the carriers and hauliers
upon whom a good deal of the internal commerce of the country
relied. The probate records of some of these men have survived.
The most illuminating are those of William Parks, a carrier who
died in 1559.[3] His house contained a shop with scales, weights and
baskets as though it were used for the collection and delivery of
goods in transit. He owed debts to at least five London merchants,
including a mercer, a salter and a pewterer. The debts owed to him
show his customers: the Bishop of Worcester owed him four separate
debts while one Worcester cloth manufacturer owed for the carriage
of two cloths to London, and two other citizens, known to be
clothiers, owed him similar sums for unspecified reasons.

Here we have the carrier taking cloths to London and returning
with the imported and luxury goods which were Worcester's main
requirements from the capital; his debts from the bishop and a
parson may indicate that he was also bringing back books from
London. Parks probably ran a regular service between Worcester
and the capital. We do not know how he transported his goods, but
John Huxley who died in 1581 owned three horses with their

packsaddles and was described as a haulier, while a carrier who died in 1605 left two horses and a waggon in his stable. A waggoner in 1613 left five horses and his waggon.[4] All of these men were of little below average means, but they did provide not only a vital commercial link but probably also the main channel by which the provinces heard the latest news and came into contact with the latest ideas, either through books or by word of mouth.

One other vital communication route remains, the river Severn, one of England's major navigable rivers at this time. Worcester, in common with other towns along the river as far up as Shrewsbury, was a minor inland port, for as far as the movement of goods was concerned, waterways generally carried far more than the road system. Despite occasional shallows, quite large boats could reach Bewdley, which always seems to have acted as the principal upstream terminus of the river traffic, with Bristol at the opposite end. The origins of the use of this important trade route lie well back in the medieval period, but its main growth must lie in the later fifteenth century onwards, for when the antiquary Leland visited Bewdley in the 1530s he was struck by its largely new buildings and the recentness of its rise to importance.[5]

The best single source of information on this river trade is the Port Books of Bristol, in which were recorded not only details of cargoes which paid customs duties, but also an abstract of the information provided by the masters of ships plying within territorial waters as part of the system designed to control exports.[6] Since voyages along the Severn which had Bristol as their origin or destination are included in the coastal traffic recorded in the port books, they give a very informative picture of the river traffic. Unfortunately this is only a selective view, for voyages along the river which did not reach Bristol are unrecorded.

The total number of voyages appearing in the books shows that the greatest part of the trade between Bristol and its Severn valley hinterland was always with ports below Worcester, and especially with Tewkesbury and Gloucester which provided very large supplies of cereals for both Bristol itself and the English and Welsh shores of the Bristol Channel. Only about a quarter of the voyages were with Worcester and the ports which involved passing through Worcester – Bewdley, Bridgnorth and Shrewsbury. Bewdley and Worcester seem to have had about an equal share of the traffic but Bridgnorth and Shrewsbury contrived to improve substantially their modest later-sixteenth-century contribution by the early years of the seven-teenth. The scale of this trade, in terms of voyages made, was not great. In 1605 between 8 April and 7 December, 178 voyages were made along the Severn towards Bristol.[7] Of this number, 46, some 26 per cent, were from ports above Tewkesbury, 24 from Worcester itself, 19 from Bewdley and 3 from Shrewsbury. This implies a boat departing from Worcester a little less often than once per week, although the boats from the upper Severn towns may well have called in at the city on their way.

The cargoes carried downstream from Worcester to Bristol were a varied assortment, but cloth and wool, with large quantities of leather, were the main contributions to the river trade. Further upstream, Bewdley sent down the products of its surrounding district, leather and skins, large amounts of wax and honey, with occasional cargoes of barrel staves. From Shrewsbury and Bridgnorth came large boatloads of wool. Although different ports shipped the specialities of their areas, from the region above Worcester came essentially raw materials for Bristol's industry – skins to be tanned, leather to be made up, wax and honey, staves for the barrels of the wine trade, wool for the cloth industry of the city and its region. Worcester, at least in the early Elizabethan period, sent its manufac-tured cloth, and wool, probably the fleeces of Worcestershire sheep.[8]

The boats brought back to Worcester a wide range of imported and manufactured articles – in 1576 the principal cargo was wine, carried by almost all on their return journey from Bristol. In addition, soap was very frequent, followed by metals such as iron and lead, oil – probably the fish oil used in the cloth industry – rosin and liquorice. The consignments to the upper Severn towns supple-ment this list, for their needs were very similar and probably part of their cargoes were landed at Worcester in any case. Grocery wares were an important element, those imported luxury goods which only a sea-port like Bristol could supply, such as the barrels of oranges which went to Bewdley with pepper and raisins, or the dye-wood and alum for the cloth industry and the canvas and linens from Ireland and the Continent. But the staple was wine, followed by grocery and mercery, soap, and raw materials for the manufacture and processing of cloth.[9]

This pattern is essentially one of Bristol drawing from its hinter-land the raw materials it required for its industries and sending back imported and manufactured goods. This was not a static situation, for between the 1580s and the first decade of the seventeenth century it is clear that this pattern was becoming very much more complex. The volume of traffic shows a clear increase but it is its content which displays the most change. Where Worcester had in the past exported wool and cloth, in 1605 these commodities are but two among a number, including skins and leather, linen cloth, hops, aquavite, wax, cheese and wool.[10] But to these generally agricultural products are added a range of manufactured goods, fair quantities of glass, brass pots, woad, nails, wick yarn and paper. The other upper Severn towns were also sending down a vastly increased quantity of manufactures, in particular the scythes and nails of the growing metal industries of north Worcestershire and south Shropshire.

Vessels brought back from Bristol far less than they had once done and the proportion of raw materials rises impressively, iron and coal, even wheat and skins, although Worcester's principal requirement remained the wine which Bristol imported from France and Spain. The early Elizabethan pattern had been a simple one of raw materials flowing downstream and imported and industrial products coming back up – almost a 'colonial' relationship between the Severn valley and Bristol; now the pattern was being partially reversed, with a mixture of raw materials and manufactures moving in both directions. This change is a reflection of the great economic developments taking place in the upper Severn valley in the later years of Elizabeth's reign, a process by which that area was becoming much more industrialized, more complex and independent of the large towns which lay downstream.

Another interesting development was the increasing size of the region which depended upon the Severn as its artery: tanners from Lichfield, Nuneaton, Leicester and south Warwickshire are prominent in 1623.[11] Occasionally the river is used as the lower portion of a trade route running down the length of the western coast of England – two shipments of Derbyshire wool in the 1580s and three cargoes of Lancashire cloth in 1572–3 passed through Worcester.[12] Thus Worcester was an important river port on the vital artery which connected Bristol with its hinterland. But the Port Books tell us nothing of the voyages which did not touch Bristol, and these may well have been even more important than the long-range traffic.

The Severn was vital to Worcester for the supply of firewood and coal and the volume of traffic in these fuels alone was very considerable, for in 1585 all boats bringing fuel to the city were to be removed from the quay within one day to make room for others once they had been unloaded. A statement drawn up in 1591 of the tolls to be charged on goods unloaded lists the payments to be made on cargoes of coal, wood, iron, perry, stone, wool, hay, straw, brick, lime and ashes, with special regulations for grain and fruit. Evidently a wide variety of bulky raw materials was supplied to the city by river, most of them in all probability from sources within the county. Similarly salt was brought from Droitwich by road and loaded into boats at Worcester to be taken downstream.[13]

The reason for this use of the river for the transport of heavy or bulky materials is a simple one: water transport was probably quicker and certainly cheaper than any other available means. The accounts of the building of the manor house at Kyre Park, in the extreme north-west of Worcestershire, provide some good examples of this.[14] In 1588, 80 tons of stone were brought from Madeley in Shropshire to Bewdley by boat and then to Kyre by road. The freight charge for the river journey works out at a little over one penny per mile per ton. The charge for the section by road is between 8*d*. and 9*d*. per mile per ton. In the same way in 1614 a ton of lead from Bristol cost 10*s*. to bring the 80 miles from Bristol and another 10*s*. for the mere seven miles from Bewdley to Kyre by road.[15] So for these long journeys the river highway might be as much as ten times as cheap as the road system. These figures explain more eloquently than anything else the reason why the Severn was so important in the economy of the whole region.

The part played by Worcester boatmen in this river trade is revealed by an examination of their wills and associated inventories. Thomas Shawe, who died in 1578, was carrying wood, especially barrel-staves and spokes, and in one instance had taken several tons of them to a Taunton man.[16] He was also delivering coal, presumably from southern Shropshire, along the Worcestershire stretch of the river. Samuel Blacknedge seems to have specialized in taking salt downriver to Gloucester, for at his death he was owed on several accounts for the transport of at least 150 tons in total.[17] He was also supplying grocery – oranges, figs and pomegranates – to a Droitwich man whose salt he carried. Presumably he had brought these goods back upriver from Gloucester or Bristol, as he did the salt fish he sometimes carried. He was also owed for the carriage of barrel-staves and coal, but in smaller quantities. Roger Brooke's storehouses contained large quantities of wood – fuel, barrel-staves and planks, with panels for building purposes, as well as coal and lead.[18] Arnold Beane seems to have had a small rope-making business – hemp is recorded as an occasional river cargo – and possessed large quantities of timber. He was indebted to men from Madeley and Broseley, both important coal mining villages, so he was probably fetching coal from them.[19] The wills of several more city boatmen mention the ownership of timber, especially coopery ware, the shaped wood for staves and spokes.

Some of these Worcester boatmen were quite comfortably wealthy; Roger Brooke for instance left property valued at over £300, and several others listed above left property of well above average value. Some of them could almost be called the river equivalents of the wholesale merchants of the seaports, for they were dealing on their own account in a wide variety of wholesale goods, and then selling them, either to shopkeepers or direct to the public. Timber and fuel in particular were sold directly by the boatmen and were not carried simply as a haulage service, and goods imported from Bristol seem to have been dealt with as wholesale investments rather than as a matter of transporting goods already owned by others. Except for the haulage of salt, these Worcester boatmen were mainly concerned with trading upriver to Bewdley and south Shropshire. We only have a fragment of their total dealings, but it seems likely that the long-range trade with Bristol was only a minor part of their activities, their principal interest being in bringing down the raw materials required by the economy of Worcester from its rural hinterland upstream.

We know from other sources that the river was used to take a very large proportion of the cloth manufactured in the city to be fulled at the mill at Hartlebury, 12 miles upriver.[20] Boats were also used for the transport of passengers on occasion, for in a breach of promise case in the bishop's court the unfortunate girl alleged that she was just leaving by Roger Brooke's boat to enter domestic service in Bristol when she received her proposal of marriage.[21]

Several of the Worcester boatmen owned little fleets – Samuel Blacknedge had four, worth £32, while Arnold Beane had six – the *Ragged Staff*, the *Old Speedwell*, the *Spy*, the *Luke*, the *Butterbox* or *Swallow* and the *Black Pear*, altogether worth £17.[22] Some of these boats must have been very small and old, and even the best of them were hardly major investments since the most valuable were priced at under £10. There is no sign of a boat-building industry in Worcester but in later years one existed in Tewkesbury.[23] At the end of the seventeenth century a traveller observed that boats were hauled upstream by gangs of six to eight men.[24] There is little contemporary Worcester evidence of the size of crews, but in 1614 a boatman was prosecuted by the church authorities for unloading his boat on a Sunday, in company with four of his "servants".[25] These may well have been the crew, but even if they were not, it indicates that the river trade provided employment for a considerable number of the poorer classes in the city, either as crew or as dockers.

The importance of this river traffic to the city is shown by the interest the corporation took in it on behalf of the community. The municipality paid for the upkeep of the quays which lay downstream from the bridge, a responsibility in existence at least by 1466, and a warehouse was maintained by the city at the quay.[26] The city also took responsibility for major improvement schemes, for in 1572 it promoted a private bill in Parliament enabling it to construct "the water-course for a new cut out of Severn". The bill was defeated at its third reading. Whatever this project was – possibly a dock of some kind to draw the boats off the main course of the river – six years later the corporation resolved to dredge the river bed at considerable expense to improve access to the quays. The upkeep of these quays was an expensive business, and in 1569 the city spent nearly £20 under this head, and mention was made that one of the quays was new.[27]

The navigation of the Severn gave rise to a long series of disputes involving the corporation and other authorities. Acts of Parliament of 1430, 1503 and 1532 had been aimed at making the Severn a free river devoid of toll barriers and other obstructions.[28] That of 1503 was specifically directed at Worcester, among other towns, forbidding it to charge tolls on boats unless it could prove its legal entitlement to do so in Star Chamber. This it succeeded in doing, for in 1504 that court decreed its confirmation of the city's right to charge tolls on wine going upriver and boats coming down.[29] The ordinances of 1496 reveal that tolls were charged on vessels going upriver and on goods loaded or unloaded. In a dispute with Bewdley in 1499 it was decided that no toll should be paid on goods which were simply carried past the city, and if city officials forced boats loaded with fuel to stop and sell their cargoes, then the owners should be compensated. A similar dispute over the forced sale of firewood bound for ports downstream was settled in 1561. In 1563 Tewkesbury complained to the Crown about Worcester's toll charges on its boats, but this seems to have been the last dispute over Worcester's right to charge tolls on boats which only passed by without stopping, and the claim seems to have been abandoned after this.[30]

In 1582 and in 1583 the corporation successfully defended in the Exchequer court its right to inspect all vessels passing by if it suspected they could be breaking the complex regulations on the movement of foodstuffs and other strategic commodities.[31] The re-definition of the toll charges on all goods loaded and unloaded at the quays, made in 1591, reveals quite high charges: a boat of between 12 and 20 tons paid one shilling for its cargo.[32] Although, as we have seen, the right to charge tolls on boats merely in transit was given up in the 1560s, charges at the quays must still have brought in a good income to the authorities; this does not appear in the city accounts so the Water Bailiff may well have used it to pay for the routine running expenses and upkeep of the port facilities.

The turn of Worcester to have its privileges themselves infringed came in 1636, when the scheme to make the Avon navigable aroused the protests of the corporation, so that in 1641 it objected in detail to the distortion and diversion of prevailing patterns of trade which it alleged would be brought about.[33] The core of the city's anxiety was that the opening up of the Avon to navigation by-passed Worcester as the point where river-borne trade was unloaded for land carriage to Warwickshire. As an example of this, Coventry traders in 1506 were importing goods from Bristol as far as Worcester and then bringing them home overland.[34] The Worcester vintners in particular were the standard wine distributors over much of Warwickshire, an area normally beyond Worcester's economic region; Thomas Bromley, a leading Worcester vintner, was owed debts at his death from Coventry, Stratford-upon-Avon, Southam and Kineton.[35] This trading bonus must have been very largely lost when the canalization of the Avon was completed in the middle years of the seventeenth century.

It is hard to assess very exactly the importance to Worcester's economy of the Severn trade, but it was certainly of very considerable significance, most crucially in the supply of raw materials, fuel and food, and in expanding the city's capacity as a regional centre for the supply and exchange of goods. In general, the city's links with its market area, and with the greater world beyond, both by land and by water, were extremely valuable; this was a major factor not only in the prosperity of Worcester, but in its very existence.

6

Markets and fairs

One essential feature of the economy of all significant towns was that they were all market centres. To them flocked country folk in order to sell their produce and to buy whatever goods they could not themselves supply and the town provided. The town acted as a centre for the exchange of two broad classes of goods, the agricultural produce of the countryside and the manufactured goods made in the town or imported to it. Worcester needed the food grown by its rural neighbours in order to live, especially since it was more industrialized and less agricultural than many English towns. It relied also on the custom of country people in its stalls and shops, for no town's citizens could survive by merely selling to each other. Many towns relied on their markets to attract to them that extra volume of business which made them more prosperous than average. Leland in his travels round England observed how some towns enjoyed more wealth than most due to the attractiveness of their markets. Worcester's prosperity owed much to its importance as a market centre and as the site of very well-attended fairs.

Worcester was entitled to hold markets by its charters: that of 1555 confirmed the by then traditional markets on Monday, Wednesday and Saturday. The Monday market seems to have declined – it was after all not a very suitable day – but the county historian Habington in the early seventeenth century mentions the Wednesday market, and the Saturday one he claims was "so great a market as scarce any markets in England equalleth it".[1] Granted a certain amount of hyperbolic local patriotism, it remains true that Worcester's flourishing market was of great importance in the local economy.

We may gather some details of the distances people travelled to attend it by examining the debt statements contained in the probate records of Worcester citizens, for these reveal the place of residence of the customers of Worcester shopkeepers, and we may be reasonably certain that the people who bought from Worcester tradesmen also traded in the market, for the two activities are so closely associated as to be complementary. The map based on this evidence shows that these customers were drawn from an elliptical area about 25 miles from west to east and about 15 miles from north to south (figure 12). Thus few people travelled more than 10 or 12 miles to the city to buy and sell, and this represents the core of Worcester's region, the area from which people looked first to the city as their centre for the selling of their produce and the purchase of the goods and services their villages could not provide. The size of this region was determined partly by the distance which people could reasonably cover on foot with their produce and purchases (15 miles was approaching the maximum in this respect) and also by the presence of other market centres.

The market towns of Droitwich, Bromsgrove, Kidderminster, Stourbridge, Halesowen and Bewdley cut off a large section of northern Worcestershire from the city's direct influence, while behind them stood Birmingham and Wolverhampton, both thriving commercial centres. This is well shown by the accounts of the Talbot estates, centred at Grafton Manor near Bromsgrove.[2] The cereals raised on these estates were sent to market almost completely at Bromsgrove, Kidderminster and Stourbridge. Purchases of a variety of goods from nails, glass and tiles to sugar and pepper came from this group of towns rather than from Worcester. To the south of Worcester a similar band of towns restrained the city's influence – Ledbury, Tewkesbury, Pershore and Evesham with Gloucester and Bristol behind them. Evesham in particular was a flourishing centre whose market Habington claimed was second only to Worcester's in its importance. The influence of the city spread further to the east and west because the nearest good market centres were further away: in the east Alcester was small and distant and in the west the more distant towns of Hereford, Leominster and Ludlow had regions which met Worcester's half-way.

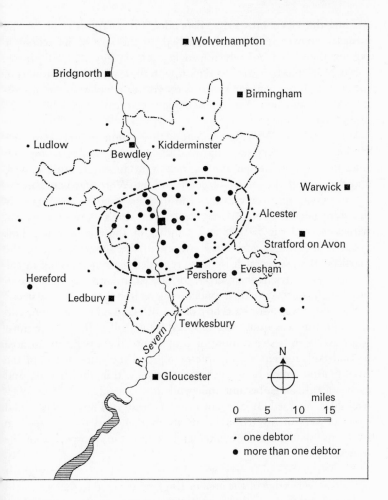

12 *Worcester's market region (based on the debt statements in the probate records, in which debts to Worcester shopkeepers are recorded).*

Thus the city's prosperity, dependent to a large extent on the attractive power of its market, relied on the size of its economic region, the area from which people came to buy and sell. If we compare Worcester's market region with those of the other towns in the county, the reason for Worcester's greater population and importance is obvious, for Worcester's region is at least treble the size of any of the others.[3]

Why should Worcester occupy this commanding position? Undoubtedly its very size improved the attractiveness of its market, since the larger the town, the less risk of produce remaining unsold, and the greater the choice of goods to buy. Worcester was also the county town, and to the assizes and quarter sessions came not only the shire gentry to act as magistrates but also a flow of jurymen, witnesses, and the friends and families of those concerned. This must have brought additional custom to the shops, if not to the markets; the assizes at least were regarded as major events in the lives of Worcestrians themselves, for one set of witnesses in a case in the church courts date their evidence by reference to the last assizes.[4]

Worcester was also the centre of the diocesan administration, and although this was quite decentralized into smaller units, there must still have been a steady flow of people into the city from an area beyond both the city's economic region and the shire, for until the Reformation much of Gloucestershire lay within the diocese, and even after this area became independent, the southern half of Warwickshire retained its allegiance to Worcester. Thus the city had other powers of attraction beside its market, and these helped to swell its sphere of influence and hence the prosperity of its tradespeople.

Worcester was also very well placed as a centre of exchange. It lay on the very edge of the area of England devoted to the open-field system of agriculture, the south-eastern quarter of the county being the only part of the shire largely devoted to it. This was symptomatic of the city's position in a borderland, not so much political as geographical and economic. To the west and north lay the Highland Zone of Britain, principally pastoral, enclosed, thinly populated and under-urbanized. To the south and east stretched the Lowland Zone with its open fields, arable, rich and heavily populated. Worcestershire lay exactly between these two broad regions, with its western half's landscape undulating, well wooded and devoted to stock-raising while the eastern portion was far more purely arable, flat and open. Between the two ran the Severn with Worcester on its banks.

Thus the city was admirably placed to act as a channel by which two contrasting regions could exchange each other's products: to its markets and fairs came cattle, sheep and horses from the west and cereals from the east, so that its market places served not only the needs of the citizens but also the basic commercial requirements of broad farming regions, a situation which provided ample opportunity for enrichment. This exchange between two distinct agricultural areas is shown by the places from which came the people who dealt in stock and cereals in Worcester market (see figure 13). The corn dealers came most frequently from the south-eastern quarter of the county – these were the men who were bringing cereals in large quantities to the city's markets and very few indeed came from the west or north. The Vale of Evesham had in fact a national reputation for its cereal production, "the granary of Worcestershire".[5]

The city authorities charged tolls on the sale of animals, and the official record of these transactions gives a good indication of where stock was coming from and who was buying it; a typical picture of the transactions taking place on a normal market day is reconstructed by combining a good number of them. The result shows the origin of the vendors of cattle and horses sold in the city's ordinary triweekly markets and the places their buyers came from during the 1550s (see figure 13). The basic pattern is that of the area to the west of the Severn sending animals to the city to be bought by people from the south and east. Most buyers came from within the shire, and almost completely from its southern half. Cattle in particular came from the west and north-west, an area stretching as far as Hereford. This area is a wider one than that already suggested as the region of Worcester shopkeepers' country customers, so it may well be that those who came to deal in the market included some drawn from a rather wider area than the regular shop clientele.

But the main point of this evidence is that Worcester drew considerable benefit from lying between two specialized agricultural regions which required a medium through which to exchange their products. One may presume that the cereals from the east were exchanged for the stock from the west and vice versa, but this is more illustrative of the principle involved than of the range of products concerned, for from the west must have come dairy

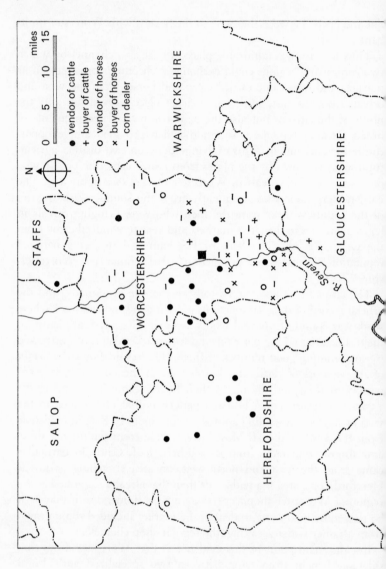

13 Worcester markets: commodity transactions.[6] *(Symbols indicate places of origin.)*

produce such as butter and cheese, wax and honey, tallow, leather and skins, wood and timber. Equally to the cereals coming from the east we must add a number of other commodities such as fruit and vegetables, hay, straw, and malt.

Thus Worcester thrived as an urban centre partly because of the range and attractiveness of its market, which depended not only on the city's size but on the fact that it was an administrative and communications centre, and ideally placed between these two regions, the one arable and other pastoral. The citizens themselves depended on the market first of all as a source of food. About half the cattle referred to above as sold in the market were brought by Worcestrians, presumably for slaughter. Worcester was more dependent than most towns on the markets for its food supply because it was so highly industrialized and agriculture was so uncommon as an activity for the citizens, even as a sideline. Without the market it would have starved; when plague in 1637 discouraged the country people from attending it, only organized charity prevented a very serious food shortage.[7] Apart from this basic function, the city profited greatly from the attractiveness of the market; the more country people came to it, whether to buy or to sell, the more there were to buy from Worcester shopkeepers and to avail themselves of those specialized services which only a town could supply – on this question of supplying rural needs towns lived or died.

The importance of the market in the life of the city is reflected in the interest the municipal authorities took in it. Above all else they were interested in maintaining a reliable flow of the cheapest possible food and drink: this aspect is dealt with more fully below in chapter 11. The corporation was also concerned with the siting of the various sub-divisions of the market and this legislation is also of interest in illustrating how fragmented and specialized an originally simple institution had become. A specific position had been assigned to the market for cattle by 1496, when Angel Lane and Dolday were reserved for English and Welsh cattle respectively.[8] These lanes were relatively uninhabited and gates were placed across the ends to keep the animals in. Sheep were sold in Broad Street, corn in the market place so named, while the 1496 ordinances reveal the existence of specific areas of streets reserved for the markets for barley, oatmeal and salt; during the sixteenth century the sites for the sale of garden produce, ironmongery, leather and objects made from wood were determined.[9]

It was a part of the corporation's legal duties to regulate the market, to prevent abuses of local or statute law and to check on the quantity and quality of goods offered for sale. These were very onerous obligations, and for most of the century they were the responsibility of the bailiffs and aldermen. The city government was also entitled to a wide range of tolls, a privilege renewed by the 1555 charter which gave it the right to receive them on all transactions in the city and within a seven-mile radius of it. Most of these dues seem to have been charged on entry into the city rather than in the market place; before 1571 the right of the bailiffs to charge these tolls seems to have been farmed out to the keepers of the city gates, but in that year the practice was forbidden.[10]

Various towns and villages around Worcester tried to escape from these tolls by claiming that they had once or did then belong to ancient demesne, and were therefore toll-free throughout the country. Droitwich, Tewkesbury and Coventry came into conflict with the city governors during the sixteenth century over this question, while proof of ancient demesne status was placed before the corporation by over 20 towns and villages in the market area of Worcester during the late Elizabethan period. The reason for this activity seems in at least some cases the result of an attempt by the civic authorities to impose tolls as a novel imposition on areas which had traditionally been free of them: these attempts all seem to have failed. Lists of the tolls payable were posted up in the market places and on the city gates, but no record survives of the exact sums charged.[11]

The administration of the market and the collection of tolls was organized from the 'toll shop' which stood in the Corn Market, rebuilt in 1602. The Guildhall was used as a market hall, for here leather was sold and stored between markets, as was also the wool and yarn used in the cloth industry.

Thus the Worcester markets were of great importance to the city, but these tri-weekly occasions are by themselves only part of the picture: the four annual fairs held at Worcester were of very considerable economic significance. As confirmed by the 1555 charter, the fairs took place on nine days around Palm Sunday, on the Friday and Saturday before Low Sunday (the first Sunday after Easter Sunday), around the Feast of the Assumption (13 to 16 August) and between 6 and 9 September. Habington states that by the early seventeenth century the August and September fairs were less important than they had once been because attendance had originally been combined with pilgrimage to the shrine of the Virgin in the cathedral, a practice firmly suppressed at the Reformation; they were also held in harvest time when few country people could spare the time to come, so the two Easter fairs were left as the main ones.[12]

The corporation records of toll payments, already referred to, give an idea of the nature of these fairs. They seem to have relied principally on the exchange of livestock, and especially horses. The crowds from the countryside came from a considerably wider area than for normal markets, this in turn promoting a generally increased demand for all the goods and services which the city could provide – the economic function of fairs was very much the same as bank holidays are in modern seaside resorts. The number of animals concerned was much larger than at markets: at the Easter fairs of 1560 nearly 1,500 sheep changed hands, while on another similar occasion 1,400 were sold.[13] The normal number of horses exchanged was between 40 and 70 at Easter, but the number of transactions involved was the largest of all and the distance travelled by both parties was usually greater than for other animals. Cattle seem to have been normally dealt with in August and September, and in 1551 these fairs saw at least 180 cattle bought and sold.[14] Although the records of the weekly markets may have been badly kept, they rarely record more than half-a-dozen transactions in livestock, so these fairs seem to have been the main medium for the exchange of farm stock over a large area.

Sheep came mainly from a fairly restricted region, as shown in figure 14, which is based on the sales at the Easter fairs of 1560 and of a somewhat later but unrecorded date.[15] They came almost completely from west of the Severn, from north-western Worcestershire and eastern Herefordshire, but one flock had covered over 70 miles from Carmarthenshire, and a few large flocks had come over 30 miles from northern Herefordshire. Their buyers came from southern Worcestershire and from Warwickshire, an area not much wider than for ordinary markets, although the number and size of transactions is much larger. This state of affairs is equally true of the cattle dealt with in the August and September fairs of 1551 (see figure 15[16]). Here the area covered is mainly the county itself, and a part of eastern Herefordshire. Very few came more than 20 miles, but the east-to-west movement is again clear.

The horse fairs attracted a much wider range of business: stock

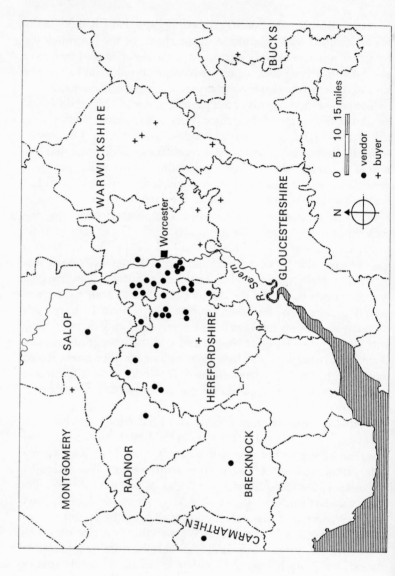

14 Worcester: sheep fairs. (Symbols indicate places of origin.)

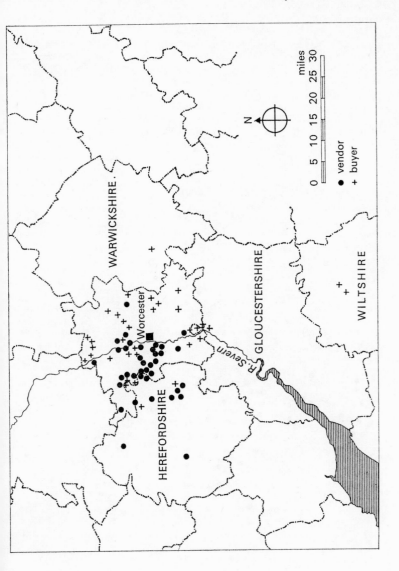

15 Worcester: cattle fairs. (Symbols indicate places of origin.)

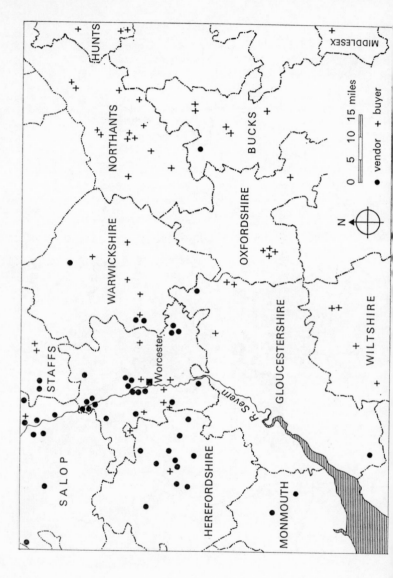

16   Worcester: horse fairs. (Symbols indicate places of origin.)

came from a greatly extended region compared with the restricted parts of western Worcestershire and eastern Herefordshire, from which most of the cattle and sheep came (see figure 16[17]). Shropshire and Monmouthshire, Staffordshire and Warwickshire supply animals, while the buyers come from a wide area of the south and east Midlands, especially the counties of Northampton, Huntingdon and Buckingham. Some of these men were dealers on quite a large scale, and were probably obtaining stock to supply the London and Home Counties market. But this should not obscure the very wide area of the east and west Midlands from which buyers and sellers made their way to Worcester market. Other fairs beside these two illustrated, received horses from most of the counties of central Wales, especially Radnor, from Lancashire and Derbyshire, and buyers from Kent and London, Rutland and Bedfordshire.

Worcester's thriving fairs were important to the city as a source of food – many of the cattle and sheep were bought by Worcester butchers as in the markets – but their main importance was that they attracted to the city a greater number of people from a wider area than did the markets. These were not just the people who came to buy and sell livestock, for we have only been looking at one aspect of the fair: many more must have come to observe, meet friends, settle debts or as a holiday expedition. This led to a general heightening of demand for all the goods which the city's shopkeepers and craftsmen sold. On these occasions much of the commercial activity of the city must have been concentrated.

The importance of the fairs is shown by a dispute within the corporation in 1561, when it was proposed to move the sites of the main parts of the fairs to the cathedral end of the High Street.[18] In September there was a heated council meeting at which a number of members, including both the aldermen, walked out of the chamber in protest against the move; this is the only case in the whole of the sixteenth century when details of voting are recorded. It appears that those members of the council who lived around the previous site of the fairs had objected to a council decision more strongly than any other group in the whole century are recorded as doing, and as a result it was decided eventually to hold the fair in each place on alternate years. The heat generated by this issue is an indication of the prosperity which proximity to the fair brought to shopkeepers.

All citizens appear to have had the right to erect stalls, for markets and fairs, in the streets and in 1561 there is a reference to shearmen, cappers, goldsmiths, glovers, brewers and bedders setting up stalls in the High Street. Others beside the shopkeepers and stallholders profited from both markets and fairs, for the innkeepers and ale-sellers in particular received a very greatly increased custom: in 1554 the number of alehouses was fixed in each ward, and those near the principal market places were allowed an increased quota because of the demand from country people attending markets and fairs.[19]

These occasions were also times when town and country mixed, when news and ideas were disseminated over a wide area of country-side around the city; here the countrymen were brought into contact with the outside world, albeit at second hand. At the markets proc-lamations were made, new laws read out and property transactions between country people made. Above all people met and talked and exchanged news – two enquiries into treasonable statements in the 1530s concerned country people who had come to market and were talking about the political situation either in an inn after they had finished their business or on the long trudge home.[20] Thus those who attended the markets and fairs went back to their villages not only with the money from their sales and the goods they had brought from Worcester shopkeepers and stallholders, they also took away for digestion and dissemination the news and new ideas about politics and religion which the city's frequent contacts with the world beyond the Worcestershire fields had brought to it.

So like all towns Worcester depended on its flourishing markets to buy its food and sell much of its own produce, and on its fairs to widen that contact with the rural masses, that exchange of goods between town and country, which was the basis of the urban economy.

7

The trades of Worcester

Before looking in detail at the various ways in which the citizens of
Worcester earned their livelihoods, we must examine the general
outline of the city's economy, and this is best done by looking at the
proportions of the various trades represented in the city. The main
evidence for this is provided by the probate records which contain
extensive details of the numbers of various tradesmen working in the
city. These records cover the period 1540 to 1620, and contain
records of some 664 men whose trade is referred to; when this total
is split into two groups at the year 1590, evidence of any trend
operating can be seen. The broad groups into which these trades can
be divided are shown in table 6. It should be emphasized that these
figures concern the self-employed citizens of Worcester only, but
that this group is a very large one and covers all those who had any
influence over the destiny of the community.

The economy of Worcester, looked at in this way, was dominated
by the cloth industry, manufacturing and processing, which
accounted for by far the largest group of tradesmen – 40 per cent or
more before 1590 and over 50 per cent after this date. Next to these
came a broad group, all of whom were concerned both in making
goods and selling those goods to a local market from their own
shops, the artisan-retailers: this group accounted for 25 per cent of
the total in the first period, dropping to 18 per cent in the second.
Next came the purely retailing trades, those shopkeepers who did not
themselves make goods but imported them from outside the city,

| | Number of wills | | Proportion (%) | |
	to 1589	1590–1620	to 1589	1590–1620
CLOTH				
Weaver/clothier	122	129	32	45
Others	3	2	1	1
Processors	34	22	9	8
			42	54
ARTISAN-RETAILERS				
Tailor	14	4	4	1
Tanner	11	7	3	3
Other leather workers	31	12	8	4
Metal workers	28	15	7	5
Other artisan-retailers	13	13	3	5
			25	18
PURE RETAILERS				
Mercer	28	4	7	1
Draper	16	3	4	1
Other distributors	5	3	1	1
			12	3
FOOD AND DRINK				
Butcher	12	17	3	6
Baker	9	9	2	3
Brewer	16	12	4	4
Rest of food and drink	10	2	3	1
			12	14
Services	23	16	6	6
Building	6	8	2	3
Total	377	287		

Table 6   Trade structure based on probate records

either from the rest of the country or from abroad. This group, 12 per cent of the total before 1590, collapses to 3 per cent afterwards. The food and drink supply trades saw a slight increase from 12 per cent, to 14 per cent. Lastly, those providing professional or other services form a small and varied group, constant in size, while the building workers complete this analysis with another very small group.

Here some significant features deserve attention. Firstly, Worcester was far more highly 'industrialized' in the relative, Tudor, sense of the word than most other provincial towns. By the end of the sixteenth century over half its self-employed tradesmen and, since the cloth industry was a relatively heavy employer of labour, well over half the total population, was concerned in the production or processing of woollen cloth. Not only was this group of tradesmen quite outstanding in size and wealth, it was also increasing its predominance during the reign of Elizabeth, when one might presume that the cloth industry should have been contracting, or at least been stagnant. This large urban textile industry contrasts strikingly with most other towns, for even Coventry in the 1520s, with its own textile trade at its peak, could only muster 33 per cent of its citizens so employed, while Norwich in the Elizabethan period, with its worsted industry of great importance, had only 17 per cent employed in it; the average proportion is probably represented by Northampton and Leicester with 13½ per cent and 8½ per cent respectively.[1]

This purely industrial element among Worcester's tradesmen is superimposed on the normal economic structure of a major provincial market centre, but here again there are some noteworthy features. The purely distributive trades, the mercers, drapers, haberdashers and the like, were subject to a disastrous decline in numbers – for example the mercers fall from making up 7 per cent of the total tradesmen to less than 1 per cent. Similarly the tailors, although not quite the same kind of trade, fall from 4 per cent to 1 per cent. These are issues which are dealt with in detail below, but it is perhaps a phenomenon not common to most towns, although there seems some trace of it at Leicester.[2] The leather industry, although important, was much less prominent than in some east Midlands towns. Other aspects of Worcester's occupational structure seem to resemble the norm: the food and drink trades for instance closely resemble the proportion in Coventry,

Leicester, Northampton and Exeter.[3] Its building industry was smaller than most of the towns cited above, but this may well be due in part to the distortion produced by comparing numbers derived from probate records with those from other towns where the freemen's register has been used.

We may put this occupational structure in perspective by comparing it with the medieval past. A Poll Tax list[4] originating in the reign of Richard II reveals something of the civic economy at the end of

	% to 1589	% 1590–1620	% late 14th century
Cloth manufacture	33	46	3
Cloth processing	9	8	11
Artisan-retailers:			
tailor	4	1	11
leather	11	7	19
metals	7	5	7
others	3	5	10
	25	18	47
Retail/distributive	12	3	7
Food and drink	12	14	20
Services	6	6	7
Building	2	3	3

Table 7 Analysis of trade structure

the fourteenth century (see table 7). Unfortunately it is only partially preserved, and since trades still tended to gather in particular areas of towns at this date some distortion may have occurred. However it indicates that the artisan-retailers then made up nearly half the total, building and services were much the same as in the sixteenth century, but food and drink, at 20 per cent, was a rather larger group than later, while the distributive trades stood, at 7 per cent, at half their later size. The most striking difference is the relatively minute size of the cloth industry, only 14 per cent of the total. This figure conceals the fact that the cloth manufacturers, the weavers formed only 3 per cent of the total, while the cloth processors, the fullers and dyers, supplied a group nearly four times as large. This would suggest that at this date Worcester was mainly concerned in the finishing of cloth produced in the countryside rather than being itself a major textile producing centre.

Thus the rise of Worcester as a highly specialized textile-producing town must be assigned to the fifteenth century, for at the end of the fourteenth century it was clearly a quite typical provincial town of moderate size, its trade structure reflecting this with its predominance of small shopkeeper-craftsmen pursuing a variety of occupations. Much of the city's later rise to wealth, and of the particular character of sixteenth-century Worcester, must be attributed to the imposition of an industrial textile manufacturing centre upon the structure of a sound market town economy.

As we have seen, the tradesmen of Worcester may be divided into two broad groups, those who both made goods and sold them, and those who dealt in materials imported from outside and did not actually make anything. This latter group, the purely distributive trades, is the first to be looked at in detail.

Of the distributive tradesmen, the mercer was certainly the most important. Next to the cloth manufacturer he was the wealthiest of all the citizens, and in more typical towns the mercer usually disposed of more wealth – and the power that accompanied wealth – than any other townsman. Despite their partial eclipse by the wealthier clothiers, the mercers of Worcester were rich by any standards and held considerable political and social power. Their riches are easily illustrated: one in 1607 left bequests in his will totalling £1,100 including £120 to charity; one inventory of property left at death in 1552 totals £357 while another of 1559 amounts to at least £400. Most mercers left inventories worth over £100, while the value of stock in the shops alone was often very high – £123 in 1552, £340 in 1556, £230 in 1583.[5]

By contemporary Worcester standards this represented an enormous capital investment in stock and tools, for the average city tradesmen had rarely more than £20 absorbed in stock or equipment, and often much less. Much of the profits of the mercer's business was necessarily re-invested in buying new stock, but much was spent on luxurious houses and furnishings. For example John Walsgrove in 1567 had retired from active trade but his house had

19 rooms opulently furnished, overflowing with cushions (many made from church vestments), supplied with glass windows (still a luxury at this date) pictures and musical instruments. His wardrobe was worth £14 and his silver and gilt plate £59. Beside this house he had a farm near Malvern with a six-roomed farmhouse and 45 acres of crops.[6]

How were mercers able to make such impressive fortunes? The basic trade of the mercer was the supply of textile fabrics, especially the expensive imported ones, and the preservation of a number of inventories which give a list of every item in stock in these shops allows an examination of the source of this wealth. Luxury cloths make up an important part of the shop goods, including velvets, silks and satins from the Mediterranean, but the total stock of other imported fabrics is often more valuable. Thus Richard Horwood had £52 worth of luxury cloths but £64 worth of the more mundane fabrics – canvas and linen from Normandy and the Low Countries in particular. Other mercers were selling large quantities of worsteds and other woollen cloths, not necessarily imported from abroad – one had £8 worth of English worsted.[7] Worcester's concentration on making high-quality broadcloth meant that often other woollens had to be brought from other parts of the country and sold by her mercers.

Yet textiles formed only the basis of the mercer's trade, for the contents of these shops extend over a very wide range of goods. Grocery of some kind was normally present, essentially the spices and other oriental produce which had to be imported, normally pepper, ginger, cloves and mace, with similar items like liquorice, treacle, marmalade, almonds, dates, saffron and sugar. The other main class of stock was haberdashery, a multiplicity of small items, usually manufactured abroad, such as pins and knives, laces, thread and buttons, purses and inkpots, paper, lace, brushes, spectacles and buckles. This very miscellaneous collection of small imported articles bulks large in all mercers' inventories, but in quantity rather than value.

Beside these principal kinds of commodity, mercers also supplied all sorts of miscellaneous wants for which no other specialized supplier existed, and in this way the contents of these shops approached the range of goods for sale in a modern department store. Lute strings and virginal wires often occur; Edward Bratt supplied dyestuffs and chemicals for the cloth processing industry;

others stocked hats and caps, parchment and frying pans, pitch and quicksilver, dog collars and saltpetre.[8] Many tended to specialize in the provision of particular classes of these goods, in addition to the normal varied range. William Robinson specialized in pewter articles – saltcellars, tin bottles and spoons, lead inkbottles. Peter Gough had opened up an apothecary's department and the list of drugs and potions in stock at his death extends over a document between eight and ten feet long.[9]

Other mercers specialized in stationery, like Thomas Heywood who had "7 primers and 2 latin books" in his shop, or Richard Horwood who stocked two dozen primers, three service books, eleven "accidence" (presumably Latin grammars), three horn books and five dozen "ABC": clearly all aimed at the schoolboy market provided by the city's two schools. Horwood was also a stockist of specialized ironmongery, for in his shop were saws and chisels, "pincers for shoemakers", goldsmith's tools, latches and locks, hawk bells, nails, tacks and chains, snuffers and five thousand hooks and eyes.[10] William Heywood had £5 worth of wax and a "wax house" and also a storehouse for "pitchers and cups". One had a storehouse for salt, another a tailor's shop: these were yet more of the many specialisms within the mercer's trade.[11]

So these tradesmen were concerned in selling a very wide range of goods, the only common factor among their crowded storerooms being the fact that nothing of all this was made in Worcester: most of the city's shopkeepers were selling the things they themselves made, leaving the mercer to cover the whole field of goods which came from other parts of the country or especially from abroad. The mercer's trade absorbed most of those who were retailing in this field, for the specialist haberdasher, grocer or stationer is rare in the city. Only one stationer's will is recorded, and one grocer too, leaving the whole field to be monopolized by the mercer.

Many mercers were so successful that they had begun to move out of the town and abandon their original business. One appears in 1579 with no shop but at least 13 houses in the city, clearly becoming an urban rentier, an unusual course for a successful Worcestrian to take. More typically, many of the others were running farms in the countryside – one in 1558 had no shop but extensive rural property, farm stock and crops. Another in 1521 refers to a farm in Presteigne, and the example of John Walsgrove's farm at Malvern has already been quoted.[12] The mercer's trade was one of the most reliable avenues of advancement through wealth to social elevation, from urban shopkeeper to country gentleman-farmer.

The haberdashers provide the only exception to the rule of the absorption of all this kind of trade into the many-sided mercer's business. The probate records of five haberdashers have survived, covering the whole period, but most of them were very poor compared with the mercers and their shop stocks were tiny.

This whole class of distributive trades seems to have undergone a decline during the later Elizabethan period. We have 23 mercers' wills from before 1580 but only eight from between 1580 and 1620. Even these eight are generally drastically poorer than the preceding ones, two of the inventories being worth under £30 in the early seventeenth century. The reason for this striking decline in the fortunes of such a flourishing and wealthy trade must lie in the nature of the market it served. The mercer relied as much as or more than most other trades on the supply of his imported goods to the surrounding country people, and especially to the wealthier yeoman-farmers and gentry. The people who could afford to buy the essentially luxurious contents of these shops were necessarily the richer classes of a wide area, and this contention is borne out by the people recorded as owing money to mercers. Peter Gough's debtors for instance were scattered all over Worcester's region, and included a random selection of many of the local landed families – Talbots, Throckmortons, Packingtons, Gowers and the Bishop of Worcester.[13]

It was on the patronage of these people that the mercer's fortune was built, not on the pins or thread he sold to his fellow citizens. And these local gentry were beginning to be much more conscious of the attractions of the capital, for in London lay the influence of Parliament, the Inns of Court with their important educational role, and the fount of fashion to which all were increasingly sensitive; more frequent visits to London could only lead to the purchase there of many of the goods sold by the Worcester mercer. The Talbots for instance were buying much of their spices and similar luxuries from London quite early in the reign of Elizabeth.[14] Since the Worcester mercer in any case drew his supplies from London wholesalers, this is suggested as the major factor behind the decline of the Worcester mercer. A contributory force may be the rise of competing suppliers in the smaller country market towns in the shire.

The other tradesman mainly concerned with distributive trade was the draper. He sold a selection of fabrics rather like that of the mercer, but with a more utilitarian bias, normally omitting the luxury fabrics, although most were still drawn from sources some distance from the city. It was normal for this trade to be split into two camps, those specializing in woollen fabrics and others concentrating on linen ones, but in Worcester only woollen drapers seem to have flourished, linens presumably being left to the mercer. The inventory of Edward Crosby gives a good idea of the draper's stock – a wide variety of coloured woollen fabrics, kerseys, cottons, Kentish cloth, friezes, flannel and a small amount of linen – in fact all the woollen textiles produced in other parts of the country but not in Worcester. He also sold some Irish rugs and women's stockings. The total value of his stock was £111 – a considerable sum.[15]

The draper was a wealthy man in the first half of the sixteenth century, not quite rivalling the mercer but approaching that standard. Wills survive for this period which mention sums of about or over £100 in at least five cases, but Crosby's business, described above, must have been the last of these opulent concerns. Of the 18 surviving drapers' wills, 14 come from before 1570, and the later ones are distinctly less affluent, a general situation very similar to the one we have already noted for the mercer. Thus we have again to account for a distributive trade in marked decline, both in the numbers engaged in it and the wealth they earned. The debts of Crosby give us some idea of his customers and so a clue to the reason for this decline.[16]

Crosby was owed money by 136 people who had bought small amounts of cloth from him, and of these at least half came from the countryside around the city. He was clearly also acting as a wholesaler, for he was selling to rural tailors, and seven of the 20 Worcester debtors whose trades are given were tailors, while the rest had bought cloth presumably to be made up into clothing either at home or by their own local tailor. Thus Crosby, and so presumably the other drapers too, relied largely upon rural custom, but from a much wider social and economic spectrum than the mercer. The reason for the draper's decline lies in the increased competition felt from a countryside of growing economic sophistication and independence.

An examination of the trades specified in the probate records and marriage bonds from the whole county shows this clearly.[17] The total number of trades mentioned in the period from the beginning of regular preservation in the 1540s until the end of the sixteenth century was divided in half exactly: the division came at the year 1580. In a static situation there should be as many instances of a particular trade in the years up to 1580 as there are in the years 1580–99. However the number of drapers mentioned in Worcester itself is halved from 6 to 3, while the drapers in the rest of the county remain static. The impressive change is in the number of tailors. Between the two periods the Worcester tailors fall from 8 to 6 but those in the shire increase from 2 to 42 – a quite remarkable growth. This great rise in the numbers of country tailors must reflect a proliferation of these tradesmen in the countryside beginning perhaps in the middle years of the sixteenth century.

This phenomenon may well be the reason for the decline of the Worcester draper: the rural tailor may well have been supplying his customers with cloth, but at any rate the fact that country people needed no longer to come to the city to obtain the services of a tailor may well have discouraged them from buying their cloth from a city draper – the two trades stood or fell together.

Thus both the purely retail, distributive trades, the mercers and drapers, show great prosperity until the reign of Elizabeth, and then experience a serious decline due to competition from London, the smaller country towns and the country villages themselves. The consequences for the whole prosperity of the city were potentially serious, but were concealed by the wealth of the cloth industry. This decline in the city's role as a distributive centre was not final, for by the eighteenth century it had recovered, if not strengthened, its original primacy.

A small number of other activities which were of a purely retailing nature deserve attention. Despite the competition of the mercers, a single stationer survived, supplied with his stock by London wholesalers.[18] He was a wealthy man with an inventory total of £185, and his premises were divided between his stationer's shop with its paper, books and parchment and the skinner's shop where parchment was prepared. He was certainly supplying books – although we are not given a list of them – as he had been paid by the Bishop for the future delivery of 49 books by "Dr Whitgift and Mr Cartwright"; he was probably fetching books to order from London rather than selling from stock. The existence of the cathedral and the clerical trade which it brought must have been a vital factor in this business.

The only grocer whose probate records have survived had a small business and an unremarkable house.[19] The number of recorded vintners is small compared with the volume of wine shipped up the Severn from Bristol but this is again a purely importing and retailing business. The vintner Edward Darnell was very wealthy – his inventory totalled £300 – but he was also involved in cloth manufacture.[20] In his wine cellar he had £40 worth of wine, he leased a tavern and so sold part of his stock there. Thomas Bromley died owing over £100 to a Bristol wine shipper, while his own debtors show him distributing his wares over a wide area of Worcester's region, especially to Warwickshire, an area normally beyond the city's influence: this result of the use of river transport has already been noted.[21] He was also supplying the Talbot household at Bromsgrove with wine on occasions, but both the last Prior of Worcester, who lived like a country gentleman, and the Talbots, generally imported their wine direct from the Bristol merchant.[22] This must have considerably narrowed the Worcester vintner's market, although the lesser gentry and the city's inns and alehouses must have remained a good business proposition.

Lastly among these retailers are those non-resident ones who were a valuable source of supply for goods not produced locally. Pedlars and other itinerants were regular visitors, for among the traders who brought their packs into the city and were obliged to pay toll on them were "kendalmen, linenmen", shoemakers, glovers and tanners. It seems that many of them were using the inns as places to sell their goods. Worcester had its own chapmen based in the city and one of these in 1491 was buying his stock wholesale from a London mercer.[23]

But most of these traders must have been strangers to the city, like Robert Secker or Clarke of Attercliffe in Yorkshire who fell ill and died in Worcester, probably in the winter of 1580–1.[24] He left three horses with their packs and a series of debts owed to him from towns beginning at Birmingham and then running through Bromsgrove, Worcester, Pershore, Evesham, Tewkesbury, then through Herefordshire to Leominster and back into Worcestershire at Clifton-on-Teme. His principal stock in trade was knives, sold apparently wholesale to local cutlers and ironmongers. Clearly this chapman was buying the knives produced in Sheffield and was selling them along a round taking in towns on a circuitous route running through Worcestershire and eastern Herefordshire. There must have been many more like him who supplied the Worcester shopkeepers as well as the citizens in general, and who attended the markets and fairs to sell to the country folk.

This completes the survey of the purely distributive element in Worcester's economy; as will be seen, most of the general run of tradesmen were selling what they themselves made, but still the mercers and drapers were an important element in the urban economy, and their marked decline in the later Elizabethan period is an important phenomenon, although probably not a marked feature of many other towns.

8

The cloth industry
part one

Of Worcester's manufacturing activities, the production of woollen cloth was by far the most important, in the number of families engaged in it, in the wealth which it produced and in its general effect on the character and prosperity of the whole community. Worcester produced broadcloth of a very high quality, principally for the export market, and this quality was often remarked upon: one Worcester clothier described himself in 1576 as the maker of "the finest cloths in the world".[1] The city lay on the edge of the region which specialized in this field, centred on Gloucestershire and Wiltshire. The Worcester industry, although making a very similar product, functioned quite independently of the main area of production, a self-contained industrial complex.

The importance of the cloth industry was, as we have seen, a fifteenth-century growth, but already in 1466 it was stated that "it is used and accustomed great clothmaking to be had within the said city and suburbs of the same, and so occupied by great part of the people there dwelling".[2] By the sixteenth century contemporaries commented on the city's main industry. According to Leland "the wealth of the town of Worcester standeth most by drapring, and no town of England, at this present time, maketh so many cloths yearly as this town doth". Camden considered the inhabitants "many in number, courteous and wealthy by the trade of clothing", while

Habington noted the social and economic predominance of the clothiers and the very high quality of the textiles produced.[3]

The manufacture of cloth was England's only great industry – what proportion of the national total of this vital export did Worcester produce? We have available two sets of statistics, one for the end of the Middle Ages and one dating from the early years of Elizabeth. In 1468–9 the aulnage returns credit Worcestershire with 477½ cloths out of a national total of over 39,000, so that the county's share was a little over 1 per cent.[4] Gloucestershire and Wiltshire produced between them over 9,000 cloths. Thus on a national scale the county's contribution was not large. What is perhaps more striking is that this is not really a county total so much as the production of a single city, for there is little evidence, at least in the sixteenth century, that the country areas were making broadcloth in significant quantities. This total of nearly 500 cloths is really the production of the city of Worcester alone, and for a single city to make so much is really quite unusual: even Norwich, much larger and more important than Worcester, was credited with only 557 cloths on this occasion.

The other basis for comparison is the figures for the number of cloths found to be of inadequate quality on the London cloth market in 1561–2.[5] Worcester's share was about 3½ per cent. The London market probably dealt with most of the high-quality cloth sold, but not so much of the lower-quality fabrics, so inflating Worcester's share, but on the other hand the quality regulations of the city were probably much more strictly enforced than in the countryside so that a smaller proportion of its cloths were found faulty. The essentially urban nature of the Worcestershire cloth manufacture is also shown, for no faulty cloth was presented from anywhere else in the shire but the city. These two surveys show that Worcester's share of the total national production was small but significant, but as this was almost completely the work of a single city, it tends to lend weight to Leland's opinion that Worcester by the sixteenth century made more cloth than any other town in the country.

The production of cloth was a long and complex process involving a number of different skills, so that its organization was necessarily complicated. The details of the organization of the Worcester industry are dealt with in greater detail below, but it is worthwhile to examine first its general structure. The text-book view of the

English broadcloth industry still tends to present two broad assumptions. The first of these is that although located in towns in the early Middle Ages, the industry soon migrated to the countryside so that by the sixteenth century it was essentially rural; the second is that it is suggested that production centred around the great clothier, operating various forms of the domestic system, owning the looms and raw materials supplied to the captive craftsmen – a prototype capitalist entrepreneur.

But Worcester's industry was very different from these stereotypes, for it was essentially urban, unaffected by any migration to the countryside and flourished in the allegedly restrictive atmosphere of a major city. In organization the industry showed every possible form, but the capitalistic domestic system in any developed sense was rare; the independent artisan of moderate means dominated this sector of the economy. In order to elucidate more closely the detailed nature of the activities which produced most of the city's wealth, the various stages taken in the making of cloth will be examined in turn.

Since Worcester produced a very high quality broadcloth, its supplies of wool were necessarily drawn from regions specializing in the very highest quality. It was stated in 1557 that the city shared the supply area of the main broadcloth-producing regions of Wiltshire and Gloucestershire – the contents of clothiers' wool stores reveal that this was, as one would expect, the area of England which enjoyed a reputation for the finest quality wool, Shropshire and Herefordshire.[6] Wool must often have been bought in large quantities; it was a seasonal commodity, and the value of that stored in some clothiers' houses is high. In 1612 one wool store was worth £130 while in 1588 another was valued at £58, figures quite typical of the larger operators.[7]

How was this wool brought to the city? There is no evidence of resident wool dealers, or of clothiers acting as middlemen. Some certainly travelled to the area of supply to buy their stocks: one weaver was owed the deposit he had placed on some wool – "I took him to lay earnest upon wool".[8] Other debts to farmers in Herefordshire or Shrewsbury do not indicate how buyer and seller came into contact with each other, but certainly the proximity of Worcester to the area producing its wool must have been a major factor in the original siting of the industry there.

The city was also a wool market in its own right. Wool was sent

from Worcestershire farms; the Talbot estates near Bromsgrove
sent quantities to Worcester market in 1575 and 1576 which fetched
prices not too far below those set by Herefordshire fleeces.[9] The
Guildhall was the market for wool and judging by the regulations
passed to control it, this was a major source of raw material for the
industry. Strangers were free to sell their wool after 10 a.m. but
only citizens could buy it until noon.[10]

The quantity of wool which passed through this market is difficult to calculate exactly, but the superintendent of the Guildhall, the
Hallkeeper, weighed all wool brought to be sold and charged a toll
on it of one penny per tod. His accounts survive between 1550–1
and 1559–60 and show an income from this source varying between
£4 and £21, but generally about £5.[11] This indicates an annual
turnover of about 15 tons, but ranging up to over 60 tons. If these
figures are correct the market could only have supplied the smaller
producers, for the great clothiers had such large stocks of wool in
their houses that the annual consumption of many of them must
have been several tons. They would be obliged to buy at source and
leave the more modest operators to rely on the market.

The first process in the production of cloth was the preparation of
yarn from the wool and spinning it ready for weaving on the loom.
Spinning was a simple process and provided a source of extra income
for many a Worcester household otherwise unconnected with cloth-
making. The number of houses containing spinning wheels is
legion. Most spinners were women, and for widows in particular,
always a large class, this income was vital. Thus when Elizabeth
Rea, widow, died in 1617 her modest dwelling contained eleven
skeins of yarn and two spinning wheels; another widow in 1611
possessed two wheels, three pounds of wool and yarn, baskets and
shears.[12] Unmarried girls do not naturally appear often in the probate records, but as the term spinster implies, they must often have
been the users of the wheels found scattered around the homes of so
many people.

Yarn produced in this way, with wool – regulations often class
the two together – was sold in the market, but yarn spun in the
countryside was also brought in and sold. A weaver in 1555 owed a
Tewkesbury woman payment for yarn supplied.[13] By 1466 there
was sufficient difficulty in getting wool spun that clothiers were
taking it into the countryside and had to be forbidden to do so when
labour was available in the city.[14] Spinners were sometimes also

mployed directly by the clothiers – the only real extension of the omestic system into the city. Only the very richest clothiers are ever ecorded as employing spinners regularly, and an even smaller umber of them actually supplied their spinners with wool. The nain practice seems to have been to spin the wool on the clothier's wn premises, and 'spinning chambers' often appear in their ouses.

The earliest reference to a clothier's spinners, implying regular mployment, is in 1568, when five women (one from the country ear Droitwich) are so described, but the regular use of spinners vorking in their own homes does not seem to have occurred until ne 1590s and even the early seventeenth century, when an improvenent in the prosperity of the industry is evident.[15] The probate ecords of unusually prosperous clothiers mention wool "at the pinners" in 1599 and 1612, a will of 1613 has a bequest to "all my pinners" in the testator's employ for over a year while one of 1617 nentions "my spinners".[16] This practice of spinners working regularly and directly for one employer seems to have been a revival in etter times of the custom of the boom period early in the sixteenth entury, as indicated by a very strict ordinance of 1558 which rohibited the use of spinners in the countryside within a 12-mile adius: beyond this area work could only be carried out in bulk and n market towns.[17] The reason for this measure is not clear but it eems to have been the result of the unstable commercial conditions f the time forcing clothiers to look for the cheapest possible labour, vhich probably lay in the countryside, and the prohibition of competition for labour would also keep costs down. In any case a depresion in the cloth trade must have hit first at those employed in these asks, people reliant upon their small earnings here to raise their ncomes to subsistence level.

The basic process of manufacture, the actual weaving of the cloth n the loom, was undertaken by the clothier or weaver. The two erms are partly interchangeable for by the turn of the sixteenth and eventeenth centuries many men of limited means styled themselves clothier' although their activities were indistinguishable from the arly Elizabethan weaver. This was probably merely part of that eneral process of social sensitivity and up-grading which took place n English society at this time, for instance in the much wider ssumption of the style 'gentleman'. The process of weaving cloth vas undertaken by a very wide range of operators from the poor,

independent weaver with one loom to the great, wealthy clothier
with three or more looms, plus one or two more weavers working for
him in their own homes, and himself acting as a dealer in the cloth
produced by smaller tradesmen. There was every variety between
these two extremes, but we may roughly consider them in two main
groups, those styling themselves as weavers or those of equivalent
status, and those whose businesses were large enough to merit the
term 'clothier'.

The majority of sixteenth-century operators were weavers. Most
of them left assets valued in their inventories at between £10 and
£30; the number of looms they possessed varied, about half having
one and half two. The quantity of wool or yarn in their houses was
small – rarely more than £10 worth and often much less. The
cloths which they were weaving do not commonly appear in the
inventories: they must have sold them to a local middleman as soon
as they were completed in order to finance the purchase of the
wool for the next one, for in many cases the total values of the inventories would not cover the cost of the materials for making one
longcloth. Thus a slump of any kind would quickly affect these
small businesses, as failure to sell the cloth they had already woven
would deprive them of all the capital needed to continue work.

Typical of these smaller operators was George Miles. When he
died in 1551 he left goods and property worth £11 11s. 8d.[18] His
house had ten rooms – large for his standing – and at the rear lay
his "working chamber" containing wool and yarn worth £3 and
a loom with its ancillary equipment valued at 25s. Some of these
inventories do not mention a loom at all, and more fail to record any
cloth, wool or yarn. A few of them may have been journeymen,
although it is unlikely that many of this class would be rich enough
to make a will, and in other cases the weaver may have been retired
on some occasions property may well have been sold off to meet the
expenses of illness and burial. The absence of any item in an inventory is not conclusive. But it serves to underline an important point,
the narrow financial margin on which these men lived, so that they
could not afford to lay in stocks of more wool than were immediately
required or to wait for any length of time before selling the cloth
they had woven. The absence of very much evidence of 'putting
out' in rich clothiers' inventories lends no support to the idea that
weavers with no looms or wool recorded in their homes were
actually working for the clothier on a domestic basis. Not all of these

weavers were in any case making the broadcloth which was the
main concern of the clothier. About a tenth of the looms recorded in
weavers' homes were narrow looms, used for making the smaller
and cheaper textiles destined, at least in this area, for the local
market rather than for export. These required less capital to make,
especially in the initial outlay on raw materials, but equally the
profit margin on them must have been smaller than on export-
quality broadcloth.

Among these modest but independent weavers there were a number of men too rich to be classed with the weavers but too poor to be
counted among the clothiers, but there is still a fairly clear division
in terms of wealth between the two groups. Just as few weavers
possessed assets worth more than £10 to £30, so most clothiers were
worth over £70, and often more than £100. In terms of wealth at
least, the two main classes of business in the cloth industry were well
differentiated. There is much less distinction between the number of
looms each group owned, for the clothier normally owned two and
sometimes three. Five are recorded in one house in 1548 and four
in 1545 but after these boom times more than three are most
unusual.[19] In this respect the clothier appears as merely a more
wealthy weaver.

The feature which swells the value of the clothier's inventory is
partly the opulence of his house and furnishings – in itself significant
– but mostly the value of the stocks of raw materials and textiles
which he held. He would very frequently have cloths being made on
the looms when the inventory was taken – a rarity for mere weavers
– so presumably the business was elaborate enough to carry on
despite the death of its head. One inventory lists nine cloths in store
at the house, worth £115.[20] The normal situation was to have a
considerable amount of wool and yarn in stock, to have cloths
uncompleted on the looms, perhaps to have one or two in store, but
more probably to have two or more at the fuller's being finished or at
London being sold. Thus Thomas Patterick had on his death in
1585 three looms with three cloths on them, three undergoing the
finishing process at the fuller's and two awaiting sale at London.
Their total value was £76, and he also owned a store of wool worth
£40. Patterick left an inventory totalling over £155, so his stocks
of wool and cloth accounted for £116 of this.[21]

The example just given could be repeated many times over: the
essential difference between the weaver and the clothier was that the

clothier had invested a much greater quantity of capital in his bus
ness, could afford to buy and store large quantities of raw material
and to have cloth lying 'idle' in the finishing processes and ;
London. Thus he could keep up continuous production, uninte
rupted by lack of sufficient capital, so that although he might hav
only two looms, the same number as the weaver, he could afford 1
keep them in continuous use, and perhaps by this means to emplc
a journeyman to work a third loom. Unlike many of the crafts (
Tudor Worcester, the textile industry demanded the use of cor
siderable quantities of capital.

Despite the general independence of production at every level, th
domestic system was present in some cases. There are however onl
seven examples of weavers who are clearly employed at home b
clothiers, or in which clothiers own looms stationed in weaver
houses. There are two cases, in 1576 and 1611, of a single loom i
each case being owned by a clothier but placed in a weaver's hous
In 1588 there occurs an example of a weaver working in his hor
on a cloth owned by a clothier and in the same year another clothic
had four cloths being manufactured for him by outside weaver
Another will of 1586 mentions cloth "at the weavers" while i
1611 and 1617 two clothiers have cloth on another weaver's loor
or mention cloth "at the weavers". The only other evidence of th
absorption of all stages of production by the clothier, apart from th
spinners mentioned above, is a clothier who had a dyer and a
"overseer" working for him in 1520 and one in 1562 who appeal
to have had a fulling mill, for he mentions "my millman".[22]

Thus the domestic system in any developed form was uncommo
in Worcester: one must contrast these isolated cases quoted abov
with the hundreds of other records of textile producers which sho
no abatement of their independent operation. The clothier relie
for expansion above the level achieved by the humble weaver not s
much on the extension of his workforce as on the continuous use (
his own quite modest number of looms, a continuum based on th
deployment of quite large amounts of capital. Another major factc
was that the clothier could act as a middleman for the sale of th
independent weaver's cloth. There is one documented case of
clothier – and a rich one at that – selling cloth to other clothiers i
the city.[23]

The vast majority of Worcester cloths were sold in London: th
smaller producer could not have afforded to wait for his cloth t

ɔ there and the proceeds to return – the great clothier must have
ɔught his cloth from him and sent it to London with his own.
'ertainly there is no evidence of full-time middlemen or London
ealers operating in the city. This practice may well account for
ɔme of the very considerable fortunes made by men who owned
nly a small number of looms and have no other conspicuous source
f income.

The wealth of these clothiers is attested by their inventories. Most
ɔtalled between £100 and £200, a very considerable financial
:atus by Worcester standards, and a few had amassed property
ɔorth between £500 and £1,000. These very rich ones were often
1ose operating some restricted version of the domestic system. Their
ɔuses were opulently appointed. When John Wilde died in 1611
is property was valued at over £600; his house had 15 well-
urnished rooms and his clothing was worth nearly £19, with ruffs,
llk garters, nightcaps and handkerchiefs. Most citizens would be
1cky to own a wardrobe worth 10s. at this time. Thomas Wilde,
lthough retired from active business before his death, had made his
ɔrtune as a clothier, buying the medieval hospital, the Command-
ry, and converting it into a dwelling-house which would have been
credit to any country gentleman. His inventory was worth £700,
is house ran to 31 rooms, the furniture reflected his solid opulence,
ɔictures and maps decorated the walls, while his personal clothing
ɔas valued at £10 and in one room lay 20 feather beds, those
tatus symbols of early modern England.[24]

After the weaving process had been completed the cloth was sent
ɔn to the fuller, usually called a 'walker' in Worcester. Here it was
hickened, sheared and cleaned so that it was only necessary to dye it
fterwards to prepare it for the customer. The walkers were a dis-
inct trade with their individual fortunes depending on whether they
emained the processors of other producers' cloth or branched out
nore widely in the cloth industry. Those who were solely cloth
inishers were no richer than the small weavers, but those who
ɔranched out into the production of cloth under their own initiative
njoyed a financial status very like that of the average clothier. The
ɔalue of the tools and equipment involved in this craft was very
mall, rarely exceeding £2. Many leased racks in gardens and vacant
ɔlots in and around the city, especially in the area of gardens where
he Black Friars had once stood against the northern wall; these
ɔacks were wooden frames on which the cloth was hung to dry in

the open air after the fulling process had been completed. Th
normal practice seems to have been for the weaver or clothier t
bring his cloth to the fuller, who carried out his duties and the
returned the cloth to its maker – the fuller retained his independenc
and very rarely became the direct employee of the clothier. Th
walker, no matter how humble, was a relatively free agent.

Some walkers may well have carried out the fulling process com
pletely on their own premises, but by the later Middle Ages it wa
customary to use water-driven machinery to beat the cloth to mat
it together. The location of the fulling mills used by the Worceste
industry is difficult to determine but normally it seems that mills i
the countryside were used, despite the legislation of 1555 and 155
forbidding the use of rural mills for processes which could be carrie
on within the city.[25] This is another example of municipal policy i
the difficult middle years of the century, aimed at maximizing
employment for the citizens by discouraging rural competition o
any kind.

There is firm documentary evidence for the use of the fulling
mill at Hartlebury which had existed on the bishop's manor since th
thirteenth century. A leading clothier bequeathed money in 161
for improving the landing stage there "that their cloths may b
landed clean". A single boat, known as the "cloth barge", was use
to take the textiles up the Severn to the mill. The use of the barge or
Sundays was an intermittent source of concern to the corporation
beginning in 1565, and the walkers were prosecuted by the ecclesi
astical authorities for working on Sundays more often than an
other trade in the earlier seventeenth century, usually in connection
with the barge.[26]

But the process of finishing cloth was not the only activity of the
walkers. A number of them had supplies of hemp in their houses and
one had a fully equipped workshop for making rope; why thi
should be associated with the walker's trade is not clear.[27] The
richest walkers were involved in the actual manufacture of the cloth
but in a fashion which is not entirely obvious. Only two of them
actually owned looms and were making cloth themselves like any
clothier.[28] Far more common, especially from the 1570s onwards,
were walkers who owned only stocks of wool and yarn and assorted
pieces of cloth. Only one is stated to have cloth "at the weavers" but
it is obvious in at least half a dozen cases that these men must have
been operating some modified form of the domestic system, since

omeone else was clearly doing the weaving for them. Two of them
lso ran dyeing businesses but it was quite natural for these two
inishing processes to be brought under single ownership.[29] Thus
he walkers were making inroads into the independence of the
veaver, but like the clothier, this was only achieved in a small
1umber of cases, at least before 1620. In most respects the walker
,imply processed the cloth its owners brought him.

The final finishing stage was that of dyeing. Most of the city's
roadcloth, like that of the rest of the region, was exported without
)eing dyed, as English dyers could not match the technical skill of
hose on the Continent. The dyer's trade in Worcester was not
herefore of great importance, and the numbers involved in it were
,mall, but there was sufficient work available at any one time to
<eep several in a state of moderate affluence. There is some indica-
:ion that the craft was not as prosperous by the end of the sixteenth
:entury as it had been in the middle years. The trade required what
was for the time a very considerable investment in equipment, plant
and raw materials. The workshops of dyers were valued at £20 in
1541, £8 in 1556 and £27 in 1601.[30] Most of this sum was accounted for by the large vats and furnaces required: only the brewers of
the city had more money invested in plant. The dyer also normally
<ept large quantities of wood, dyestuffs and chemicals; Bertram
Cox had in 1556 a shop containing £10 worth of wood and stocks
of madder (a red dye) galls, coppras and alum together valued at over
£19.[31]

The relationships prevailing between the dyer and the other
elements in the cloth trade are complex ones. The normal procedure
seems, as with other stages in the industry, to have been for the
owner of the cloth to bring it to the dyer and collect it from him and
pay him when the work was completed. But in one case a dyer was
owed money by two walkers, suggesting that the walker was taking
responsibility for both of the cloth finishing processes on the
clothier's behalf. There are also two instances in which the trades of
walker and dyer are combined and two other dyers are recorded as
owning stores of wool, yarn or cloth in their homes – in one case
worth £35. These latter men seem to have been manufacturing
cloth by the putting-out system. In another case a clothier has a dyer
as one of his employees.[32] Thus upon the basic system of the dyer as
an independent craftsman is superimposed a typically obscure but
small number of variations, every stage from the dyer as the

entrepreneur responsible for the whole cloth-making process to the dyer completely subordinated to the clothier, all tending to mask the general independence of the average craftsmen.

Cloth was not solely produced by one of the tradesmen described above. There are cases of a wide variety of tradesmen, otherwise unconnected with the textile trade, whose homes contain looms or large stocks of wool or yarn and who were clearly making significant quantities of cloth. A butcher, smith, tailor, glover, brewer, barber, fishmonger and shoemaker are but a selection of them.[33] These appear to be mainly men who had taken up cloth production as a sideline when the industry was at its most prosperous before the crisis of the 1550s, for there are 11 cases of this kind in probate records drawn up before the mid-1560s and only three after this period. The increase in detailed control and regulation of the industry which was so pronounced in these crisis years in the middle of the century may also have tended to discourage dabbling of this kind.

Thus cloth was produced in a complex series of ways, but this complexity should not be allowed to obscure the basic system of a series of independent craftsmen passing the work on to each other through the various stages of manufacture. The various other types of organization outlined above were merely variations on this theme. This great variety of systems of production existing side by side, combined with a basic structure of independent artisans, does in fact seem to have been the norm in the West of England broadcloth industry, for both Devon and Wiltshire had broadly similar patterns of production.[34]

9

The cloth industry

part two

Compared with the complexity of the manufacture of cloth outlined in the last chapter, the marketing of the finished textiles was much more straightforward. The vast majority of the city's cloths was sent to London for sale. A small and dwindling quantity went down the Severn to Bristol, but the capital remained always the centre for the sale of almost all the export-quality production. This is shown by numerous references in inventories to cloth at London as yet unsold. Cloths were sent to London by the regular carrier service – one carrier was owed at his death by three clothiers for the carriage of their cloths there.[1] Although this must have been the principal form of transport employed, clothiers, especially the great ones, undertook their own transport since packcloths (for packhorses) appear in their inventories. One employed a carter and cart driver.[2]

For some clothiers, regular journeys to London to sell their cloth in person were part of their business routine: one clothier bequeathed a coat which he was accustomed to ride to London in, another had a wooden chest "at the Castle in Wood Street" in London as if he were a sufficiently regular visitor to keep a reserve of property there. Yet another had a London agent who acted for him and who received a bequest for his "pains in selling my cloth".[3] Many of the smaller manufacturers must have sold their cloth to Worcester's larger clothiers, because they could not afford to wait for a sale in

London. In 1564 John English was accused by his fellow clothiers of "harmful dealing" in cloth, apparently by buying up cloth in Worcester and re-selling it in London.[4] Quite what was so objectionable in this is not clear. There is no evidence in the second half of the sixteenth century of anyone from Worcester participating directly in the export trade itself, for they all sold their cloth to wholesalers who then shipped it abroad.

However in the first half of the century there is clear evidence that some Worcester men had become cloth merchants in their own right and were personally engaged in the export trade. By a happy chance the account book of one of these men, William Mucklowe, made in 1511, has been preserved by his family.[5] Mucklowe is described elsewhere as a mercer, and this was certainly one of his commercial roles, but his principal business was the sale of high-quality broadcloth in the Low Countries. Since he was based in Worcester it seems inevitable that he was exporting Worcester cloth, after first buying it on the spot from the producers, and bringing back imports for his mercer's shop. His accounts are full of mathematical inconsistencies – this one expects – but a general idea of the nature of his activities can be gleaned from them.

They are the accounts of his sales and purchases at two of the Flemish fairs of 1511, the spring market at Bergen-op-Zoom and the more important summer fair at Antwerp. Mucklowe took 478 cloths to these fairs, mostly shortcloths, and failed to sell nearly 100 of them. Those cloths he did sell were disposed of in 39 separate transactions, most of them of moderate size, and to men who came mostly from Antwerp but occasionally from Brussels. In the smaller transactions cash was normally paid, and in the rest a deposit of between a quarter and a half of the full price was paid and the remainder promised for the next market. From the fairs Mucklowe received £786 in cash and £147 in barter – goods he needed to import to England. There remained the sum of £814 due to be paid to him at the next fair, and against this he could set the £246 received from debts contracted in the same way previously. This gave him on paper a total income of just over £2,000 and of this £1,200 was actually to hand. The scale of Mucklowe's business was thus large, for this represented only six months' work, albeit the busiest half of the year, and he was probably personally responsible for something of the order of 2 per cent of London's total cloth exports.[6]

The money he made in the Low Countries he sent back to England as either cash, bills, or imported goods. In this case he transferred £400 to London and there paid back debts and interest of nearly £500 in addition; over £360 was spent in Flanders on a wide range of mercery which ran through cloth in large quantities, linens and canvases from the Low Countries themselves, velvets, satins and damasks from the Mediterranean and Near East; grocery played an important part with nearly two tons of sugar, plus pepper and other spices, treacle and ginger. Haberdashery followed, with pins and needles, bells and girdles, pouches and thread, brushes, swan feathers, spectacles, wire, knives, leather buckets, brown paper and what appear to be two small cannon. This collection covered virtually all the common stock of the Worcester mercer-grocer-haberdasher, although spices were a little under-represented. All these goods were shipped back to London, spread among six ships for safety.

Unfortunately we do not know what Mucklowe's profit was, for we are not told what he originally paid for his cloth or what income he managed to get from his imported mercery. What is clear is that Mucklowe must have exported in one year a large proportion of the total production of the city's looms. How he originally arrived at this dominant position in Worcester's economy is a matter for conjecture – he may have begun as a clothier, been drawn into direct exporting and then into mercery as a way of exploiting his access to the market of origin of much of the mercer's stock; on the other hand, and this seems rather more likely, he may have begun as a mercer and from the large profits derived from this trade and his contacts with both Worcester clothiers and London wholesale mercer-cloth exporters, from whom he would have bought his stock, he may have risen to act as a middleman for the former and a colleague for the latter.

Whatever his career, Mucklowe was a phenomenon of considerable importance in Worcester. When he died in 1529 his inventory totalled £830, despite the fact that he had already retired from active trade.[7] By Worcester standards, especially at this early date, this was a very impressive fortune. He was bailiff of Worcester on three occasions between 1499 and 1517 and was influential enough in 1528 to be claiming patronage from the Crown on the grounds of his service to it and to Wolsey: perhaps he had been engaged on diplomatic work in Flanders.[8] Mucklowe may well have been the dominant force in the sale of Worcester cloth in his lifetime, but after his death there is no evidence that any other citizen carried on his work – his own family became lesser gentry. The little commercial empire which he had built up – he was an immigrant to the city from a rural yeoman family – died with him. In any case it is unlikely that he could have withstood for long the pressures which were making London, and so Londoners, the sole outlet for the city's broadcloth. Mucklowe's own relations with London are obscure: he was certainly working closely with the London mercer-cloth exporters but there is no evidence that he ever belonged to any company or commercial organization in the capital. However it seems almost certain that he would have used the port of London.

Beside this uniquely well-documented example there are other indications that Worcester people were exporting cloth themselves. One other citizen called himself a "merchant" in his will of 1518, and he may well have been functioning like Mucklowe. The wills of two London members of the Mercers' Company, which was largely concerned with exporting broadcloth, are indicative: the first, dated 1512, is that of John Robbins, who was also a wool exporter, and mentions a house owned in Worcester beside making a bequest to the cathedral; the second was made by John Thomas, a very rich London mercer, who died at much the same time and made generous charitable bequests to Worcester and also left quite large sums to two Worcester weavers and a fuller: the context suggests that these Worcester cloth craftsmen were his employees.[9] Robbins may well have moved from Worcester to London and severed most of his links with the city, but Thomas seems to have been still running his clothier's business in Worcester while exporting from London.

The close relationship between the Mercer's Company and the export trade renders it highly probable that these men were acting in a capacity similar to that of Mucklowe but had moved their centre of operations to London instead of remaining Worcester-based as Mucklowe did, probably to his disadvantage. The essential point is that these were Worcester men exporting Worcester cloth, and that they were all operating in the first half of the sixteenth century. After their time, Londoners took complete control over this stage of the industry, probably due to the great commercial advantages of a base in the capital – it is a general feature of the commercial history of the time that London was greatly strengthening its hold over the trade of wide areas of the provinces which had recently been more independent. A contributory factor must have been the boom conditions prevailing earlier in the sixteenth century which would have supplied Worcester businessmen with capital on a more generous scale than was possible in later years.

We have seen how important the cloth industry was to the economic well-being of Worcester. Unfortunately it was a trade subject both to frequent fluctuations in activity, i.e. to booms and slumps, and to a long-term decline between the sixteenth and eighteenth centuries. How did these factors affect the industry in Worcester? The first depression of which there is evidence took place in the later 1550s. In 1557 the corporation complained to the central government that 200 looms were idle and that the number of unemployed and their dependants had reached the alarming total of 1,000.[10] This seems to have been a sober and accurate estimate, for the situation was serious enough not require the usual exaggeration, while the quoted number of unemployed seems to tally well with a precise survey already made by the corporation. This means that over 20 per cent of the inhabitants were in serious difficulties.

The explanation for this slump advanced at the time was that the statute of 1551 required Worcester cloth to be of a higher quality than the rest of the West of England broadcloths; this is dealt with below. This grievance was soon remedied and the position, judging by the absence of complaint or serious unemployment, seems to have improved. In the 1570s trade was described as "not so good as it hath been" and it was alleged that the industry was undergoing a long-term decline: in living memory the number of looms in use had fallen from 380 to 160.[11] The source for this second statement is a highly rhetorical one, unreliable in other respects from a numerical point of view, but the general impression may well be a fair one. In the early seventeenth century matters seem to have worsened. In 1622 the city was said to be seriously impoverished due to its reliance on the textile trade, and there are a number of other indications of difficulty about this time.[12]

These references are not really very satisfactory: pleas of disastrous impoverishment and impending ruin are very common in this period in complaints to the central government from all kinds of sectional interests. Fortunately we have two series of statistics which give a better idea of the state of the industry. The first of these is the annual number of new apprentices taken on by weavers and clothiers (figure 17). It seems a legitimate presumption that these reflect the vitality and prospects of the industry at the time. It is unfortunate that these

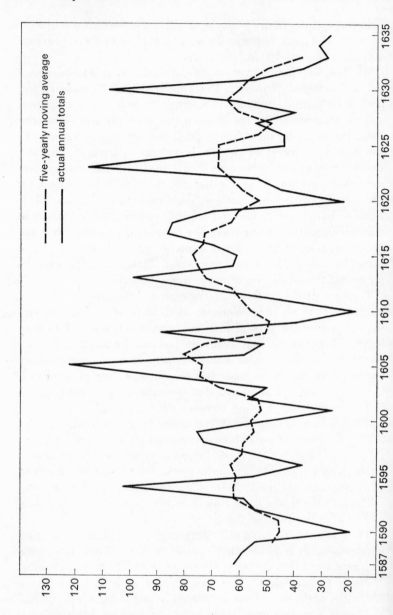

17 Cloth manufacturers' new apprentices: actual annual totals and five-yearly moving averages, 1587–1635.

records do not begin until 1587–8 and end in 1635: however they are probably highly accurate as the apprenticeship regulations were strictly enforced. The graph shows how these figures give a good indication of what was happening, although there is a wide variation from year to year which may reflect the extremely sensitive nature of the industry to trade cycles.

The broad pattern seems to be one of healthy recovery in the 1590s followed by a slight recession at the turn of the century and a quick recovery. The 1610s saw a more stable level higher than any sustained for any considerable period of time before and although the earlier 1620s see a more unsettled time, they do not show the serious situation indicated by other sources. A really serious decline sets in in the mid-1620s and was very serious by the mid-1630s: because the series ends here we do not know how this particular depression, more serious than any other indicated here, ended. The picture shown here is definitely not one of steady decline: viewed in a long-term perspective the number of apprentices taken on did not vary much over the whole period, although it is subject to short term variations. If anything, there is an upward trend visible over the period up to 1625. However, while for the cloth industry merely to hold its own was a considerable achievement in the conditions of the time, in view of the ever-increasing population of the city it is clear that since the number of new apprentices remains stable, the proportion of the inhabitants engaged in the textile industry must have shrunk, and new forms of employment would have had to be found.

The other series of statistics is derived from the Hallkeeper's accounts indicating the amount of wool sold in the city market (figure 18). If these figures are at all reliable, it seems justified to assume that the wool market reflects demand for raw material and so the condition of the industry. The figures indicate that the late 1540s were very slack, followed by a very significant improvement in the 1550s, which continued until the early 1560s. This was marked by great violence in fluctuation, as the very high wool sales for 1553–4 and 1559 indicate. After the early 1560s a period of decline and stagnation set in which reached its peak in the mid and later 1570s. A striking recovery took place in about 1590, when the volume of wool sold may well have nearly doubled, but this was falling away again by 1600. The accounts for the early seventeenth century are missing: but it is encouraging to see the trends in these

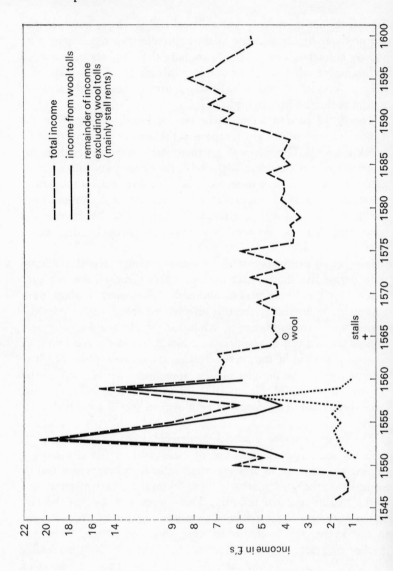

18 Hallkeeper's accounts: sources of income 1546–1600.

statistics confirming those in the apprenticeship figures for the period in which they overlap.

The trouble of the 1550s, apparently due as much to violent fluctuation in output as to a simple slump, can be confirmed from documentary sources, while the long static period which followed it is a confirmation of the quoted contemporary observations that a long-term, but mild, recession was going on. Thus the period 1546–90 was one, if not of actual slump, at least of static output and adaptation to changed conditions. It is also perhaps significant to note that the period of maximum population growth in the city and its region coincides with this static period in its principal source of employment and wealth. This is the background against which much of Worcester's history must be seen.

What of the cloth industry in the first half of the sixteenth century? If it had followed the national trend, it would have been a boom period, in which the town would have prospered greatly. There is evidence of this prosperity in wills – new houses being built for example – but there is no possible way of arriving at anything more than this general impression of affluence, as the climax of a rising late-medieval tide. It is quite possible that the industry had a more highly capitalist organization at this time – for instance the city government was forced to legislate against cloth producers' employees being paid in truck and not in money, but the surviving documentary evidence is simply too slight for any firm conclusions to be drawn.[13]

The Worcester cloth industry was regulated and controlled at three different levels – by the central government, by the city government, and by the guilds and companies concerned in it. The principal Act of Parliament which affected the industry was that of 1533.[14] This stated that the urban cloth industry of Worcestershire was being severely damaged by competition from the countryside and that in future only in the city of Worcester and the market towns of Evesham, Droitwich, Kidderminster and Bromsgrove might cloth-making be practised. The very considerable effect of this statute is considered below. A statute of 1551, which regulated the cloth industry on a national scale in an attempt to stave off a slump by enforced quality standards, prescribed that "long Worcesters" and "short Worcesters" should be considerably heavier for the same given area of cloth than the rest of the western broadcloth producing area, Gloucestershire and Wiltshire.[15]

This measure aroused considerable protest from Worcester, which found itself out-priced and so capable of competing only in the small, very high-quality market: unemployment, it claimed, had become very serious for this reason. The only alternative was to break the quality regulations, and one Worcester clothier was prosecuted by the Crown in 1555 for selling cloth in London which was slightly too light. The corporation sent deputations to the Privy Council on three occasions between 1555 and 1557, at considerable expense, an indication of the seriousness with which it viewed the situation. Their efforts were successful and in 1557 another Act modified the imbalance by reducing the weight of the long Worcesters, although it also lowered the weight of their competitors.[16] This seems to have satisfied the city, which was at least assured of producing the highest quality of all the West of England broadcloths, and may in any case have blamed the 1551 Act for a depression due to more fundamental causes. This Act brought to an end specific parliamentary control of Worcester's industry.

The city authorities were equally aware of the need to regulate the manufacture in the middle of the century. Much of this regulation was the result of the relevant national statutes: the corporation appointed committees to examine them and to draw up the requisite local measures. Thus in 1557 official searchers were appointed to examine all cloths. The walker was obliged to bring all his cloths to the Guildhall to be checked when still wet and unshrunk, and the searchers had full authority to enter the houses of both weavers and walkers to ensure that their equipment was of a proper standard. The 1557 Act which was, as has been seen, partly designed to help the city, was received favourably, and a new committee was set up. Cloths were now to be brought by the walker to the Guildhall to be checked both when wet and when dry, but inspection could be carried out on his own premises if he possessed accurate weights and measures. In 1562 clothiers were forbidden to put their distinguishing mark on the cloth produced by anyone outside the city – a measure to keep up the quality of the city's cloth and also an indication that Worcester clothiers may have been acting as middlemen in buying up rural cloth. Lastly in 1563 regulations were drawn up to ensure that weavers used correct techniques to produce cloth of adequate length.[17]

The city's regulations were supported by prosecutions of offenders. A weaver who put inferior quality wool in the middle of his cloth and good quality along the edges (a common device at the time) was punished in 1561. In 1564 a clothworker who had been improperly apprenticed but was working independently was prosecuted and suspended for seven years.[18]

The point behind all this legislation was that the slump of the 1550s had been partially blamed on the poor quality of English cloth; Worcester more than any other area depended on the preservation of its reputation for very high quality. It is significant that only one of these many regulations ever mentions the Company of Weavers – the matter was of such crucial importance that it was the concern of the city government, not a mere craft organization. The legislation seems to have been effective, for after 1563 there is no more: the task of creating machinery for the strict enforcement of minimum quality standards had been completed.

Much of the legislation which controlled the urban cloth industry has been criticized as restrictive in outlook, designed to limit production, keep up prices and exclude the newcomer. This may possibly be true in some cases; in Worcester its object was to assist the recovery of the industry, and to stabilize and expand sales. The control of quality through inspection and the apprenticeship system was the only sure way to help the industry. Control and regulation was a matter of maintaining high quality, not one of restriction or dampening enterprise.

Much of the routine control of textile production was left to the craft organization itself. There appear to have been separate guilds or companies for the separate trades within the industry throughout most of the sixteenth century, although their earlier history is most obscure. In 1575 the clothiers vainly petitioned for a new charter, and in 1590 the weavers, walkers and clothiers were combined together by royal charter to produce a single company, the Clothiers', which thus combined all the important trades concerned.[19] The motive for this may have been a desire for fully co-ordinated control, especially as this period saw a general diversification of enterprise within the trade, with, for instance, walkers acting as clothiers.

The charter of 1590 gives valuable information on the organization of this company. It states that a new organization was required because of the inefficiency of the old system; the new company was to be administered by a master and four wardens, elected annually, and a group of thirty "Assistants". These together would make regulations and punish offenders, generally controlling and supervising the industry, and in particular the apprenticeship system. An attempt was made to see that all interests were fairly represented: of the men nominated as the first governing body, two of the wardens were weavers and two walkers, while the assistants consisted of 18 weavers, 8 walkers and 4 clothiers. If in practice the great clothier came to dominate the craft, the organization of the Clothiers' Company was designed to frustrate this trend.

The company was chiefly concerned with the control of apprentices and journeymen. It enforced the seven-year term with painstaking care, and often obliged an apprentice to work out his full term, even if only a few weeks remained. There seems to have been a good deal of exchange of apprentices between masters, not all due to death or retirement, and these were carefully recorded by the company.[20] The journeymen were also carefully controlled, their position protected against the use of apprentice labour and of strangers from outside the town. The company allowed stranger journeymen to work, but only on payment of a fee: 18 were licensed in 1588.[21] The journeymen certainly resented this manipulation by their employers and in 1605 attempted to form their own organization, but the Clothiers petitioned the Crown to prevent them breaking away. In 1619 they were agitating again, this time for better wages.[22] The provocation for this outbreak of unrest against the employers seems to have been prosperity, not depression: the journeymen wanted to share in the profits of the recovery which began in the 1590s.

The company administered at least four revolving loan funds left as charities. These amounted in total to at least £200 and were available to men setting up on their own for the first time. The system was a valuable one, especially since capital was so much more vital in this trade than in most others.[23]

Thus the cloth industry was regulated at all levels, but there is little evidence that it was excessively self-interested or opposed to enterprise. The object in most cases was to assure sales by the maintenance of high quality. There is little evidence of any reason why the urban industry should have been excessively handicapped, at least in the goods in which Worcester specialized. Regulations helped rather than hindered the city's economy.

The issue of the rise of rural industry and rural competition is a familiar theme in the literature of the early textile industry. Generally the growth of a cloth industry in the countryside was a death blow to urban cloth production. Yet Worcester prospered, all circumstances considered, while despite the growth of rural weavers during the sixteenth century, the countryside never presented any effective competition. There are a number of references to the existence of rural competition – for instance the use by Worcester clothiers of spinners or other workpeople from outside the city was discouraged in 1466 and 1558.[24] Undoubtedly a critical factor was the Worcestershire Cloth Act of 1533, referred to above. By strictly limiting the production of cloth to Worcester and four other market towns it could not eradicate the country weaver altogether – and it certainly did not – but it did create an atmosphere of disapproval and ensured that conspicuous offenders, such as any nascent group of rural clothiers, could be suppressed. The Worcester clothiers certainly considered that the Act was the basis of their prosperity, for when in 1575 the corporation was attempting to prove that a particular clothier was a citizen although he denied it, its main argument was that his family had grown rich on the basis of the protection which the Act gave to citizen clothiers.[25]

Despite the city's faith in the advantages accruing from this Act, mere prohibition is slight evidence. But the clothiers fined in London in 1561–2, mentioned above, were all from the city: not a single one came from outside it in the county. However in 1561 a man from Hartlebury was fined £80 for making 40 cloths outside a market town.[26] The significant fact here is that the prosecution was brought, showing that the regulations were being enforced.

There is little evidence of the existence of any major cloth producers in any part of the county including the market towns. Even ignoring the looser use of the term 'clothier' in the early seventeenth century, few exist in wills and inventories of the period. Such major cloth producers as there are come from the other market towns prescribed in the 1533 Act. In Bromsgrove and Kidderminster clothiers produced mainly narrow cloths, not the broadcloth which would compete with Worcester.

A survey of 47 country and small-town weavers' inventories for the period 1552–1600 and 14 for 1615–20 shows that most of them were not well off by Worcester standards. Their stock of materials was slight, their looms, although often three or four in number, were normally narrow ones. Very few indeed had any cloth actually in their houses when the inventory was made – this reflects the restricted nature of their business and perhaps some reliance on clothiers from the market towns or from Worcester. The majority were producing narrow cloth: this meant that they were in no way competing with the urban industry. Worcester specialized in high-quality broadcloth which these country weavers were unable to produce, for lack of both equipment and capital resources. They were making low-quality cloth, linen as well as woollen, for local consumption.

However the number of weavers in the countryside did clearly increase. Impressive evidence has been produced of a dramatic increase in the number of rural as compared with urban weavers in the later sixteenth and earlier seventeenth centuries.[27] This is certainly true on the basis of the evidence supplied, but this may merely reflect an increase in specialization and professionalization. Nearly all the rural weavers whose inventories were examined had quite considerable stocks of animals and were farming on a modest scale. A minor shift in the balance of emphasis, perhaps an increase in the amount of effort put into weaving, could result in an apparently striking increase in the number of weavers. Thus, whether as a result of the 1533 Act or not, the rural weavers were not competing with the city industry in either products or markets: the city reigned supreme.

Worcester's economy therefore rested on the basis of the production of broadcloth of quantity and quality. Half of her citizens were engaged in the industry, which was a source of great wealth to a few and of a moderately high standard of living to many. It did not show any well-developed form of the domestic system, but rested on the voluntary co-operation of a large number of independent artisans. It was closely regulated but with the object of raising quality not stifling enterprise. It was untroubled by rural competition. Only the eventual decline of the export market for its particular specialized product led to the eventual ending of the industry in Worcester during the eighteenth century.

The principal activities of the textile industry have already been covered, but they may be joined by a number of other trades directly connected or associated with the main cloth manufacturers. The capper occupied a position between the manufacturing and distributive trades. Normally he both manufactured headgear and sold finished products imported from elsewhere. There is only one surviving capper's inventory after the 1560s and this one is very impoverished so it seems that the highly specialized capping industry of Bewdley and Kidderminster had destroyed the trade in the other towns of the region, at least as a manufacturing occupation.[28]

A craftsman ancillary to the cloth manufacturer was the card-maker, who made the combs used to untangle the separate fibres of wool before it was spun. The demand for these was slight and the number of recorded cardmakers in the city was small. Normally they had in their modest houses supplies of the main raw materials, boards, leather and wire. All these items came down the river from northern Worcestershire, which was the city's basic supply for all these materials: probably there was very serious competition from cardmakers nearer the sources of raw material in the countryside.

Lastly, the knitting of stockings was an occupation for some of the very poor. One unmarried woman left in 1575, in her two-roomed house, 11 pairs of knitted stockings and four knitted night-caps, plus a little wool. In 1591 all knitters of stockings were called before the bailiffs to check on their honesty because some of them had been acting as receivers of stolen yarn – the presumption here was that, like spinning, this was an occupation followed by the very poor. A single hosier's inventory is preserved, but this is most uninformative.[29]

A single carpet-weaver was recorded in 1591 with completed carpets and coverlets in his "ware shop". There must have been considerable demand for these furnishing fabrics in the city, judging by the contents of many of the houses, but the native manufacture seems to have declined since the later fifteenth century when the carpet-weavers seem to have been an important craft. Probably the specialized competition of Kidderminster, already severe by the later sixteenth century, was crucial here.[30] Many of the minor textile trades seem to have been discouraged from growing in the city by the great specialization in broadcloth. Evesham, for example, was a centre of silk-weaving from an early date while Worcester took no part in it as yet. The adverse effects of this were not really felt until the cloth industry went into more serious decline in the later seventeenth century; then the lack of any industry which could be stimulated to compensate for the decline in broadcloth was deeply felt for a time.

10

Shopkeeper-artisans

The majority of Worcester's citizens were concerned in the production of goods, but only the cloth trades could really be called
industrial, for only there were the producing and retailing elements
separated. Most other people made things and sold them too, so we
must now examine the rest of the trades which maintained a large
proportion of the city's inhabitants. The small artisan-retailer was the
basis of most urban economies, and perhaps the largest group involved here is that which depended on the production and processing
of leather and goods made from leather, a vital commodity for a
multitude of purposes in early modern England, and a group of
trades which is often under-rated in studies of the subject. It is
possible to divide the trades involved roughly into two groups, those
which processed the skins into leather and those making up the
leather into finished goods.

Of the leather producers, the tanner is the most important. The
tanner received raw hides and processed them, chiefly by steeping
them in chemicals, until they could be sold to be made up into
leather articles. At least 16 tanners occur in the probate records but
there is a wide variety in their wealth. Some were extremely rich –
Richard Badland's inventory was valued at £969 while another
tanner bequeathed over £500 in his will, and was employing
three apprentices and three male employees, a large working force
by Worcester standards.[1] Both these men stood among the very
wealthiest of their generation, but they were exceptional: the normal

anner's inventory varied from £60 to £90, a comfortable amount
)ut not an outstanding one.

The business of tanning required a good deal of capital since the
engthy process necessitated having a great many hides at various
stages of completion in order that a steady supply should be available
'or sale. One tanner in 1576 had £46 worth of hides and leather in
his possession out of a total inventory value of £91, another £42
worth out of £79, another £82 out of a total of £136.[2] Tanning
was one of the few trades in Worcester where investment of capital
on this scale was necessary. The value of the equipment was not
high. The contents of one tan-house, which amounted in 1556 to
17 vats, 3 lime pits and other plant, was valued at under £5.[3] Some
tanners had much less than this invested in equipment, which was
in any case fairly simple. The other principal raw material required
was oak bark, the source of the tannin in which the hides and skins
were steeped. Normally large stocks of this vital commodity were
kept. Bark had to be supplied from the countryside and a tanner in
one instance owned a large amount still to be brought from a
distance; in another case a tanner bequeathed a contractual arrangement for the supply of bark.[4] It was ground up in a 'bark mill',
normally of little value, but occasionally housed in its own building,
the 'mill-house'.

The tanner usually sold his leather as it lay in the tan-house, for
there is only one case of one running a shop with leather for sale in
it.[5] The tanner's main customers were shoemakers – this is shown
by the description of the leather in preparation, which was
often described as shoemaker's leather, and presumably some of the
thicker hide went into soles and boots too. Shoemakers, and occasionally saddlers, figure prominently among tanners' debtors. Thus the
tanner's was a trade which required relatively high capital investment but repaid it on a moderate scale. Despite some outstanding
exceptions, the draper or mercer could have the same sum invested
in his business and yet be considerably more prosperous. The
Worcester tanners were chiefly concentrated in the parish of St
Clements, beside the river and about as far from the centre of the
city as was possible.

Tanning was by no means necessarily an urban occupation and
there was considerable distribution of the industry throughout the
countryside and smaller towns of the shire, but there is no evidence
that this balance was altering in any way.[6] Probably, although

distance from some raw materials handicapped the city tanners, they benefited from proximity to the market and especially to the butchers who would be important suppliers of hides, and they would also have access to the cargoes of skins which came down the river from the north. But as will be seen below, the country tanners still supplied much leather to the city.

The city was notably lacking in processors of the more supple leathers, the curriers and whittawers: only a single currier is recorded and he was operating on a small scale; the absence of this branch of the trade is difficult to explain.[7]

Those engaged in making up and selling leather articles form a large group. Of these the shoemakers were numerically the most important. In terms of wealth however the shoemaker was one of the most humble of all the city's independent tradesmen. The great majority of their inventories were valued at about £5 in the 1550s rising to about £10 in the early seventeenth century. Between a quarter and a half of these totals was normally made up by his stock of made shoes, with tools normally being valued at only a few shillings. The range of goods for sale was very limited, the normal categories being men's, women's, and children's shoes and a small number of boots. Although the shoemaker was thus living only a short way above subsistence level, a small number were able to make themselves very respectably wealthy: one in 1574 was worth over £115 and had a total shop stock of made-up articles and skins of about £34, but this was quite exceptional.[8]

If a shoemaker rose above the average low level of wealth he did so by diversifying his activities, as in the case of one who had taken up farming on a small scale, another who owned a mill and was processing malt, one whose brewing business was on a far larger scale than his shoemaking, or still another who owned a weaving loom.[9] Such diversification seems to have been very common among the leather trades as a whole: it is clear that this particular occupation by itself provided little opportunity for financial advancement and many were forced to take on more than one trade to make any progress.

The shoemakers seem never to have produced their own leather, and they bought their supplies from the tanner; judging by their debt statements many bought from tanners from the countryside as much as from the city suppliers.

Only one cobbler's inventory has been preserved and this was very modest with a two-roomed house with its contents valued at £3 18s. 4d.[10] Probably most cobblers, with even fewer opportunities than the shoemakers, were so poor that they left no will.

The corvisor's trade also was closely allied to that of the shoemaker. It should have covered the production of a much wider range of leather goods than the shoemaker's but there is little evidence that it did in fact do so. Where the contents of shops are listed they appear to be mostly boots and shoes. However, the corvisor must have extended his activities somewhat beyond making shoes, for the normal inventory is substantially wealthier than the shoemaker's, often between £20 and £40. Possibly they were also currying leather – the absence of this trade has been observed above – for one corvisor was currying not only his own leather but leather for sale.[11]

Only three glover's inventories occur: this is surprising, for in the eighteenth and nineteenth centuries gloving became one of the principal industries of the town, replacing the position cloth had once held, and the manufacture remains important at the present day. There is no sign of this concentration before the Civil War, and although the evidence is very scanty, there seems to have been a wide variation in the profitability of the trade. One inventory was valued at only £6, but another glover at the same time owned five houses, had skins and purses as well as gloves in his shop, was processing his own skins into leather by currying rather than tanning, and was also producing cloth.[12]

The saddlers form the last trade in this group. Like the glover, the saddler ranged from the adequately provided to the well off – none was either as poor as the shoemaker or strikingly rich. However, there seems here too to have been an appreciable amount of diversification, especially into participation in the cloth industry or in brewing; the wealthier saddler seems to have been rarely concerned solely in his own trade. In any case the saddler had more opportunity for making money through the fact that his customers were normally the wealthier classes in town and country – one list of debts includes an impressive sprinkling of the names of near-by gentry families, and any trader who could supply this market normally prospered more than his fellows.[13] The saddler, like the others, does not seem to have extended his stock of goods very much; even a wealthy one only sold spurs in addition to saddles and their associated equipment.

The leather industry was as susceptible as any to the regulation of authority, whether central or local. The leather searchers were appointed every year with the other corporation officials, and the task of the normal regulation of the industry seems to have fallen to them and to the central government, which passed a very comprehensive act in 1563 under which the tanners of Worcester were being prosecuted in 1582.[14] Any faulty leather suspected by the searchers was referred to a jury – one in 1602 was composed of three tanners and three shoemakers – who on the basis of their expert knowledge judged whether the complaint was well-founded.[15] The preserved accounts of these leather trials principally concern leather produced by non-resident tanners and there is reason to suppose that the searchers and juries were a good deal less enthusiastic to proceed against their fellow citizens. In 1565 a rare prosecution of tanners from the city itself was initiated by "Parker the informer" – presumably a common informer – and not the city or trade officials.[16]

The corporation was also responsible for the regulation of the city's leather market. This was held in the Guildhall and detailed regulations were produced for the control of strangers bringing leather to it. It is obvious from this, and from the permission granted to foreign shoemakers to buy from foreign tanners, that the city was an important market for the exchange of leather, not only for the supply of the city but also for shoemakers outside it.[17] This is confirmed by the origins of leather seized because it was faulty – Great Malvern, Clifton-on-Teme, and even Shrewsbury appear here.[18] Reference has already been made to the very considerable trade in skins and leather along the Severn. The corporation was also called upon to arbitrate between the various branches of the leather industry in 1572–4. The company of shoemakers and corvisors complained that a number of cobblers had set up in business without being freemen, a contravention of the city's basic rule that no one might carry out any form of trade on his own account without being formally admitted to the freedom.[19] But the cobblers, who must have been a new trade previously monopolized by the shoemakers, were only one of a number of loosely organized or new trades which tried to evade the necessity of acquiring citizenship and through this greater subservience to the corporation.

The next main division of Worcester's producer-retailers is the metal trades, and of these the most important was the smith. In terms of wealth the smiths break down into two clear groups of

about equal size. One was distinctly poor, with inventories worth
£5 or a little more. The other group was of well above average
wealth, its inventories being worth at least £25 and up to £50 or
more. There were very few who fell between the two divisions. The
poor group seems to have been principally occupied with shoeing
horses and other simple repair tasks – one was owed money for
mending a church bell-clapper.[20] Their stocks of tools and iron
were very limited.

The more wealthy group were acting as ironmongers and manufacturers of a wide range of small iron goods, such as hinges, locks,
chains and edge tools. Often they bought their iron in bulk – stocks
were worth up to £10 and their equipment at least £5, compared
with the few shillings of the poor blacksmiths. These wealthy smiths
seem also to have been partly acting purely as retailers, for one owed
a "kendalman" £2 as if he had been buying knives or some similar
product from such an itinerant pedlar as has already been described.[21] Although there is no sign of a decline in the profitability of
the smith's trade, the numbers engaged in it dropped. Between
1558 and 1568 seven smiths died and left probate records, yet between 1570 and 1620 there are only six more. This indicates that
the generation dying off in the 1550s and 1560s was not being replaced on anything like the same scale, and in 1566 the corporation
allowed a smith to enter the city and the freedom on favourable
terms because Worcester was "destitute" of a good smith.[22]

The reason for this decline in the number of smiths is probably
complex. He was the artisan most commonly found in the ordinary
country village, so that only for specialized ironmongery could
these urban smiths extend their customers beyond the citizens and
travellers. In addition a whole range of specialist ferrous-goods producers was growing up in the north Worcestershire–Black Country
–Birmingham area. Against this competition the Worcester smiths
tended to fall off in numbers, although those who remained managed
to keep up their standard of living.

The ironmonger was rare in Worcester, presumably because the
wealthier smiths siphoned off most of his trade, and only one is
recorded. The other main trade concerned in making and selling
iron goods was the cutler, another trade of above-average wealth,
although small in numbers. The contents of their shops show that
making knives was not their principal occupation at all – possibly
the smiths and pedlars were too active here – and instead they

specialized in making swords and daggers. Thus in 1572 one shop contained five dozen dagger blades and four sword blades a against only two dozen knives, and another shop in the early seven teenth century held only swords and daggers.[23] The dagger, if no the sword, was a common article of dress in the city at this time, anc in addition the soldiers which the city and county had so often tc supply and equip must have provided a good market. The sword ir particular must have been bought by the wealthy classes of the country, always the most profitable source of income for the urbar artisan.

Cutlers had retail shops as well as their workshops or forges unlike the smiths who usually employed one room for both smithy and shop. There is no evidence that the cutlers suffered a decline resembling in any way that of the smiths. A single wiredrawer i recorded: he was apparently principally concerned in making fish hooks.[24] One would expect more of this wire-producing industry since wire was required by the cardmakers to supply the cloth trade but it must have been imported from north Worcestershire where the industry was well established.[25]

Other metals were worked besides iron. The pewterer was the most important producer in this group. The inventories of Worcester citizens, especially the better off, show how important was the pro duction of pewter and brass tableware and utensils of every kind - many houses had their butteries stacked high with them, since the use of pottery was uncommon. Although no pewterer was especially wealthy, most were comfortably prosperous. Most of them had a shop where finished goods were sold and also one or more workshop where they were made.

Some establishments were relatively very large – Harry Green left a "warehouse" which must have served as a shop, three general workshops and a casting workshop, all obviously in full use.[26] This was by Worcester standards a very large industrial establishment, especially as Green also had another workshop for casting bells, making a total of five workshops as well as the retail shop. Invest ment in industrial plant too was relatively heavy, involving a large number of moulds for casting the pewter and brass articles – Green had £30 worth of tools and equipment.

The goods sold by the pewterer covered a wide range. They con sisted firstly of goods actually made from pewter – Green's shop contained drinking pots, salts, spoons, bottles, chafing dishes, a

mortar, candlesticks and plates. In addition, the pewterer made and
sold brass goods, especially kettles and pots. This was at least as
important a part of the trade as pewter goods, for these brass con-
tainers were the principal means of boiling and cooking in Worcester
homes. Iron cooking utensils are rarely found, and pottery was
equally uncommon – the average Worcestrian's meal was cooked in
the pewterer's products and often eaten or drunk out of them too.

The city's pewter industry also included the only bell-founder of
whom we have definite proof – bell-founding had been a medieval
industry in the city. Nicholas Green, who died in 1541, ran both a
pewterer's and a bell-founding business, both, judging by the capital
invested in them, of roughly equal importance.[27] When he died he
was owed money by ten sets of parochial church wardens, covering
a wide area of the diocese but excluding Warwickshire. This was
considerably wider than the normal commercial region of Worcester,
and reached from Sedgeley in south Staffordshire to Blockley in
north Gloucestershire and stretched into Herefordshire. In this way
the possession of a highly specialized trade like bell-founding
brought business to the city from beyond its normal range. Green
was also unusually wealthy, with an inventory worth £155. When
his son Harry died in 1569 he had greatly expanded the pewter
business to replace an obvious decline in bell-founding since the
Reformation, but he still kept on a separate "Bell House" with
equipment still clearly in use.[28] The final extinction of this bell-
founding business came by 1571, when Harry Green's widow died.
She was keeping the pewter business going with the help of four
employees but the stock of bell-casting equipment had almost
disappeared.[29]

The goldsmith is the last of these metal-working artisans. The one
clear list of shop goods that survives indicates that goldsmiths in fact
worked principally in silver – two silver barrels, three bowls, two
salt-cellars, 24 spoons and pins, thimbles, rings and clasps – all in
silver, and only seven rings in gold.[30] The plate which is a common
feature of wealthy households and the half-dozen spoons which
appear in many more humble ones, indicate that the use of gold was
quite unusual except in personal jewellery. This particular goldsmith was quite wealthy, with goods worth £115, but others were
far more modest – £55 in 1587 and even £3 in 1551.[31] Thus the
goldsmith was not the very wealthy figure he may once have been
in the medieval past. In 1563 a goldsmith surrendered his freedom

and left the town for lack of work, a most unusual event in an'
trade.[32] Thus the craftsmen working in metals form a very varied
group within the city's economy, important both as producers and a
retailers of what they made, and of very varying economic fortunes

Another small group of tradesmen in Worcester was formed b'
those working on articles made from wood – the turner, and th'
hooper or cooper. The numbers engaged in these trades was ver'
small, but their wealth was above average, although not strikingl'
so, with inventories usually of over £40. The turner, although as th'
name implies principally engaged in working wood on the lathe
seems to have occupied himself with a wide range of products. On'
was making spokes, weaver's shuttles, bow staves, and arrow shaft
as well as his more usual treen ware for the kitchen.[33] The hoope'
or cooper concentrated more on his main activity, the making o'
staves for barrels, but one was making spokes for cart wheels too
Diversification was as common in this trade as it was in others – on'
cooper is described as a dyer, although he had no dyeing equipment
while one of the turners was leasing a mill and lands near the cit'
and owned a fair quantity of malt.[34]

The scarcity of members of these trades is explained by the larg'
quantities of barrel staves and spokes which came down the rive'
ready-made from the Wyre Forest area round Bewdley, often a basi'
cargo for the Worcester boatmen who sold them in the city. The cit'
producers would have great difficulty in competing with this supply
since the forest workers had much lower transport costs for thei'
raw materials. These trades, although a significant element in th'
economy, were kept down in numbers and wealth by the keenness o'
rural competition. This is another illustration of the fact tha'
although the Severn basin brought prosperity to the city in man'
ways, with its relative ease of transport of bulky materials along th'
river, it also exposed Worcester to competition from specialized
workers over an area much wider than would normally affect ai
English city.

Another small group of tradesmen served the needs of thos'
requiring hunting equipment – the bowyer, fletcher and gunsmith
The demand, even from within the city, for hunting equipment wa'
quite considerable; bows and arrows were quite frequentl'
bequeathed in wills. There is no clear indication of any decline ii
these traders during the period under review. The bowyers wer'
very few and we have little information on their activities. Th'

fletcher's trade was larger and one had quite a large establishment, with his shop where he both sold and worked and two upstairs rooms used to store £7 worth of timber and his feathers.[35] His wood was being brought from west Worcestershire and south Shropshire, and he had bought 10,000 feathers from a man from Yardley in the extreme north-east of his own county. The wealth of both bowyers and fletchers in terms of inventoried value seems to have been fairly static and about average.

A partial explanation for this is the replacement of bows and arrows by guns for both sporting and military purposes – in many ways it is surprising that the older trades held on for so long. A gunsmith was present in the city by the Elizabethan period, and died in 1598.[36] His inventory shows him to have been mainly supplying sporting guns – his shop contained five fowling pieces and three "birding" pieces. He also supplied powder flasks and touch-boxes, three "stone-bows" and four crossbows. He must have been in part aiming at the market provided by the raising of soldiers in city and shire, for his stocks of 40 powder flasks and 72 touch-boxes seem much larger than his gun sales would support, and he also owned odd quantities of armour, a sword and some daggers. He was also acting as a locksmith (a skill very similar to his main one) for he had in his shop a stock of seven locks and keys. He must have been an immigrant from the metal-working areas of north Worcestershire, for he owned extensive property in that region. These hunting supply trades are perhaps the best examples of Worcester artisans being supplied with raw materials, often over long distances, from the countryside and selling the manufactured goods back to the country people.

We may next turn to the supply of retail clothing, to the tailor. The main requisite here was skill; tools and equipment were worth a few shillings at the most. The customer must usually have brought his own cloth to the tailor, for in only one case did a tailor possess any stock of cloth himself. In this single instance he had odd lengths of kersey, flannel and canvas, rabbit and kid skins and had in stock three new doublets, one of which was made of "goat skins with blue lace".[37] In all other cases the tailor was either using the customer's own materials, or was buying from the mercer or draper with a specific customer in mind. The opportunities for diversification for the tailors were slight – one raised his fortunes very substantially by branching out into the cloth industry, but this is the only example.[38]

The tailors were a failing trade; the normal inventory value of about £20, quite respectable in the 1550s, was still the same in the early seventeenth century, when inventory values of other trades had undergone substantial increases. The number of tailors shows a marked decline too. We have nine probate records from 1540–59 but only seven from 1560–1620. On the basis of the comparison outlined on page 90 there was 8 city tailors recorded in the period up till 1580 and 6 between 1580 and 1600. In the shire there are 2 before 1580 and the striking total of 42 after that date. This very remarkable growth of tailors resident in the countryside is continued into the early seventeenth century, but it is not absolutely conclusive in that it may well partly show merely an increasing professionalism among many tailors who were farming a little less than they had once done. However the rise of severe rural competition for the urban tailor is indisputable.

There now follows a miscellaneous group of tradesmen responsible for producing and selling a varied range of goods. The principal one of these is the chandler. The most striking feature of the chandlery trade was that, unlike some others, it was subject to a great increase in the late Elizabethan period. From 1610 to 1620 we have seven chandlers' probate records, yet before this only two are recorded. Until the 1580s butchers and barbers seem to have been making candles on a small scale: their complete loss of this trade in the mid-Elizabethan period may be part cause, part result of the rise of the chandler. The wealth of this mushrooming trade was also marked. Of these nine chandlers four left inventories or bequests totalling over £100 each, while the rest were generally of above average wealth. The reason for this marked growth in the number of chandlers and their fairly impressive wealth is difficult to detect. The price of candles was regulated by the community more often than that of any other commodity. Legislation was passed to restrict sales of candles to persons outside the town in 1568 and 1588, and these facts together suggest that there was a serious shortage of sources of artificial light, from which the chandler may well have profited, despite attempts at price fixing and regulation.[39] The explanation may well be an increase in demand, itself arising partly from an increased population and also from an increasing consumption of candles by the individual, connected with a greater need for artificial light.

In any case the chandler's business, although basically the conversion of animal fat into candles and their sale, was by no means confined to this. Although the number of wax, as opposed to tallow, candles sold was small, the sale of honey was usual, and in one case the chandler kept his own bees: this was a natural extension of the wax trade.[40] Equally natural was an extension of an interest in the making of candle wicks to the manufacture of cord, bowstrings, thread and even rope, which were all common. The sale of soap was also an understandable development, as soap was made from tallow, and similarly the appearance of candlesticks in these shop stocks is equally natural. However, the Worcester chandler supplied a further range of goods quite unconnected with candles – raw materials such as chalk, glue, pitch, tar, resin, ashes and reddle.[41] Most chandlers sold ground mustard, for which they kept a mill and some seed. One of the most common of these sidelines was the sale of pottery, usually pots, cups and trenchers. These were all imported, as pottery was not made in the city, partly from the potters' village of Hanley Castle on the Worcester side of the Malvern Hills, and also in large quantities from "Wegbury" which may well be Wednesbury in south Staffordshire.[42]

In addition scythe-sharpening stones, mouse-traps, perry and ver-juice occur at least twice each.[43] Perhaps the common factor shared by this varied collection of items was that they were all imported, like the tallow and wicks which were the chandler's main-stay, from the surrounding countryside, and were largely household requirements not generally available from any other tradesmen. The chandler was given the opportunity not only to acquire miscellaneous rural products, but also to sell them when no one else in the city specialized in these particular lines. In any case the value of a com-plete shop stock of these miscellaneous commodities did not approach the value of the raw materials for candles, so that making these remained the principal activity of the chandler. But the marked increase in both the number and the profitability of chandler's businesses in the later Elizabethan period is a significant economic phenomenon to set beside the decline to be seen in so many of the basic trades outlined above. It is perhaps noteworthy in this respect that the chandler, unlike many of the distributive and productive trades, was not particularly dependent on rural customers.

The rest of Worcester's craftsmen-retailers may be briefly dealt with. Rope-making does not seem to have supported many specialized tradesmen: the two main examples were fullers who also ran small ropeworks.[44] The making of tiles was a more important trade. Tilemaking seems to have been practised on a small scale by a number of people in various trades – for instance a brewer-farmer-clothier in 1560 and another clothier in 1611. Two more individuals possessed "tile-houses" which were presumably for small-scale production.[45] However at least two citizens were producing tiles on a large scale, both in the fields somewhere to the north-east of the city. Philip Dedicote, who had prospered and moved into the dissolved hospital of St Oswald, owned a total of 67,000 bricks and tiles at his death, valued at £20. John Marson seems to have been the main Worcester tile-maker during the Elizabethan period. He died with goods worth nearly £200, and was obviously farming the land on the outskirts of the city and raising large crops of cereals.[46] However his brick-oven, all the other equipment and stock of bricks and tiles were worth £20. Worcester was supplying tiles to Hartlebury and to Bromsgrove, so that a wide area of the city's region, and beyond, was being supplied by the tile-makers of Worcester.[47]

This completes the survey of the artisan-retailers, those who made things and then sold them. We must now turn to another important group, which cannot be very strictly classified with either those producing and retailing goods or those providing services. This group is formed by those who supplied food and drink.

II

Agriculture, food and drink and the service trades

Agriculture seems at first sight an unlikely division of the urban economy, but in most provincial towns there was a strong element farming the land surrounding the town either as its sole livelihood or as a most important adjunct to its shopkeeping or industrial activities. In both Warwick and Leicester, admittedly smaller towns with rather sluggish economies, agriculture played a most important part in the finances of a large proportion of townsmen at all income levels.[1] Compared with these towns, Worcester emerges as much more markedly urban and industrial in character, for agriculture was such a minor part of its economy that it is difficult to find any large-scale farmers at all. The reason for this probably lies less in its size than in the predominance of the cloth industry and the lack of common fields around the city.

There does exist a group of men whom we could legitimately describe as farmers, but it is almost completely composed of wealthy tradesmen who have moved into farming as a supplementary or minor aspect of their principal business. There are only about 20 examples of this extant in our period, such as the tanner who in 1615 owned five acres of crops near the city, or the mercer with £25 worth of stock and crops in 1558 or a bell-founder-pewterer with a mill, crops and 50 animals in 1541.[2]

These examples could be multiplied, but only a very few owned independent, respectably-sized farms in the countryside. A clothier held a farm with its own buildings, 120 acres of crops and 45 animals, while a mercer owned a farm near Malvern with its buildings, 48 acres of crops and 33 animals.[3] This small group was composed principally of men retired from active trade; although still resident in the city they were clearly undergoing the transition from prosperous citizen to country gentleman-farmer. The reason for their agrarian activities were far more social than economic; they were investing the profits from their businesses in land as a source of respectability and family permanence rather than in order to earn a living.

The rather larger group which dabbled in agriculture on a much smaller scale than these rich and successful citizens was not of great importance to the economy: its members had not invested large amounts of either time or money in their farming ventures and numerically the group as a whole was still a small one. The wealth of its members was however above average, few having inventories valued at under £100. For them agriculture was another of those forms of economic diversification noted so often already among the city's traders. The odd small field here and there around the city, with half a dozen cattle or a few acres of mixed cereals provided them with a small but valuable source of additional income, useful when they had expanded their businesses as far as they could, and perhaps partly acquired for social reasons.

The ownership of a few animals, as opposed to growing crops, was more popular among citizens in the middle and lower income groups. For example a smith had 13 sheep, a pig and some poultry, a brewer owned a horse and five cattle, a baker a single cow.[4] Obviously stock needed far less time than crop-raising, so that tradesmen who were occupied with their main business for much of the day could still keep a few animals to swell the family budget. This group of people keeping animals of some sort in small numbers is larger than those dabbling in arable or mixed farming, but still represents less than one tenth of the population. In particular the keeping of pigs was a common practice, so frequent indeed within the built-up area of the city and in odd open spaces around or just inside the walls that the corporation was forced to fight a perpetual battle to try to diminish the nuisance caused by pigs wandering the streets or kept in already crowded residential areas.

The city possessed no open, cultivated common fields at all. The main cultivated area lay on the north-eastern and eastern side of the walls, but appears to have been completely split up into enclosed, privately-owned fields. A few more small enclosed fields lay on the eastern bank of the Severn upstream from the bridge, but apart from these areas, some of them at least turned over to pasture, there were large expanses of grassland enclosed on the south and east, stretching away from the road to Alcester and Stratford-upon-Avon. A wide region more distant from the city lacked any large village, within a five- or six-mile radius of Worcester, in such parishes as St John-in-Bedwardine, Warndon and Claines; here citizens dabbling in farming on a moderate scale leased many fields. The only genuine common field which the city still retained was the common meadow, Pitchcroft, between the road to the north and the Severn. Even this seems to have been partly divided into small pasture fields by the end of the sixteenth century.

The main problem about Pitchcroft was that of over-stocking. In 1568 a maximum – a 'stint' – of 20 sheep (or 30 for butchers) was imposed, and repeated the following year. In 1579 a new committee was appointed to examine protests received from the users of the fields. These were apparently directed against the people who lived outside the city boundary along the road to the north. The issue at stake here is not clear but seems to be connected with enclosure.[5]

There appears to have been common ground in the Losemore area in 1539, but as there is no later mention of any need to regulate its use, it may well have been enclosed too.[6] Since there is no mention of leased fields in the inventories of many citizens owning animals, they must have relied principally on the common meadow and on their own gardens. The number of gardens scattered around the city was large, and although some of them were leased, they could only have provided enough land for raising vegetables or a small number of poultry and pigs. Many inventories suggest that they were not cultivated at all, but were used to keep horses or pigs, and for the storage or disposal of unwanted objects.

There remains a small group of people for whom agriculture was something approaching a full-time occupation. A single grazier is recorded early in the century, but generally the butchers do not seem to have branched out into cattle-raising as did their counterparts in the east Midlands. This leaves about a dozen examples of people described as "yeoman" or more rarely "husbandman" in their probate records. In most cases they were drawn from the parishes nearest the cultivated fields along the city's eastern wall, and they appear to have been the only citizens for whom farming was a permanent occupation. Although some of them were fairly wealthy, most of the money was invested in crops or stock and their homes display a standard of comfort appreciably below average. To these men we must add a very small group described as gardeners: only two inventories have been preserved and both are rather poor.[7] Since one of the homes contained garden tools we must presume that these men tended the gardens of others since neither appears to have held any land.

A point which emerges from an examination of this agricultural activity is that it seems to have been on the increase. The wills of yeomen and husbandmen supply eight examples dated from 1600 and 1620 and only four previous to this. This example is confirmed by the other agricultural amateurs. The explanation may be due to the failure of some trades to maintain their profitability – drapers, tailors and smiths, for instance – thus forcing them to find some supplementary source of income. Other explanations might be that the sharply rising price of food was forcing more townsmen to raise their own, while alternatively prosperity for others would have enabled more to dabble in farming. Different reasons must apply to different groups within the community.

The poor were hit hardest by the rising food prices of the period, and here we would expect the greatest amount of part-time food production, but many of the people of Worcester remained absolutely dependent on the market for their food supply. The lack of any evidence for extensive agricultural activity in the city indicates that for the majority all food had to be brought in at current market prices. This distinguished Worcester from many other towns of roughly similar size in Britain, showing it to be far more industrialized and far more distinct from the country village in its economic structure than the normal run of provincial cities.

The food and drink trades

We must now turn to the food and drink trades proper, and first of all to the butcher. This was one of the most common trades, with at least 30 well represented in the probate records. The range of wealth covered by the butchers was so great that it is difficult to

roduce any significant generalization, but it seems likely that
roadly speaking they were a little more wealthy than average dur-
ng the sixteenth century, but by the early seventeenth an even
reater diversity of wealth is seen, with inventories ranging in value
rom £3 to £489, suggesting that a polarization was taking place,
vith one group rather poorer than earlier and another of very
narked riches. Perhaps the ever-increasing price of food created
onditions in which the enterprising few did well and the rest found
usiness increasingly difficult.

There is no evidence that butchers were acting as graziers at all,
marked contrast with east Midland towns like Leicester where the
utcher-grazier emerged as a local figure of great economic impor-
ance.[8] The Worcester butchers instead kept a small number of
nimals at any one time to act as a pool and ensure a steady supply
f meat, so that of the many inventories which record the presence
f stock, few note more than 8 or 10 cattle or 20 sheep, and many
ad none at all. A small number had branched out into farming:
ne had attached to his city house a small farm with 25 cattle, 10
igs and £9 worth of crops.[9] Another, the wealthiest of all these
utchers, kept near the city 111 sheep, 75 cattle and 57 acres of
rops.[10] In both these cases it will be seen that there is no real
mphasis on stock-raising, for crops have a high priority – they
epresent the sort of general economic diversification we have noted
o often with other trades.

The Worcester butchers appear in the market and fair records
uying sheep in numbers of up to hundreds at a time, but that these
vere destined for fairly immediate slaughter is shown by the absence
f such large flocks in the inventories. Most of the slaughtering must
ave taken place at the rear of the butcher's own house for only two
re recorded as owning slaughter-houses and the trade had to be
orbidden to slaughter animals in the streets. Two sidelines apart
rom the sale of meat could add to the profitability of a butcher's
hop. The first was that he could sell the skins and hides he amassed
o the tanner in the section of the city market set aside for this pur-
ose, or better still he could act as a leather dealer in his own right
y having the skins made into leather by the tanner and then himself
elling the finished product. One butcher is stated to have 13 hides
eing processed for him by a tanner, another has six tanned calfskins
n his possession while a third is owed money by a glover from
Droitwich.[11] The second opening was the making and selling of

candles: one butcher in 1570 had all the necessary equipment –
tallow, wick yarn and candle moulds – and was further encroaching
on the trade of the chandler with stocks of pitch and earthenware
Another had stocks of candles, tallow and soap in 1566.[12] By th
middle of the Elizabethan period the rise of the chandler deprive
the butcher of his opportunity here, but he could still sell his tallow
to the chandler.

The bakers of Worcester were fewer in numbers than the butcher
but their improving riches as the century draws to a close provide
an interesting parallel to the butchers' similar profit drawn from
food shortages. The bakers who died before 1590 show inventor
values which are about average, ranging from £20 to £40. But i
the 1590s a distinct improvement sets in which by the early seven
teenth century has raised the average inventory value to over £100
This must reflect a marked improvement in the baker's busines
during the later Elizabethan period, probably again connected wit
the ever-rising demand for, and price of, food. There may too hav
been a slight increase in the numbers of bakers trading in the city

The equipment required by the baker was minimal, principall
only the oven, but here, as in some other trades, an increase i
investment in plant can be seen towards the end of the sixteent
century, for an oven was valued in 1609 at £3 where some decade
before a few shillings would have sufficed, and the use of expensiv
brass furnaces can be seen in other inventories.[13] Little storage spac
was required, for the quantity of cereals in stock at any time seem
to have been only enough to carry on between markets. The failur
or inability of the bakers to stockpile grain meant that the price o
bread necessarily closely reflected the prevailing market costs o
cereals, liable to very severe fluctuation after the not infrequen
poor harvests of the time. Opportunities for economic diversification
such a conspicuous feature of other trades, must have been limite
for the baker, for only a small number branched out into the makin
of malt, and none at all farmed.

The fishmongers formed a small and rather poor group, hit har
by the Reformation and the subsequent decline in effective enforce
ment of fish-days, for the only inventories valued at over £100 dat
from 1524 and 1535.[14] The fishmonger's main stock was compose
of preserved fish, reflecting a relatively high investment in sho
stock: one shop contained £30 worth of salt fish and another £2
worth.[15] This concentration on imported food meant that the fish

monger's customers were drawn to a marked degree from the countryside compared with the other food dealers, because the country folk themselves supplied most of their other food requirements. However the large country households – like those of Prior More and the Talbots – bought their salt fish direct from either London or Stourbridge fair near Cambridge.[16] The declining market for fish is shown by the fact that the last two fishmongers whose probate records survive, in 1578 and 1587, were both engaged in cloth manufacture on a small scale; the absence of any records after 1587 suggests that those who carried on were poor and few in number.

The River Severn itself was a valuable source of food, with a number of fishermen eking out a meagre living upon its waters. Here again their modest wealth dropped while that of others rose. One such fisherman in 1552 owned five boats and £5 worth of nets, but by the later years of the century one small boat and a few shillings worth of nets were the best they could muster.[17] We are not told where these fishermen sold their catches, but since they did not own shops they must have used market stalls, which are known to have sold fresh fish.

The last of these tradesmen to be considered is the brewer. The poorest brewer was wealthier than average and the richest were among the most wealthy men in the city. One who died in 1608 left bequests worth over £1,500, and there are at least three more inventories valued at over £200 and numerous ones which exceed £100.[18] Nearly all the Worcester brewers made their own malt, with malt mills, horses to work them, grain and malt owned by most of them. Usually the amount of capital invested here was not great, although one brewer had £97 worth of malt in store at his death; malt mills were usually valued at between £2 and £4 and stocks of cereals and malt rarely absorbed more than £10.[19] The principal investment of the brewer was in the apparatus used in the actual brewing process, furnaces and vats being the main items. Normally these account for between £10 and £20 in the brewer's inventory, although in one case in 1608 the total value of the brewery equipment was £32, and including the malt mill, £42.[20] Although there is a distinct increase in the capital invested in this industrial plant, it is no greater than the increase in the total wealth of the brewer. For example the capital invested in the two brass furnaces, apparently stock equipment in a reasonably sized brewery, is £6 13s. 4d. in 1551, £8 10s. 0d. in 1593 and £20 10s. 0d. i 1608.[21] Although not an impressive sum, the amount the brewe had invested in industrial plant, as opposed to stock-in-trade o raw materials, was probably larger than in any of the other trade in the city.

The brewer normally sold his products wholesale rather tha retailing them himself: the latter practice was in any case forbidde by the corporation. There is one case of a brewer (a most prosperou one) with his own shop, although this may have only been necessar because of the number of wholesale customers.[22] Despite the amour of capital which his wealth provided, the brewer was not likely t diversify his economic activities in the way that so many of th tradesmen did. A few – a surprisingly small proportion – wei engaged in farming in a small way. One was a "brewer an surgeon" but the main sideline was the cloth industry.[23]

The malt-maker never really established himself as an indeper dent trader, as he did in many towns. Even in 1496 it was claime that the brewers were making so much of their own malt tha country people and city malt-makers were being put out c business.[24] However, despite the brewer's absorption of most of thi activity, a few survived. The will of one is recorded, while in 158 a weaver was making malt and the growth of malt-makers practis ing their trade without being freemen caused some concern to th corporation.[25] The distilling of beer and ale into a drink with more potent alcoholic content, rather like gin, is rare as an indeper dent trade, the only example being in 1611, but it was occasionall practised by mercers and apothecaries, although the market for thi could never have been very great.[26]

This completes our survey of those trades concerned in the manu facture and sale of food and drink. Perhaps the most importan feature which emerges is the relative wealth of these trades – botl baker and brewer, and many butchers, were clearly making a ver good living and this can only be interpreted in terms of increase demand due to population growth. Despite rising prices and th efforts of local authorities to keep down those of food in particular there were clearly substantial opportunities for profit in these trades

Local government took greater interest in the supply of food an drink to and by the people under its care than perhaps in any othe branch of the city's economy. A number of broad principles can b seen at work. Firstly the city's market must exist primarily to serv ne citizens alone: food or other supplies must be available only to ne inhabitants, until they have had adequate time to buy what they eed, and dealers in foodstuffs, such as bakers and brewers, were ot allowed to buy up their requirements until the ordinary citizens ad had time to buy. The purchase of food by outsiders was at all imes discouraged.

The second broad class of regulation was aimed at the control of he quality and prices of foodstuffs. Although formal and detailed ttempts at price-fixing were only resorted to in emergencies, at east after the middle of the sixteenth century, the ale tasters con- inued with their work and the assize of bread was also enforced; this eneral supervision of the prices and quality of consumables was the rincipal duty of the city aldermen. Part of this concern was con- ected with the ever-present Tudor wariness – at times verging on eurosis – over the risk of popular unrest and disturbances, as well s a general paternalism. Thus in 1570 and in 1590 brewers were pecifically instructed to maintain a supply of cheap beer for the oor.[27] Brewers were generally allowed to make two or three lifferent grades of beer so that cheap drink was available at all times vithout crippling the profitability of the business.

As a corollary to this control, trades had to be strictly supervised o ensure that the regulations were properly observed. Butchers vere restricted to particular areas of the city and by the later years of the century were forbidden to keep more than one shop.[28] Similarly fishmongers were confined to a single street although this nay well have been mainly designed to limit the inevitable nuisance of such a trade.[29] Normally a considerable measure of control was eft to the various guilds and trading companies, but the regulation of the brewing trade was considered so vital that the trade company vas not allowed to admit new members until the corporation's assent had been received, quite unnecessary in any other trade.[30]

Attempts to prevent profiteering and cornering of the market in food ('forestalling' and 'regrating') were regularly punished, and it is perhaps significant that of 16 men fined in 1555 for these offences, only four were actually members of the regular food-supply trades: a wide variety of tradesmen were dabbling in this branch of the economy, many of them perhaps alehouse keepers and victual- lers.[31] Suspicion of profiteering may well explain the determination to keep beer production separate from its retailing, for by the 1560s no brewer was allowed to retail his own products, although this

regulation does not seem to have been in force at the end of th
fifteenth century.[32]

Legislation was also required to protect the city's food trader
against competition from the countryside, as in an order of 158
which excluded all bread and cakes baked outside the city from sal
within it.[33] In times of high prices or scarcity the authorities coul
act to alleviate the situation, as in the famines of 1556–7 and 1597
They could also stop any diversion of food to inessential purposes, a
in 1586 and 1614 when they banned the making of barley int
malt; they could also enforce more stringently and with increase
penalties the normal controls over prices and quality.[34] The enfor
ing of this large corpus of miscellaneous regulations on the foo
and drink trades was a constant problem, a continual battle agains
the evasion and lethargy which always threatened to depress th
whole policy into a mere licensing system. Occasionally vigorou
drives were made to enforce the regulations, as in 1550 when trade
men were threatened with disfranchisement – which would hav
banned them from all trade within the city – if they broke thes
regulations continually.[35]

The basic problem behind all these efforts was the constant pres
sure of demand, due to population growth and immigratior
exceeding the limited supply of food available. However, grante
the essential liability of the system to inefficiency except in period
of increased stress, the regulatory machinery was neither strikingl
self-interested nor dampeningly protectionist.

The service trades

This completes our survey of the trades in the city concerned witl
food and drink production, and we must now turn to a mucl
smaller group, but a most important one: those men who earnec
their livings by the provision of services of one kind or anothei
either to their fellow citizens or to outsiders and the country folk
Closely allied to the traders just outlined above were those servic
trades which provided hospitality of some sort, most prominentl
the innkeepers; this trade was quite distinct from the alehous
keepers and victuallers, and was so treated in contemporary legis
lation. The inn, unlike the other sources of refreshment, wa
required to keep some accommodation for travellers and thei

orses, and the general class of the establishment was markedly
iigher. In 1555, when the corporation took on the task of licensing
uch premises, there were ten inns in the city; they were called The
Cardinal's Hat, Lion, Bull, White Hart, Talbot, Antelope,
Hickock's House, The Bell, Griffin and Saracen's Head.[36] All
idditions to this number, and there were very few, needed the
iuthority's approval.

Innkeeping seems to have grown appreciably either in wealth or
n social standing during the Elizabethan period, for of the seven
innkeepers whose probate records survive, only one is dated earlier
han 1585. Similarly the inventories show considerable wealth, none
of them being valued at under £100. One innkeeper owned land
worth £200 in 1602, while the inventory of another was valued at
over £300 in 1585.[37] This affluence may reflect the increasing
iumber of travellers on the roads of Elizabethan England, a state of
iffairs which the city was well placed to exploit. In any case these
inns were places of entertainment for the wealthier classes inside the
city – the corporation for instance entertained visitors from Droitwich on official business in the Antelope.[38] Facilities for visitors
were not particularly impressive; one inn had only 16 beds, another,
he largest, 11 bedrooms for hire and about another five rooms for
sleeping, but sharing of rooms was always quite normal, for the inn
with 11 bedrooms had a stock of 95 pairs of sheets – and Tudor
Englishmen were not particularly concerned about dirty linen.[39]
All the inns had stables and residential accommodation for the
ostlers. The main investment for the innkeeper was in a large store
of linen – £60 worth in one case.[40] Country gentry in Worcestershire had not yet begun to keep town houses at this date, but some
of them may well have had a standing arrangement at one of the
inns for accommodation when required, for one inn had a 'Sheriff's
Chamber' and 'Blount's Chamber' and two others named, but not
after recognizable county families.[41]

Far below the ranks of the innkeepers came the alehouse keepers,
with their more obscure colleagues the victuallers. There was no
clear distinction between the two except that alehouse keeping was
very rarely a full-time occupation, for we have no probate records
at all from people who are so described. This fact is underlined by a
list of alehouses keepers and victuallers of 1555 when 44 were
licensed and described as belonging to almost all of the more humble
of the city's trades.[42] This number had risen to 58 by 1590. In the

rest of the shire there were stated to be 447 in 1577, so in propor
tion to its population the city had much more than its fair share.⁴
Only the victuallers seem to have followed at times a full-time trade
but their inventories do not make clear the exact nature of thei
activities, beyond recording the presence of drink in their cellars
All this largely spare-time activity must have been a valuabl
source of supplementary income to this relatively large group o
citizens.

The country people attending markets and fairs formed a
important section of the clientele of these establishments and th
corporation, although generally concerned to keep down their num
bers, admitted the need for a higher proportion near the marke
places.⁴⁴ This was necessarily so, for there existed an alehouse o
victualling establishment for about every hundred of the total resi
dent population, not to mention the inns, a far greater proportio
than the citizens themselves could possibly keep in business. Th
alehouses were important meeting points for country and town, th
significance of which emerges when we consider the number o
treason and similar cases which began as conversations in suc
establishments on market days: here was one good justification fo
the strict policy of licensing and supervision followed by the eve
wary authorities. Such houses were also the principal breeding place
of minor offences such as the playing of unlawful games and drink
ing or idleness at church services, or even sexual immoralit
for organizing which one alehouse keeper was banned for life fron
the trade.⁴⁵ The inn or alehouse was also used for commercial trans
actions, thus undermining the control over such activities possibl
in the open market, and so this was discouraged.

The barber's was a trade which did not produce much wealth i
pursued as a tradesman's sole occupation. Inventory values rise fron
about £15 in the 1550s to £20 at the end of the century: clearl
the barber was among the poorer of the city's independent traders
But a barber who was solely dependent on his own trade for hi
income was the exception rather than the rule, for most of them ha
some kind of sideline which raised them above the level just indi
cated, often to an inventory value of between £40 and £100. I
many cases this extra activity was a chandler's shop combined wit
their barbering establishment. Barbers of this kind seem to hav
dealt in all the main ranges of chandlery, and by the late seven
teenth century common interests brought the barbers to amalgamat

with the Chandlers' Company.[46] Another sideline was cloth manufacture, for we have examples of two barbers clearly either weaving
themselves or acting as clothiers and having the cloth made and
finished elsewhere.[47] Yet another barber was an alehouse keeper,
and was the wealthiest of them all. These men who had diversified
their economic activities into some of the more lucrative of
Worcester's trades comprised all the wealthy barbers and achieved
a standard of living comparable to many other trades.

There are indications however that the barbers were a declining
trade in the city. All the wealthier examples referred to above come
from the early Elizabethan period, and the later ones, although not
actually conspicuously poor, are much less well-off than they had
once been; significantly, no barbers at all occur in the probate
records of the first 20 years of the seventeenth century. The reason
for this decline must be sought under two main heads. Firstly it has
already been shown that the chandlers made a striking advance in
the later Elizabethan period, and this must have removed the basic
sideline of the barber (indeed many barbers may have altered the
balance of their business activities somewhat and turned themselves
into 'chandlers'). Secondly the countryside may well have become
more independent of the town in this respect, as in a number of
other cases of declining trades examined above. No evidence exists
of any medical activities by the barbers, but if these ever existed they
too may have been in decline. Thus the barbers are yet another
example of a Worcester trade in eclipse, forced first of all to diversify in order to make a good living, and then to diversify in order
to survive.

Worcester had a small group of professional men, lawyers, doctors and schoolmasters. The lawyers depended to a large extent on
acting as civil servants for the episcopal administration – the Regis-
trar or Chancellor of the diocese was an important figure in the city.
The Warmstrey family were registrars for nearly a century, from
1544 to 1641.[48] Their wills do not reflect great wealth, for William
in 1581 left bequests of about £50 and Robert in 1600 bequests
totalling about £100, with the addition of some landed property.[49]
The Warmstreys, perhaps because of their long-standing connection
with the city, were more integrated into the life of the community
than most of the cathedral dignitaries, Robert becoming a member
of the city council and all of them marrying into the families of the
leading citizens. The chancellors were normally much richer men

- John Langford left in 1579 bequests of over £170 and extensive lands, apparently inherited from his father in Ludlow.[50] Nicholas Archbold who died in 1618 owned a most impressive house in the cathedral precincts, with many rooms, pictures, musical instruments and clocks. His inventory was valued at £816, one of the highest in existence, mainly due to the possession of tithes and leases rented from the cathedral estates.[51] One Guthlac Folliot described himself as a "notary public" but he lived in the cathedral precincts and he too was probably a legal official attached to the episcopal administration; although his inventory totalled only £62, he was dabbling in farming and had a large house.[52]

The wealth of these officials seems to a considerable extent to have depended upon their access to the administration of the estates of the Church, for they seem to have been the frequent recipients of leases of parts of the cathedral, or more rarely the episcopal, estates: one may presume that they were drawn up on terms greatly favouring the tenant. Another legal office in the city was that of town clerk; he was usually (although not invariably) a man with legal training, and his was always a position of high financial and social status.[53] That there were other practising lawyers in the city is clear from miscellaneous references in the municipal records to the behaviour of the attorneys appearing in the city courts, and from the fact that the Talbots were employing two Worcester lawyers to attend to their local business.[54] Unfortunately no probate records are apparent, possibly because these men had gentry status and tried to live outside the city boundaries. It seems likely, and there are some references to support it, that the town clerks and ecclesiastical legal officials also kept up private legal practices, for the quantity of legal work available in the city must have been large; besides the shire quarter sessions and assizes there were the church courts and the city courts, which latter were in continual use and were the scene of interminable actions for debt, judging by the frequency with which such cases are mentioned in probate records.

The medical profession – if it deserves such a distinguished title at this date – was an occupation of only modest importance in the city. The doctor's patients must largely have belonged to the wealthy gentry families of the countryside, and it is significant that of the two doctors' wills which survive, one lived in the cathedral precincts, outside the jurisdiction of the city, and the other had a country house which he obviously lived in, as well as his Worcester house. A third reference to a doctor places him in the village of St Johns, just beyond the city boundary again.[55]

The doctor we know most about, "Thomas Hare, Doctor of Physic", was a wealthy man with extensive lands, bequests of over £90, and sufficient social standing to have the dean of the cathedral as his friend; the other doctor whose will we have, Thomas Hood, was far less affluent.[56] John Halsey was another Worcester doctor; in 1580 he brought an action for slander and defamation of character because his treatment of an Evesham woman had led to some unappreciative comments on his methods from her family; soon he was in the Fleet prison in London, a convicted Catholic recusant and "a great seducer of others": his goods were then said to be worth £400.[57] References to the services of a doctor in debt statements after death and related documents are so rare that it is clear that most people never consulted one (probably to their advantage); where such references do exist they are confined to the wealthier groups, like the cathedral prebendary in the 1570s who owed £1 to a local doctor for "his counsel, consolances, confection and for his diligence in oftentimes visiting the testator in his sickness".[58]

Probably most of the citizens did their own doctoring, with no more deleterious effects than resulted from the effects of Dr Hare and his colleagues, and here the city's apothecaries came into their own. Their numbers were very limited, and Peter Gough in the 1570s combined his business with being a mercer. His stock of drugs and other concoctions is very extensive, and he was owed money for supplying five separate surgeons living in the countryside. Like Gough, whose inventory was worth nearly £150, another of the city's apothecaries who died in 1524 was of above average wealth with extensive holdings of urban property.[59]

The schoolmasters were another small professional group but their role will be considered below in chapter 19.

Lastly we come to a group of workers which it is difficult to assign very aptly to any other division, the building trades. Apart from a single tiler, all the surviving records for this group concern woodworkers – joiners, carpenters and a sawyer. The joiners and carpenters can for convenience be considered as a single group, but one of very varied wealth, from £2 to £97 in terms of inventory totals, so clearly the trade offered a wide range of opportunity to its members. The exact nature of these businesses is difficult to reconstruct – in one case the testator is owed money both for wages and for the supply of ready-made timber items.[60] Another carpenter seems mainly engaged in making furniture, for in his two shops were five beds in varying stages of completion, a clothes press and two pairs of pillars, supposedly for a four-poster bed, all these made mainly out of walnut and oak.[61] Besides this he had stocks of panels and rails and other items which suggest that he was at least in part also working on outside jobs for others.

Some of these woodworkers found alternative outlets for their talents, for Anthony Tolly worked as a monumental mason, while another carpenter was also engaged as a fisherman and as a musician too.[62] These records must ignore a large number of traders who were operating on a smaller scale, possibly without a permanent base, for the quantity of building and repairs done in the city would require a considerably larger number of workers than the probate records reveal, although other sources are no more helpful: perhaps many were based in the countryside and worked over a large area.

Last of all the glazier must be examined, a relatively new trade. There are indications of the presence of a glazier in the city in the 1570s and before 1620, but it is a trade which does not seem to have settled here in any numbers.[63] The town of Evesham seems, judging from the probate records, to have been more of a glass-supplying centre than was Worcester, while Stourbridge had its glass industry founded by alien refugees in this period. The scattering of all building workers, and in particular carpenters, throughout the countryside is a striking feature of the early years of the seventeenth century.

This complete our survey of the trades and professions followed in Worcester during the period in question. We must now turn to some more general considerations arising from a study of the civic economy.

12

Economic organization and control

The various trades of Worcester were organized in guilds or companies. The activities of these bodies is difficult to describe because their records are either lost or very scanty, partly due to their extinction as useful bodies in the eighteenth century and partly because they often operated on a personal and informal level which discouraged the creation of elaborate records. The companies of the later sixteenth century were for the most part simply the pre-Reformation craft guilds with the religious element amputated, although there is little evidence on the medieval guild structure.

In 1577 there were twelve principal companies, the mercers, the drapers and tailors, the tallow chandlers, the brewers, the bakers, the butchers and vintners, the shoemakers, the fishmongers, the smiths and cutlers, the tanners and saddlers, the glovers, and the innkeepers and victuallers.[1] Here the combination of very small trades with larger, closely related ones is quite natural, although why the saddlers should combine with the tanners rather than the shoemakers, or the vintners with the butchers is not very obvious; it suggests that perhaps the social compatibility of the members, based on their financial standing, and not purely trading considerations, were paramount. The exclusion of the trades concerned with the cloth industry from this list is due to the accidental circumstances of its compilation. To all these was added in 1598 the ironmongers, but a number of trades seem to have been left without any formal craft machinery throughout the period – the coopers for example.[2]

Some of the companies which did exist must have had a very small membership, probably less than six or so for the lesser trades like the glovers: such organizations must have led very informal lives and their influence outside the trade concerned was inevitably extremely slight.

The organization of these bodies is normally recorded in the 'books' or regulations issued to them by the corporation. Most had one or two wardens as executive officers, possibly a steward acting as treasurer and a small body of ordinary members who formed a sort of advisory committee. Thus the corvisors had in 1504 a master, two wardens and three 'assistants' and the bakers two wardens and a treasurer.[3] The cloth trades, as befitted the dominant business of the city, were reincorporated in 1590 into the Clothiers' Company, amalgamating the weavers, clothiers and fullers into a single craft organization. It had a master, four wardens and 30 assistants.[4] The principal interest, of the clothiers at least, lay in the strict regulation of the apprenticeship system. This, combined perhaps with general social functions, must have been the main concern of all of them.

Normally the corporation entrusted these craft bodies with a large measure of autonomy in handling the affairs of the trade concerned, and in this way they relieved the municipal administration of a good deal of routine regulation. But the civic authorities did intervene occasionally both to issue general declarations of policy, on apprenticeship for example, and in specific cases where either a company was damaging the common good or where there were disputes between different branches of trades. So when in the 1570s there was a dispute between the shoemakers and the self-employed cobblers over where the demarcation between their businesses lay, the corporation stepped in to arbitrate; in 1570 the drapers tried to prevent a mercer selling flannel or linen cloth, forcing the city council to decide that such items might be sold by any of the retailing trades in the city. New members were normally admitted by the companies themselves, but the brewers, and occasionally butchers and bakers, were first licensed by the corporation to ensure that only those men who would respect the common good in the much-regulated food trades were allowed to set up in business.[5]

It is difficult to discover what the guilds and companies meant in the lives of their members. References to them in wills are quite uncommon, and only occur with any frequency in the 1550s and 1560s, with a slight resurgence of interest in the early seventeenth century. These bequests usually take the form of small sums of money to buy the members drink and entertainment on the day of the testator's funeral: a will of 1523 for instance mentions a meal of "powder beef and mustard with bread and ale".[6] As time passes the bequests tend to turn away from the convivial towards the more practical, like a gift of £1 to company funds or the bequest of £3 to help buy a new funeral pall for the company's members.[7] The paucity of such references would suggest that at no time during our period, before or after the Reformation, did these bodies make a particularly strong social appeal to their members; there is little evidence that sentiment was aroused or that they did very much more than act as petty regulatory bodies.

However there are some examples of companies acting outside the strictly economic sphere. There is evidence that they did provide some sort of a burial service for their members. The weavers and drapers and tailors raised a subscription for the assistance of Geneva in 1583.[8] The companies also formed a convenient way of dividing up the citizens on formal or ceremonial occasions, as for example when Queen Elizabeth arrived in 1575, to find the citizens drawn up into the various occupations, each with its streamers.[9] On only one occasion did the corporation try to tax the inhabitants through the companies.[10] These few occasions when the company played a social rather than an economic role were exceptions to the general rule, but this should not obscure the large amount of routine, largely unrecorded administrative work carried out by these bodies.

It should be noted that the diversification of economic activity so often noted above could only serve to weaken the craft organizations; when it was common for any businessman to dabble in one or more extra trades beside his own, control and regulation, even the whole basis of the companies, was undermined. Whether this diversity was a new departure or not is not at all clear, but certainly it riddled the whole system of guilds and companies, regulation, apprenticeship and control with inconsistencies and unworkable impracticalities which tend to make the whole system look like a sham, a front of theory and pious pronouncements behind which the business of actually earning a living went on with only partial regard for the highly organized and profusely legislated régime which is all that the modern observer can see.

The role of the municipal authorities in the organization of the economy has been considered above when dealing with the individual trades, but in general its actions do not support the contention that much local – and indeed national – legislation was restrictive and monopolistic in nature. Little evidence can be produced of any policy of maintaining the crafts as closed groups – indeed examples have been given of the corporation stepping in to prevent sectional interests becoming too exclusive. The maintenance of the apprenticeship and quality regulations was an obvious necessity, especially in the cloth trade. The rise of rural industry and of the competitive influence of the smaller country towns seem to have been more closely related to the rise of larger and more sophisticated markets than to any policy of excessive regulation in the towns. In an age when paternalism was taken for granted in many branches of national life, the economy was generally, and often needfully, regulated by the authorities. Worcester's economic regulation, whether by local government or by the craft organizations themselves, cannot be very strongly criticized.

Several of the broad issues underlying the economic structure of the city are worthy of comment. Firstly we should note the relative ease with which it was possible to set up in business from the point of view of capital. The amount required was rarely large, for in many of the more humble crafts a few shillings would suffice for both tools and materials, and even in such branches as cloth-making or mercery when at least £10 or £15 was required, a number of charitable loan funds were available to aid the young man setting up in independent business. Once the seven-year apprenticeship period was completed there was no insuperable barrier to his doing so. In any case the quantity of business negotiated on credit was very great – the extent of the debts listed in many wills and inventories, in particular those of shopkeepers with large retail interests like mercers and drapers, shows how often credit was available as a normal part of commercial procedures. Finance was also available from a relatively large class of retired tradespeople and from professional men, such as the cathedral dignitaries. Often these people were largely living on the profit derived from lending quite large sums of money; assuming that the high interest rates could be afforded, there could be little difficulty involved in established tradesmen raising capital. However all these businesses had a high degree of risk inherent in them: many tradesmen listed an alarmingly high proportion of their debts as 'desperate', that is, virtually hopeless. The risk, and actual loss, for tradespeople extending credit or loan facilities was very considerable, and partly explains the prevailing high rates of interest.

During this discussion of the economy, very little has been said about the city's 'working class', the people who were employed by this large and totally dominant group of self-employed traders and manufacturers. The main justification for this neglect is that there exists very little information on the subject. The only group we know a little about are the 'free-lance' labourers. From their probate records it appears that their wealth was slight – inventory values vary from £2 to £6, with one more affluent at £14, chiefly contributed by a few farm animals.[11] Their homes were extremely simple, consisting of one, or at the most two, rooms, supplied with only the barely essential furniture and kitchen equipment. Thus one had two beds, some pots and dishes, a table and form, and two chairs, all seemingly in the same room.[12] His clothing was worth 6s. and his "working tools" 2s. However not all these labourers were living at absolute subsistence level, for one could bequeath £16 and keep a domestic servant.[13] These men must have been employed on a wide variety of tasks, working in the fields, on building-sites or on the quay. Labourers were required to stand at the Grass Cross at the town centre with their tools in their hands ready to be hired if they had no work, by 5 a.m. in summer and 6 a.m. in winter.[14] The casual labourers, despite attempts at wage freezing, were probably better able to exploit prevailing conditions to their own advantage than were many other wage earners.

The position of the large group of journeymen and similar employees of artisans is difficult to reconstruct, for we have no probate records at all originating from such people, and since they were employed and paid on a quarterly, or even longer basis, their wage rates were probably kept down more successfully than those of the building workers or the labourers. This class must have lived in conditions of almost unrelieved squalor, judging by the very modest households which some of their employers among the poorer independent tradesmen left. But some journeymen lived on their employers' premises since 'journeymen's chambers' occur in inventories, although not with great frequency. The number of unmarried journeymen could not have been large. Except for a single instance early in the seventeenth century there is no record of rebellion or attempts to form a journeymen's organization.[15]

The apprentices formed a distinct group within the city, with its numbers at any one time running into several hundreds. In all but the smaller businesses it was normal to keep as many apprentices as there were adult employees, and numbers ran up to three per master, but rarely beyond that number. In the later sixteenth century the apprenticeship regulations were strictly enforced, especially in the cloth industry. This was no new departure, for even in 1466 the seven-year term had to be strictly adhered to if the freedom of the city was desired.[16] The municipal authorities took a strong interest in the whole question, formally registering and enrolling all indentures. In 1561, even before the passing of the Statute of Artificers, the city was making a complete survey of the number of apprentices kept by each master, ensuring that the maximum numbers per business were not exceeded, apparently aiming at minimizing unemployment among journeymen.[17] Disputes between apprentices and their masters were rare, but one case in 1566 brought in the civic authorities to protect a glover's apprentice from "unlawful correction" and an inadequate diet.[18]

Apprentices' bedrooms often turn up in inventories, but many would have been the sons of townsmen and would have lived at home: the weavers normally (but not invariably) had their sons apprenticed to themselves. As with the journeymen, this group must have contained a high proportion of immigrants, probably more than in any other group within the city.

The total number of employees within any particular business is difficult to discover in most cases, but the probate records suggest that even in the larger businesses it was rarely more than four or five, and was often less; on the other hand even the poorest tradesman employed at least one person. But it remains true that the employed, a submerged and concealed group within the city, were an important part of its population, at least in terms of numbers, for with their families they probably accounted for between a half and a third of the inhabitants.

Another large group about which we know all too little were the domestic servants. Most wealthy households had several women employed in this capacity, and even quite humble homes boasted at least one. Many of them were resident on the premises and maidservants' bedrooms frequently appear in inventories. This group must have been largely formed by immigrants, certainly to the point at which it caused the authorities some concern. Maidservants were only to be hired on terms of a contract of at least one year's duration, and were to be provided by the employer with keep and lodging; this ordinance, first made in 1565, was repeated in 1568 and 1585.[19] The cathedral manorial court, governing the cathedral precincts, was equally concerned over the matter, and waged a continual offensive against those who gave lodging to unmarried girls relying on manual labour for their income.[20] The reason for this concern may well have been partly moral and partly designed to discourage potential recipients of poor relief, but it shows incidentally the existence of a large class of young women moving into the city in search of work in domestic service.

What then were the elements of strength and weakness in Worcester's economic position? Its greatest apparent strength was a cloth industry which, despite some contraction in the later sixteenth century, was still in a healthy state in the earlier seventeenth century and still brought great wealth to the area, a wealth which could lubricate a wide range of other trades which depended upon the local consumer. The city also had, and has always since possessed, certain basic commercial advantages which would maintain its prosperity: the navigable Severn, the road system and bridge, a prosperous rural region dependent upon it. It was quite capable of functioning as an important regional centre, and when the more glamorous cloth industry faded away later in the seventeenth century, the city did not undergo any long-term decline, for even the disappearance of its staple trade could not destroy the fundamental strength of its regional position.

However there were signs appearing by the later sixteenth century which indicate that Worcester, if not in actual decline, was failing to keep up the vigorous role which it had until recently played. The excessive reliance on cloth entailed a constant risk both of temporary depression and of more permanent decline. Secondly, and perhaps just as important, the city's economic domination of its region seemed to be slipping. Economic self-sufficiency in the countryside and small country towns was growing again, a situation probably in abeyance since the thirteenth century. The broadening sophistication of the rural economy, partly caused by land shortage which forced the countryman to exploit every possible source of alternative revenue, hit those urban traders most closely dependent on rural custom – the mercers, drapers, tailors and smiths for instance. In addition a number of new trades seemed to settle in the country towns more willingly than in the city – silk weaving and glazing in

Evesham for example. Fortunately the dynamic north Worcester
shire towns, such as Bromsgrove, whose growth in the century
between Reformation and Civil War was very striking, were
already outside Worcester's main market region, although it may
well be that in the later Middle Ages this was not so.

The ever-increasing influence of London was another force which
was undermining the fundamental regional influence of the provincial city. The establishment of a 'metropolitan economy' could only
weaken some aspects of the position of many regional centres within
a moderate distance of the capital. The Talbots, typical perhaps of
many of the county families, were buying an increasing amount of
their more specialized requirements from London rather than from
nearer home. A quite ordinary Worcester family was buying a
wedding dress direct from London in the 1590s.[21] In any case
nearly all imported goods, and those made outside the region, seem
to have been bought from London wholesalers – Bristol's function
in this respect was still to come, despite the excellent communica
tions which existed along the Severn. Thus it was that the con
spicuous prosperity of the cloth industry concealed a basically
sound economic position but one which was subject to increasing
competition. Worcester's future depended on the survival of the
textile manufacture for as long as possible and on maintaining its
position as a regional centre. In fact it was able to do both with
conspicuous success.

13

Standards of living

One of the basic themes of the economic history of the period 1540–1640 is that this century may well have seen a significant rise in the standard of living of at least a large section of the population. Does this detailed study of one provincial city confirm or qualify this generalization? Certainly a cursory examination of surviving inventories seems to support the idea: the quantity of furniture and furnishings, of linen and household utensils, of miscellaneous luxuries like window curtains, cushions, ornaments, watches and clocks, books and pictures all help to build up a convincing picture of a rising tide of affluence.

The use of glass in windows is a good illustration of this trend, and lends itself to fairly firm numerical analysis. In the two decades of the 1550s and 1560s only six inventories refer to window glass but in the 1570s 13 out of 95 do so, in the 1580s 16 out of 88 and in the 1590s 28 out of 93. By the early years of the seventeenth century they are so common that they are no longer regarded as moveable property and are no longer listed separately. The dating of this quite impressive spread of comfort should be pushed back a little before the house owner's death, so that we may estimate that there was a sudden increase in the later 1560s, and that the pace of installation accelerated strikingly from the late 1580s onwards.

A partial explanation of this phenomenon may be that the price of glass fell, for glass in the inventories of the 1560s is valued at about 7*d*. per square foot, a figure which was brought down to 4*d*.

by the 1570s, and kept there for the rest of the century when the
price of some other industrial commodities tended to increase. So
cost may be a factor in the earlier spread of the use of glass in
windows, but it does not seem to be very vital in explaining the later
proliferation of its use. Here we have definite evidence to support
the general impression of prosperity and rising standards of living -
Worcester houses became more comfortable and pleasant to live in
and their owners could afford to make the improvement.

But this evidence is far from conclusive. The increasing use of
glass concerned, even in the 1590s, only about a third of the inven
tories, and the inventories themselves probably represent little more
than 5 per cent of the adult population – and the richest 5 per cent
at that. This means that we can only show that about 2 per cent of
the population of Worcester were able to improve their homes in
this way.

We can extend our information on this whole question very con
siderably by analysing the total values recorded in all the inven
tories. There are some 817 inventories extant for the period
concerned so this is a very considerable sample, and only a slight
degree of adjustment has been necessary to ensure that they are all
fully comparable. Tables 8 and 9 show the result of analysing these
figures. The average value shows a distinct increase over the period
from about £40 in 1550–69 to nearly £60 in 1600–19. The figure
from before 1550, although less reliable than the later ones, shows a
very great increase – almost doubling – around the middle years of
the century. In short, the average inventory value nearly doubles
between the 1530s and 1550s, continues at about the same level in
the 1560s, increases by a quarter in the 1570s, and then stays rea
sonably stable until the early seventeenth century when it rises
again by about a fifth.

Before too many conclusions are drawn from this it would be pru
dent to observe that inflation must be constantly reckoned with
when assessing these figures. The goods listed in inventories are
mostly manufactured ones, and the prices awarded to them seem to
be an accurate reflection of the current market level, so that if we
compare the rising average value of inventories with the rising prices
of manufactured goods, we should be able to see whether in fact the
citizens of Worcester were becoming richer in 'real' terms.[1] The
result is the somewhat surprising one that if we take inflation into
account in this way, the average Worcester testator owned property

Total number of inventories	Date	Average total value	Index of average total	Price index Industrial	Price index Food
78	1529–49	£22.7	56	65	63
118	1550–9	£41.2	100	100	100
58	1560–9	£37.6	92	92	117
95	1570–9	£50.9	123	119	108
88	1580–9	£44.3	107	123	123
93	1590–9	£51.0	124	128	168
124	1600–9	£59.6	144	137	167
161	1610–19	£58.8	143	147	185

Table 8   Value of probate inventories

N.B. In all index figures 1550–9 = 100

	Proportion of total number of inventory totals at various levels of wealth			
	£0–9	£10–39	£40–99	£100+
1529–49	46%	39%	12%	3%
1550–9	37	31	20	11
1560–9	33	42	19	7
1570–9	35	35	15	15
1580–9	30	40	19	10
1590–9	33	32	16	18
1600–9	27	36	20	16
1610–19	26	42	16	16

Table 9   Distribution of probate inventory totals

of almost exactly the same 'real' value in the early seventeenth century as he had done in the mid-sixteenth.

This judgment needs a little qualification. Not all the items in the inventories – farming stock for instance – could be described as manufactured articles, and also we do not know if the prices of the particular items in the inventories which can be described as 'manufactured' moved in the same way as the small sample used to compile the price index, but neither of these sources of error should be of great importance. Thus this large sample of the fortunes of 'upper-class' citizens suggests that there was no increase in real wealth at all. Indeed if we compare the increase in the average valuation of inventories with the increasing price of food, it becomes clear that although incomes seem to keep pace with inflated prices between 1530 and 1580, from the 1580s onwards food prices rise appreciably faster than the assets of this class; the balance seems to be righting itself again early in the seventeenth century.

These figures are not seriously affected by any trend for inventories to be made by a wider social class as time goes on – there could be a dilution of the average values by the inclusion of more poor people, but this does not seem to have been the case. Indeed the only movement which seems at all evident is for the small group of the very rich to grow a little and the very poor tradesman to become less common, but these trends only affect a small minority: for the great majority of the citizens of Worcester the financial situation was one of stability; most economic groups held their own, and perhaps only the very wealthy saw their position improve appreciably. The majority stayed as it had been in the mid-sixteenth century, relatively and absolutely.

How then are we to explain the evidence of increasing comfort, and even luxury, in Worcester homes? Two trends seem to be at work: the first is the tendency for the very richest group in Worcester society to grow in both size and wealth – if this were so it would help to account for some of the impressive inventories described above, for the inventories are drawn from a small and possibly unrepresentative part of the population. The second trend is a change not so much in the wealth of the community as in the way it spent its wealth. Early in the sixteenth century much money was kept in cash or plate or was invested in loans and real estate, but as the century progressed there seems to have been a drift towards converting this wealth into the paraphernalia of domestic comfort. There is plenty of evidence, both national and local, of an increasing consciousness of social pressures, of more awareness of, and greater competition for, social status, of a rising need to make a physical exhibition of social and financial standing. Thus houses become more showily wealthy not because their owners are necessarily any

icher, but because they feel the need to register and advertise their
ocial status in this way.

It has already been observed that this evidence drawn from inven-
ories only covers the class of self-employed tradespeople and so only
minority. This group was however utterly predominant in every
ection of the city's life, so that its importance is far greater than its
umbers would suggest: the prosperity of this group must mirror
he economic fortunes of the community as a whole. It is far more
lifficult to estimate the trend of the living standards of the 'working
lass', but judging by the price and wage data considered above, its
osition was at least as bad as, and possibly a little worse than in
he rest of the country.[2] But there does exist one way of estimating
he movement of living standards within the community as a whole
the mortality rates for children already given.[3] These statistics
nust reflect the general level of hygiene, nutrition and housing, that
s they provide some sort of index of some aspects of the living stan-
lards of everyone, not just the rich. Generally speaking, these
igures indicate a deterioration between the mid-sixteenth and the
arlier seventeenth centuries. They also indicate that the trend was
ecoming more hopeful in the countryside while getting worse in
he town, the difference perhaps between food-producing communi-
ies and food-buying ones, for rocketing food prices necessarily hit
own worse than country; the price and availability of food re-
nains the major key to urban living standards.

It would be wise not to over-exaggerate the stagnation or even
lecline of standards of living indicated by all this information, but
t remains true that Worcester provides us with very little evidence
f any general rise in living standards or any clear change in the
listribution of wealth. The very rich became rather richer, the wage
arner rather poorer, and the large and important class between the
wo extremes contrived, by running hard, to remain standing still.

Housing

Ve have already seen that the period under review saw both a
lrastic increase in Worcester's population and an absence of
mprovement of living standards and prosperity; these two themes
re brought together in an examination of housing. How was this
apidly growing population housed? Does a decline in housing

conditions help to explain falling standards of health? The solution to the problem of housing a growing population took two main forms, firstly a major programme of building and rebuilding, both within the walls and in the suburbs, and secondly the modification of existing houses so that they could absorb more people, chiefly by placing more than one family per house.

As far as the rebuilding programme is concerned, we may divide it into two separate phases, the first in the late fifteenth and early sixteenth centuries, and the second beginning in about 1560. Of the first phase we know little. New Street, as the name implies, was a piece of late medieval property development, shown by the fact that the religious houses held no property here, while they owned houses scattered throughout the older streets; the blocks of property owned by the original speculators were still in existence in the sixteenth century where in all the other city streets only single houses, and not contiguous rows of buildings, were owned by individual citizens. All this suggests that the development of the street was a very recent affair, probably occurring late in the fifteenth century.[4] Other incidental references to new houses or blocks of them are placed in Baxter Street (1524), Newport Street (1524) and Woodstathe Street (1512).[5]

These references indicate that the vacant areas between the main streets and the walls were still being built up at the end of the Middle Ages; probably the resumption of building activity at this time was the result of population pressure and prosperity, for the booming cloth industry was probably approaching its peak in these years, drawing into the city both wealth and immigrants. Most towns were probably still filling in the gaps left by the economic and demographic difficulties of the later Middle Ages, but Worcester seems to have recovered more quickly than did many cities, so that by the later years of the fifteenth century it had begun to demand new houses and so create the first building boom, of which our knowledge is so fragmentary. After this period there was a lull when very little building seems to have been undertaken, extending roughly from 1520 to 1560, explained by the levelling off of the cloth boom and possibly by an easing of demand due to renewed epidemics and a reduced flow of immigrants.

As has already been observed, there was a good deal of vacant land within the walls in the mid-sixteenth century, particularly along the small lanes just within them, and it was in these areas oupled with some suburban development, that building took place n the later sixteenth and earlier seventeenth centuries. Information drawn from wills indicates that building may well have started again on a significant scale by the 1570s. The first references to recently completed or proposed new homes occur in 1576, 1579 and 1582.[6] Most of this new building, especially in the early seventeenth century, seems to have taken place in the suburbs. A new house is mentioned in the eastern suburbs in 1609, and in 1614 a rich clothier refers to his eight newly built houses in the suburbs, two at St Martin's Gate and six in the Frog Lane area.[7] In 1609 it was claimed that "there are of late many small cottages erected and built within this city and suburbs of the same, as in Foregate Street by one Mr Jennings, a minister, and by diverse other persons".[8] These cottages were intended for the poor, since the corporation was concerned about their occupiers adding to the poor relief burden. It was not until early in the seventeenth century that building outside the walled area grew to any extent, and not until this period that the demand for new housing was great enough to make the provision of homes for the poorer classes a profitable source of investment revenue for the rich.

It is possible to illustrate the growth in building activity during the Elizabethan period from other sources. The corporation granted leases which involved an obligation to build new houses on vacant plots owned by them on seven occasions between 1562 and 1601.[9] In 1570 a proclamation was made under the statute of 1540 which had ordered the rebuilding of houses on derelict land under penalty of confiscation.[10] There is more, if circumstantial, evidence of a building boom at this time. A long series of bye-laws was enacted to try to control the indiscriminate digging of sand, gravel and clay from the waste ground and unfrequented roads around the perimeter of the built-up area, materials which were extensively used in building operations, as contemporary accounts show. Six of these laws were passed between 1562 and 1573, until in 1574 the cathedral authorities were officially approached for a lease of suitable land to provide the citizens with these materials. Similar legislation in 1562 and 1570 dealt with the problem of saw pits and piled timber obstructing the highways.[11]

All this evidence, circumstantial as some of it is, suggests that there was a major wave of building activity beginning in the early years of Elizabeth's reign. This is somewhat earlier than the dates

we have for the fresh building of whole houses, and indicates tha
the early part of the building boom was concerned with the rebuild
ing of old houses on the same site, and with repair, extension and
improvement of existing houses. Then, in the 1570s came the
extension of the built-up area, predominantly in vacant areas within
the walls, followed by suburban development for the poor in the
early years of the following century. This major phase in the
rebuilding and extension of an English city may be compared with
a similar movement already known to have occurred in the English
countryside.[12]

The problem of providing homes for an ever-increasing popula
tion was not – indeed could not be – confined to the extension of
old buildings and the provision of new ones, for the evidence out
lined above does not suggest that the quantity of new housing unit
provided could even begin to match the expansion of population
which we know took place. Instead, a good deal of sub-division of
existing buildings must have gone on, to supply the poorer classes
in particular. This trend is necessarily difficult to document very
satisfactorily, and in any case must have mainly taken place in the
first half of the seventeenth century. Certainly the cathedral authori
ties, as the governors of the exempt area of the city around the
cathedral, show a keen awareness of the problem, since the sub
division of the large number of houses owned by them and rented
out involved the deterioration of their property and brought no
profit to themselves. Their concern is expressed in 1600 and
becomes keen in 1601, when four tenants were accused of dividing
their houses into two units, and one more tenant was said to have
split his house into four separate homes. At a later court another
tenant was alleged to have divided the rectory building into three.[1]
Sub-division was clearly prevalent by the early years of the seven
teenth century, and we may presume that although it was punished
or controlled by the authorities, they were powerless to stamp out a
trend dictated by economic circumstances.

This process of multi-occupation of existing houses is the only
explanation of the fact that new or improved houses cannot have
existed in sufficient numbers to house the expanding population of
the city. The trend is a significant phenomenon in itself, for it shows
that one direct result of population growth must have been a serious
decline in housing standards, and of the general standard of living
and health, pronounced by the early years of the seventeenth century

mong the poor. It may well help to explain the frequency of
pidemics and the poor general survival rate of children in these
ears as compared with the early Elizabethan period.

One important general point to emerge from all this is that, as in
. number of other cases, problems arising from population growth
lid not really become acute until the early Stuart period. Pressure
or new housing could not have been very strong until the middle
ears of Elizabeth's reign for it is not until this time that this impor-
ant programme of building, rebuilding and multi-occupation
ecomes clear. The number of the city's inhabitants had probably
een growing for 60 years before anything very striking was done,
o there was probably a surplus of houses to be taken up at first. But
ven by the middle years of the sixteenth century there was already
. housing shortage, so that despite the temporary relief provided by
he grave epidemics of the 1550s, the building boom, when it did
ome, came as only a partial solution to an increasing problem of
vercrowding.

It is difficult to understand why a greater number of wealthy
itizens – and they were in plentiful supply – did not invest their
noney in housing development; there are relatively few examples
f their having done so. Quite possibly the return on money used
n this way was unattractive, but more important seems to have
een the fact that investment in real estate almost always took place
n the countryside with the attraction of the social status to be
lerived from owning rural acres as opposed to town cottages. This
nust partially explain the inadequacy of the community's response
o the problem of providing for an increasingly badly housed popu-
ation, for although the response in terms of new houses is a major
tep in the development of the city, it was not enough to prevent a
lecline in living standards, a rise in disease, and so a check to fur-
her growth, apart from an immeasurable degree of suffering.

The poor

The problem of poverty affected Worcester, along with every other
ixteenth-century community. The city was more susceptible both
o vagrancy and to unemployment due to depression in the cloth
rade than were many towns. The problem, and attempts made to
olve it may be considered under two main heads, the distinction

contemporaries themselves made between the 'deserving', native poor and the vagrant outsiders.

Unemployment was a constant risk in a city so highly dependent on the cloth trade as was Worcester. The trade was always at risk from commercial fluctuations on the Continent which led to slumps in the production regions; these depressions greatly increased the number of people unable to support themselves while reducing the ability of the rest of the community to help them. There was also a permanent element which needed help: the old, widowed and sick in particular. This hard core of people more or less permanently dependent on community assistance of some kind was relatively small in size since the number of elderly people in the population was much less than in our own times. A survey of the "poor and impotent" of the city in 1563 revealed a total number of 88 individuals in need of support, consisting of 53 women living alone, 22 men living alone, six married couples and one child.[14] Here the vast majority must be elderly – this is shown by the small number of married couples with children.

There is no other strictly comparable evidence from later on to suggest whether this figure rose or not, but in a period of very high food prices in 1597 the most prosperous of the Worcester citizens took into their homes "above two hundred poor and aged persons" and supported them.[15] This suggests that the size of this group of people which was chronically unable to support itself without some outside help always amounted to about 2 per cent of the population. Some inventories of people near this level have survived, often widows without relatives: they lived in one room, with a bed, a few cooking utensils, a table and one set of virtually worthless clothing.

To this 'hard core' we may add a larger group who lived sufficiently near subsistence level to require public assistance in times of extreme scarcity or high prices of food and fuel, or those solely dependent on wages and so liable to unemployment, particularly in the cloth trade. Of the unemployed we have some statistics. A survey of 1556 or 1557 of the "blind, lame, impotent, sick and those that are unable to get their livings without the charitable alms of the people" reveals the alarming total of 734 individuals, composed of 138 single women, 66 single men, 34 married couples without children, 78 couples with children and their 325 children, plus 8 which cannot be clearly distinguished.[16] This number is clearly made up of our 'hard core' and its fringes, plus a large number of nemployed, indicated by the high incidence of couples with dependent children.

In a letter of April 1557 the corporation claimed that the depression in the cloth trade had created a total of 1,000 people on poor relief, compared with 700 a year previously.[17] This latter figure may well refer to the survey referred to above; those in need of relief from public funds probably included some 20 per cent of the inhabitants, an alarming figure. Although the survey of 1563 which has already been described indicates that this critical situation had by then completely vanished, the clothing industry remained at constant risk of further bouts of serious unemployment, although later instances do not appear to have been serious enough to warrant action by the municipal authorities.

Occasional large-scale relief operations by the community were required by two other disasters to which urban life was subject: plague and famine. The epidemics of Worcester have already been described; the practice of isolating infected households entailed the supply to them of food, fuel and other domestic requirements until contact with the rest of the community could be resumed. Isolation of whole households is first mentioned in 1593–4, and was continued in 1603–4 and 1609.[18]

Famine was the other natural calamity which forced the civic authorities to give relief to some of the citizens. The city found itself obliged to supply food under a public relief scheme in 1556–7 and 1597. In the winter of 1556–7 £133 was spent on rye bought at Bristol, and some similar action seems to have been taken during the previous year, in conjunction with the magistrates of the county who helped the city with money "for the relief of the poor within our city, being a godly purpose and a godly mission".[19] In 1597 the high price of food led to the corporation spending £1,800 on Baltic corn at London so that it could be sold on the market at 10 per cent or 20 per cent below the current price.[20] This was much the largest financial transaction of any kind undertaken by the corporation during the century; as the corn was sold at a loss, the cost of this food subsidy had to be recovered by gifts from the rich, £214 from citizens and £340 from people living in the county, including the cathedral precincts: those in need in the countryside were presumably helped by being allowed to buy the subsidized corn with the citizens. During this particular crisis the numbers of the chronic poor rose appreciably, so that for several months special measures

were introduced to help them; the bad harvest which had caused
high food prices inevitably entailed a period of general difficulty in
an economy dominated by agriculture. All these measures were a
further burden on a city whose financial resources were already
strained to a painful degree.

Beside these special efforts in times of crisis, the expense of poor
relief at difficult times could be considerable. The cost of aiding
the unemployed of 1556–7 involved raising a total of about £1 per
week from at least 250 households at individual sums ranging from
½*d.* to 2*d.* per week, with about 20 rich households supplying the
needy with food from their own kitchens.[21] The greatly reduced
need of 1563 was met by a levy on 330 households.[22] It is difficult
to say how regularly a rate was levied on the wealthy to help the
poor, but it is only mentioned on one other occasion, in 1553, so it
was at this time probably only an emergency measure.[23]

The years after 1570 were the ones when the community was first
faced with the problem of finding regular, permanent ways of
helping those chronically incapable of supporting themselves. In
1573 the corporation began to assign half the fines for criminal
offences to poor relief.[24] This scheme did not continue, probably
because this revenue was the traditional perquisite of the officials
responsible for the administration of justice. In 1577 a survey was
made of the "poor, impotent, blind and lame" in order to impress
the county authorities with the size of the problem and ask them
either to help the city or license these unfortunate people to beg in
the countryside, a piece of blackmail which does not seem to have
worked. That year a committee was set up to find new ways of
relieving the poor, and early in 1578 a man was brought from
outside the city who was "expert in setting on work idle children
and persons". This seems to have been connected with the first
workhouse scheme described below.[25] The success of these efforts is
not recorded, and no final arrangement appears to have been
developed.

Apart from these attempts by the corporation to tackle the problem of the 'deserving' poor as a whole, a number of more specialized
and less public agencies did valuable work. Very often the city
financial officials made informal grants to the poor and sick from
the surplus of their year's accounts. A series of almshouses made a
limited but important contribution; the Trinity Guild maintained
almshouses before the Reformation, and these were refounded by

royal charter in 1561 with room for 48 old or poor people.[26] The elementary school which had also been supported by the Guild was combined with the almshouses in a joint foundation which was administered by the "Six Masters" appointed by the corporation. Their treasurers' accounts show that they not only spent £5 to £6 yearly on keeping the poor in the almshouses, but also gave out annually to the poor of the city at large between £10 and £20.[27]

In the hard times of the 1590s they paid for the burial of the poor, for clothing, made extra large general payments and in some cases supplied poor households with regular weekly sums. In 1600 they were giving between 4*d.* and 8*d.* per week to seven people, four of them widows, for periods of between 18 weeks and a year. Help was given towards placing boys in apprenticeship – "towards the placing of his son and apparelling him 5*s.*". In 1602 plague sufferers were aided, and a prisoner in the town gaol was given clothing. Some children were sent to London, presumably for apprenticeship and domestic service. In 1605 a poor weaver was helped to send his daughter to London, assistance was given to a sick man to travel to Bath for cure and "five poor Irish men in distress" were given 6*d.*[28] Similar help was provided by two more sets of almshouses, Walsgrove's founded in 1567 for four people, and Inglethorpe's (1618) endowed to support six men and one woman.

The cathedral too was obliged by its foundation charter to distribute considerable sums to the poor – £40 was prescribed in 1545. In 1587 it was stated that this money was to be distributed as 48*s.* to prisoners in the gaols and 6*d.* per week to 20 poor householders, leaving £11 to be used as occasion required.[29] The churchwardens of each parish were in theory required to provide for the relief of the poor, but the wardens' accounts of St Andrew's do not record any significant contribution except in 1595–6 when 9*s.* 3*d.* was removed from the poorbox and used for burying the poor, helping the sick and aiding with 8*d.* per week a woman whose husband had been "taken away" to join the navy.[30] It is quite possible that some informal parochial help was given, but very probable that it did not amount to very much, especially as the tendency for concentration of the rich and poor in different parishes entailed that those areas with most need had least resources, and vice versa.

Thus a number of public and semi-public institutions in the city provided a partial solution to the problem, but private charity was

still left with a very large part to play. Some aspects of this important subject are dealt with below, but it should be noted here that
in the mid-sixteenth century and the first two decades of the seventeenth, when the need was probably at its greatest, the amount of
money bequeathed to the poor reached an average total of about
£20 per year, or about 8s. per week.[31] This might have raised the
chronic poor to subsistence level when combined with the institutional
help outlined above, but it would have been quite incapable of
meeting any extra demands.

The flow of relief from this source was also sporadic and
unreliable, and during the 1570s to 1590s was only available in a
greatly reduced volume, averaging only about £5 per year.
Normally these bequests consisted of sums of a pound or more
which were given out by the executors at or just after the funeral,
so they tended to be indiscriminate, the only usual qualification
being that the recipients should be the testator's own parishioners.
Some more specialized objects were occasionally included, such as
'poor maidens' who were given a small sum as a substitute for a
dowry. Loan funds were more frequently instituted, a set sum of
money being entrusted to the corporation or a craft company to be
lent out to young men beginning their careers, without interest or at
a low rate: these were perhaps the most useful long-term contribution made by private charity to the diminution of poverty.

Thus the city grappled with the problem of helping those who
could not help themselves because of unemployment, epidemic,
famine or chronic inability due to sickness or old age. The contribution made by private individuals through charity was a vital one, for
without it the efforts of the institutions, whose resources were
limited and the corporation, which tended to act only in emergencies, would not have been enough. As it was, it is unlikely that more
than a few died from hunger, although this should not conceal the
misery of many hundreds clinging precariously to a life devoted to
finding the next meal.

The problem of vagrancy, the influx of beggars and other
itinerants without means of support, was a general one, and worse
for the towns because they offered some kind of concealment and
an income from either crime or charity. Worcester was placed in an
unfortunate position because it was so near Wales, whose poverty
drove so many on to the roads; in 1584 it was stated that the number of poor people flocking to the city was large and increasing,

coming "the most part forth of Wales".[32] The problem was not simply one of either supporting or removing these people, for it was believed – and with justification – that crime and vagrancy were closely related phenomena.[33]

A strict régime awaited the vagrant. In 1556 a beadle was appointed to remove all vagrants; for identification purposes he wore a blue and white garment. In 1566 and 1568 a weekly search of the city was ordered, carried out by the beadle and constables. Also in 1568 a scheme was introduced whereby all vagrants so caught were to be produced before two worthy citizens of the parish concerned, who were to decide what was to be done in the first instance. Evidently this was designed to stop such cases clogging the mechanism of the courts, as they seem to have done elsewhere.[34]

A major concern was the risk of vagrants settling long enough to become a legitimate burden on poor relief funds. Accordingly in 1555 all "inmakes" – lodgers – were to be removed, and citizens not conforming to this order were to be disfranchised on the second offence. The bailiffs' permission was required before "strangers or foreign poor folks" could be leased property worth ten shillings or less per annum in 1562, and in 1573 regular reports were to be made by the ward constables to the bailiffs on all tenants of houses rented at less than 13s. 4d. yearly. This vigilance was continued into the seventeenth century when in 1609 the proliferation of small cottages in the suburbs was condemned because it encouraged the settlement of vagrants who might become a burden on the poor rates; the builders of such accommodation were to guarantee that this would not occur, or demolish them.[35]

In the courts of the Dean and Chapter, by which the area around the cathedral was governed, a continual battle was waged against the risk of vagrants settling. In 1600 ten sub-tenants were discovered and their hosts fined and usually about this time two or three tenants would be fined at every court for taking in lodgers, and the bye-law forbidding this would be repeated. In 1600 this prohibition was extended to receiving domestic servants or other unmarried female manual labour.[36] This campaign against the infiltration of people without means from the countryside was continued well into the seventeenth century. Thus vagrants were never allowed to settle down even had they wished, and the city concerned itself principally with pushing the responsibility onto other shoulders.

The setting up of a workhouse was first mooted in 1578, when a plan to construct a joint establishment with the shire was abandoned and a separate city one was decided upon. At the same time all newcomers who had lived in the city for less than three years were to be expelled, in company with all lodgers. This general project never seems to have been carried through, for the city accounts contain no record of the cost of building or maintaining the workhouse. However a 'house of correction' was built or adapted in 1597, and an overseer was appointed, and in the following year a levy was organized for building and maintaining it.[37]

It appears that this was a completely new project without a predecessor, but the use of the building seems to have lapsed, for in 1613 it was ordered that it was to be repaired so that it could be used again, and the following year another building was converted to house it. In 1620 the house of correction contained "one great pair of stocks and one chain of iron with other irons", the personal property of a testator, probably the overseer.[38] So the workhouse never seems to have been an important feature of the official treatment of vagabonds until the very end of the sixteenth century, and even then its use tended to be intermittent. Possibly some sort of joint measure was worked out with the shire authorities, but it was more likely that the resident poor never needed to be sent there and the vagrants were more conveniently (and more cheaply) ejected into the shire whenever they appeared.

There was remarkably little enterprise about the city's treatment of the problems of poverty. Unlike some towns – Norwich for instance – the methods later adopted by the central government were not first pioneered by the municipality, and Worcester's measures were mostly provoked by the national legislation which empowered them to take action. The only exception to this was the compulsory rating of 1553 and 1556–7 which preceded the statute of 1563 which formally authorized local government to take such action. Probably the explanation lies in the wealth of Worcester's upper class, especially its clothiers, which provided through private and public charity sufficient resources for the maintenance of the 'deserving' poor, while the vagrants could be pushed out into other hands in the county. However, this does not alter the basic fact that population growth and economic readjustment placed a serious financial and administrative burden on Worcester's government and citizens.

14

Society

The citizens of Worcester belonged to a series of social groups whose importance to the individual grew as their size diminished. The largest social unit of which the citizen would have been strongly aware was the city itself. Here there was a very real sense of community, hedged with legal and administrative supports. Those who came from beyond its walls were referred to as 'strangers' or 'foreigners' and only freemen, that is the class of self-employed traders who had been formally admitted to the freedom, could trade within the city; outsiders were only allowed to do so when their activities were conspicuously useful to the community. Freemen who went to live outside the boundaries were disfranchised after one year's absence.

However, city and countryside were not separated by a barrier as rigid as the legal distinctness and exclusiveness of the municipality might suggest. Intermarriage at all levels with country families was quite common, while the close economic partnership symbolized by the markets and fairs has already been described. But despite this, urban and rural society were organized along different lines, although they were not as different as external appearances suggest. Society in the town was much more open, and although still hierarchical, it was related in a fairly simple way to differing levels of wealth, and not to the ownership of land or any social prestige implicit in a particular style of life or a family name. So despite the presence of a wide community of interest between city and country,

Worcester remained a distinct social unit, conscious of its separateness, deeply aware of the different nature of its social system when compared with the countryside beyond its walls, a separateness confirmed and protected by its clearly demarcated legal and administrative independence.

At the next level below the city as a whole, the individual citizen belonged to a broad social group based on the wealth he owned – 'class' is a term too loaded with post-industrial implications to use of wealth-groupings which were the reflection of a very different economic, and so social, order. The graduations within urban society, between the rich member of the corporation and the obscure recipient of poor relief, were perhaps more extreme than in the countryside, if only because physical proximity made them more glaringly obvious, and certainly the intermediate levels between these two poles were often more subtle and complex than those beyond the walls.

We may learn a good deal more about the social structure of the city by looking at the record of the subsidy of 1525, the second instalment of the most comprehensive tax of the sixteenth century (see table 10[1]). The sub-division of the graduations of wealth reflected here is a hazardous task, for dividing lines must always be rather arbitrary. At the peak of the pyramid stood a comparatively small group of men assessed at £20 or more in goods, 6 per cent of the total and comprehending some 30 individuals. These men dominated the political, economic and social life of the city; as they held most of its riches so they monopolized its political power through their control of the self-perpetuating corporation. But there is no very clear distinction in terms of wealth between this group and the next, a broad middle section of the spectrum formed by the self-employed tradesmen, making up nearly 30 per cent of the total. These were the backbone of the town's economy. Below this group comes a transitional one, assessed at £2 in goods, really too poor to be classed as part of the 'middle class' but probably mostly self-employed; these men, totalling nearly one-fifth of the taxpayers, have been assigned to the 'working class' – reluctantly, because financial standing seems to have been a little more important than economic independence – but they might as easily be regarded as a distinct group in their own right. Below these again comes the real lower 'class', including nearly half the taxable population, and assessed only upon wages.

So these tax assessments allow the population to be classified firstly into two separate groups, the self-employed and the employees, and then into subdivisions based on wealth, with a group which tends to fall between the two. But the subsidy ignored a large number of the inhabitants because of their poverty. Since we know with a fair measure of reliability that there were 937 households in the city in 1563, we are entitled to assume that there were about 800 or more

Assessment		Number of taxpayers	Percentage of total
Goods	£50+	5	1
Goods	£40–9	4	1
Goods	£30–9	11	2
Goods	£20–9	11	2
			6
Goods	£11–19	32	6
Goods	£10	16	3
Goods	£7–8	9	2
Goods	£6	12	2
Goods	£5	19	4
Goods	£4	27	6
Goods	£3	27	6
			29
Goods	£2	90	18
Goods	£1	6	1
Profits	£1	53	11
Wages	£2	10	2
Wages	£1	167	32
			66
		499	

Table 10   Social structure: the 1525 subsidy

in 1525, which would lead us to the presumption that there are some 300 households missing from the tax assessment because of their poverty.[2] This forces us to modify the estimates given above of the relative size of the various social groups within the city population as a whole, as opposed to those within the tax assessment. With this in mind, the upper 'class' emerges with about 30 families (4 per cent), to which must be added a middle group of independent tradesmen of 140 families (18 per cent), a transitional body of self-employed men little better off than the wage earners of 100 (13 per cent), and a group of employees and poor of 530 families (66 per cent).

This provides us with a basic two-class society, a 'working class' comprehending some 80 per cent of the population and a 'middle/upper class' containing the remaining 20 per cent. The graduations within this upper group were extensive, but it is probably unwise to draw any firm division within it. It was not difficult to rise from the middle group to the upper one, for there was no distinct social barrier here, and in a city like Worcester hard work, ability and luck could bring unlimited advancement. There is certainly no evidence in wills and similar evidence that any firm frontier existed between these two sub-groups, and friendships, inter-marriage and similar social connections were very frequent. Within this broad division, wealth, and the social and political power which were in towns the direct and virtually automatic concomitants of wealth, was the only important graduating factor: social mobility within the group was necessarily high.

A very real social division within urban society lay between the independent tradesmen and their employees, the latter joined with those whose financial standing resembled that of the wage-earner. The distinction was a fairly rigid one, because of the legal requirement that all those engaged in independent trade should be freemen, a rule which was strictly enforced throughout the period under review. Thus the only way to break through this barrier was to set up in trade, but the freedom of the city could only be generally acquired by purchase or through a seven-year apprenticeship to a freeman. During the second half of the sixteenth century the admission fee stood at £4 or thereabouts, a very steep increase on the 13s. 4d. required during the first half of the century and which must have discouraged many would-be traders: this is proved by the relatively small numbers of men who acquired their freedom in this way.[3] The only alternative was apprenticeship or possibly marriage to a freeman's widow; the sons of freemen inherited their father's position. Apprenticeship would have been a discouragement to many poor families because it entailed a potential breadwinner working for seven years without wages, and even after apprenticeship some amount of capital was required in many trades. Although charities existed to lend capital to young traders, the disincentive must remain considerable, so that shortage of money and lack of citizenship must have prevented the majority from trying to cross this dividing line.

In some ways contact between employers and employees was small: the paternalism of the rich traders encouraged them to refer to their employees in their wills, but this is much rarer among the less wealthy majority. So this urban society was grouped along fairly simple economic lines, but these classifications were blurred drastically by other factors. The small size of the community forced upon it an intimacy which none could avoid. Although rich and poor tended to live in distinct quarters, these tended to be very close together, and no physical factor (like modern railway tracks) existed to prevent the citizens being mixed together in their everyday life by the essential character of the environment in which they lived. In particular, the fact that employer and employee tended to work in close proximity to each other – and even live in the same large household – prevented any wide rift between income or status groups.

A rather different sort of social grouping was formed by the parish. Primarily a religious and administrative unit, the urban parish was a very distinct community to those living in it. The frequency of bequests in wills which were confined to the testator's own parishioners are a tribute to this feeling, and frequently friends and relations all lived within the same small area. The weekly services at the parish church imparted a very real and tangible communal sense to this grouping, but it was in any case inevitable in a town of Worcester's size that the community needed to be broken down into more intimate units. The parishes in their turn must have been broken down into street communities. Despite the tendency for the rich and the poor to live in partly separate areas, the parishes often ran right across this partial zoning by social class, so that they brought together most sections of the community in a single social meeting place, the parish church at service time.

The broad trend of social zoning was for the rich to live along the main commercial streets as close to the centre of the city as possible, since all combined their place of work and their home in the same building. Thus the two principal shopping streets, High Street and Broad Street, were the centre of concentration for the rich. But the parish boundaries did not respect this grouping, and often ran quite counter to this pattern. Returning again to the 1525 subsidy, the topographical distribution of rich and poor areas is clearly shown. The central area is the richest, with a higher amount of taxation paid than the population of the parishes of St Helen and All Saints would suggest. On the other hand the peripheral parish of St Martin's pays only 11 per cent of the taxation although it contains 25 per cent of the taxpayers. The similarly situated parishes of St Clement, St Andrew and St Peter show the same phenomenon. If we compare the distribution of households contributing to the poor relief schemes of the 1550s and 1560s with that of those receiving relief, it is soon apparent that the central parishes of All Saints and St Helen have twice as many rich families as poor ones while in the peripheral parishes the situation is almost exactly reversed with twice as many families receiving relief as contribute to its cost. This disparity must have increased as homes were built expressly for the poor in the suburban areas in the later sixteenth and earlier seventeenth centuries.[4]

However, we should not make too much of all this, for the rich parishes often extended beyond the main streets into the poorer lanes, and there were always wealthy families living in even the poorest parishes. Although this tendency for rich and poor to live in different areas is a genuine and significant one, there was no clear dividing line between the zones, so that all classes mixed in most parts of the town to a greater or lesser degree: the age of the physical separation of the urban classes was still to come. In any case the various zones remained very close to each other, for from the rich parish of St Helen through the poverty of St Andrew and back to the wealth of All Saints was only a walk of two or three minutes.

The crowded and compressed nature of the city's built-up area also contributed to the fusion of different social groups, forcing people into close contact with their neighbours. This emerges very clearly from evidence given in the Bishop's Consistory Court in cases of defamation of character or immorality – everyone knew everyone else's business, and privacy or any kind of withdrawal of contact with neighbours, rich or poor, was a physical impossibility.[5] The social group formed by the street or group of buildings was an inescapable fact of urban life. Thus although the classes were to some extent segregated in different areas, the small and compressed nature of the city made this trend of limited significance in the issuing of urban society: throughout, the feature to be stressed is the degree of contact and intimate intermingling between the various social groups which was caused by the urban environment.

Next to this grouping by physical, geographical factors comes grouping by trades. There is little evidence that the craft guild, later on the trade company, was a very powerful unit. The number of sixteenth-century references to these bodies in wills is very small, and although their economic significance was still considerable, their social importance seems to have declined greatly, perhaps with their religious role. In the second half of the century there are very few mentions of them in wills at all, and those that do exist suggest that their main social importance was the provision of impressive funerals for their members. Funerals were major social occasions, on which large sums of money were lavished, but this could hardly justify assigning to the trade organizations an important social role. However, many wills show that the testator's friends were mostly drawn from among the members of his own trade, as well as those trusted and respected as executors or overseers. Clearly, inside a particular occupation there were very close links, but these were left at a personal level, rather than being expressed in the life of the craft organizations as institutions.

The smallest group to which the citizen of Worcester belonged was the family, the most powerful but least studied of all these groups. It is extremely difficult to produce very much documentation on the role of the urban family, but a few points may be made. First of all the family was a large unit: it contained not only blood relations – cousins in particular – but also the apprentices and domestic servants found in most of the wealthier families' households. However, relatively few well-established city families contained more than one adult generation: the problem of looking after the old rarely occurred, for parents frequently died before their children were even mature. Where a widow survived she was sometimes accommodated by assigning to her a part of the family house; the widow without a family to support her remained the largest chronic burden on the poor relief service. Generally speaking the family was a highly cohesive unit, and settled its own problems within itself – for instance when an aggrieved husband tried to get his neighbours to bear witness to his wife's adultery, they told him that this was a task for his own family, "his own brethren, who in such cases ought to stick unto him".[6] Most families were also economic units since son would work for their father and would be apprenticed to him so that they could take over when he died. Younger children would undertake simple mechanical tasks from an early age, and probate records indicate that widows often continued to administer their husband's business (they had probably assisted in this during his lifetime).

Compared with rural families, sixteenth-century town families died out or disappeared very quickly: it is difficult to find many examples of fourth-generation citizens. Probably the sense of social inferiority under which all townsmen laboured, and which drove them back to the countryside as soon as possible, combined with the appreciably higher mortality rates in urban areas, had much to do with this, but a contributory factor was the rarity of the principle of primogeniture in disposing of property at the death of the head of the family. The normal practice was to try to divide up an estate as equally as possible between all the children, and although businesses were normally transmitted entire, they were usually denuded of all capital in order to compensate the other children. This meant that each generation had to build up once more the achievement of the previous one; although good for the economy this situation discouraged the formation of lasting urban dynasties.

One of the most interesting issues in the social history of this period is the question of mobility – the transmuting of the old order by the rise and fall of individuals within it. Sixteenth-century England provided great opportunities for social advancement to the successful few in a society which was relatively 'open'. The town provided one of the best jumping-off grounds for the social climber for here wealth could be made much more quickly than in the countryside, and wealth, in sufficient quantity, was an acceptable *entrée* to the higher classes if tactfully veiled. So the towns drew to them immigrants in large numbers, poor and with a hopeless future on the land. Most of them did little better in the city, but a few made a distinguished success of their business careers and founded a powerful urban family, which would then usually be drawn back to the land. It is this catalytic function of towns in the mechanism of social change, their ability to turn poor immigrant to wealthy towns man to gentleman-farmer, which is one of the most interesting and important issues in urban social history.

Worcester was the goal of a continuing stream of immigrants from the countryside, like all other towns at this time, and indeed at most times. As has already been indicated, an important part of the growth of the city's total population was the inflow of migrants from the easily overcrowded rural areas, and since this growth is itself such an important phenomenon, the issue of immigration has a general as well as a social significance. Unfortunately it is particularly difficult to document it to a satisfactory degree. In many towns a register of freemen exists which does at least provide for the successful immigrant who was self-employed a record of his place of origin and trade. No such record now exists for Worcester, although there must have been one at the time since it was necessary to have written proof that any individual was properly admitted to the freedom and so entitled to trade on his own account. There are however some indirect clues which act as a poor but necessary substitute. For these purposes we may divide immigrants into two groups: firstly those who eventually became freemen, either through purchase or apprenticeship, and secondly those who came as wage-earners and remained employees for the rest of their lives, and so never needed to acquire the freedom.

The numbers of those who bought their freedom were never large; an annual average of five in the 1560s drops to about three in the 1590s. The entrance fee in the first half of the sixteenth century amounted to only 13s. 4d. but in 1555 it was raised to £5, although £4 seems to have been the most which was ever extracted in practice.[7] This appears to have been a deliberate attempt to exclude the immigrant in a period of economic difficulty. It was a large sum to expect the usual run of migrants to pay, and in fact the limited numbers who elected to enter in this way were allowed to pay in instalments, spread over two to four years in the 1560s but extending over as many as ten years as the century drew to a close. But this was always the means of entry for a minority – far more came in via an apprenticeship.

This is shown by a fragmentary record of the names of those who acquired the freedom in four separate years in the sixteenth century. In 1564–5, 1575–6 and 1582–3 totals of from 13 to 22 freemen were admitted by apprenticeship and only one or two by purchase. Interestingly, in 1522, the only other year for which this information exists, 11 men were admitted by purchase and only eight through apprenticeship.[8] If this reflects the usual situation in the first half of the century, then far more migrants moved in as adults and bought the freedom than when the price was higher later on, and the total number of new entrants in proportion to the size of the population was substantially greater than in later years. We may assume that the boom conditions of the cloth industry and the as yet under-populated state of the city led to migration in greater numbers, unobstructed by those already present in the city. This situation was brought firmly to an end by the economic crisis of the mid-sixteenth century.

So we may estimate that in the latter part of the century between 15 and 25 people were acquiring the freedom as outsiders every year. This is not a very impressive total, but it compares well with Leicester, where the figure is about 20, and Exeter with 28.[9] A far greater number of immigrants must have entered the city as employees, people looking for work and not aspiring to trade on their own account and so not requiring the freedom of the city. About these people we know very little, but they must have swelled very considerably the size of the poorer classes. The only direct contemporary reference to these people is a statement in 1584 that the number of poor people entering the city and trying to settle was increasing and that they came "the most part forth of Wales".[10] This movement is confirmed by references to 'Welshmen' as labourers on building sites and other casual work.

The local authorities, as has already been seen, were continually campaigning to stop poor people settling in the city and becoming potential recipients of poor relief funds, and they were particularly anxious to prevent the leasing of cheap housing to migrants. But we have no means of estimating the numbers of these people so that we can only judge by the concern of the corporation that the phenomenon was a considerable one. As to the origin of these would-be migrants, there is again no direct information. As far as immigrant apprentices were concerned – and this was the most important way in which the upper class received new blood – it is possible to gain some idea of their origins by looking at the birthplace of Bristol apprentices.[11] Here the boys from rural Worcestershire were mostly drawn from parishes bordering the Severn, and a far higher proportion went to masters in the wood and leather manufacturing trades than the relative importance of these trades in Bristol would suggest. It may be inferred from this that apprentices tended to come from areas where the town craftsmen in the course of their business were likely to establish personal contact with the family of the prospective migrant apprentice. Thus we should expect a high proportion of Worcester apprentices to come from homes in villages along the Severn valley, and from Herefordshire and Shropshire where the wool for Worcester's cloth industry was produced.

Some circumstantial evidence of the general origin of migrants of all ages may be derived from incidental references in wills to relatives, property and birthplaces outside Worcester, or to bequests to parishes in the countryside. If these are mapped (see figure 19) they show that the migrants come from an area between 10 and 25 miles from the city. Only a minority come from further afield, and here there is perhaps a slight predominance of people from the west, and possibly the north. In Shrewsbury, a town in a very similar geographical position, there is a much clearer movement from the west and north towards the south and east.[12]

We may also compare the situation in medieval Worcester, where the surnames recorded in tax lists of about 1300 indicate the birthplace of citizens at that date. The distribution of these surnames based on place-names indicates a movement into the city from the north and west, apart from one of the early settled areas immediately to the east.[13] This migration of people from the poorer, easily overpopulated highland zone in the west and north is only to be expected. Worcester, situated almost exactly on the border of this region and on major communication routes, was a natural target for people looking to a town for a better future or merely to find employment.

Immigration was a major factor in the population growth of the city and perhaps also in the continuance of a large class of townsmen living near the limits of subsistence. In an age of population stagnation, towns relied on immigration to counteract the effects of their high death rates, but in a period of natural growth such as the sixteenth century, immigration swelled the already growing urban population into a serious problem. But they also contributed to the fluidity and vigour of urban life compared with the countryside by supplying a continuous stream of new blood, not all of which remained in the lower social strata, apart from providing city employers with a large and willing pool of labour. From the immigrants' own point of view the very existence of cities like Worcester provided much the most readily available channel for social and economic advancement.

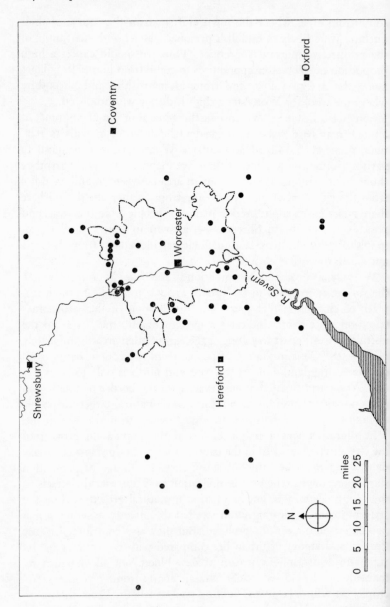

19   Origins of sixteenth-century immigrants to Worcester.

How did the mechanism of social and financial improvement
function in Worcester? The first stage was the acquisition of
wealth through independent trade enabling the immigrant, or his
son, to enter the upper class, and so the oligarchy which controlled
the corporation. It is possible to find out a good deal about this upper
group because it forms a manageable number of families whose
dominating position in the city has left its mark in the records. If we
define this upper, ruling group as the members of the corporation's
senior body, the Twentyfour, this provides us with 78 men between
1540 and 1600. For 71 of these individuals some personal information can be gleaned. Of this number, some 34 were the sons or
grandsons of citizens, although rarely citizens of great wealth or
distinction. But the remaining 37 names represent families quite
unrecorded in the city before these individuals emerge to wealth
and power: the size of this group may be partly due to our
ignorance, but it remains clear that a very high proportion, perhaps
as much as half, of the wealthy, and so ruling, class of the city was
of very recent origin as town dwellers.

Another clue is afforded by the city accounts, which record the
names of those who bought the freedom as newcomers each year:
among these occur the names of eight future members of the corporation, and most of these men had joined the Twentyfour within
ten years of entering the city as immigrants. Another significant fact
about these migrants with meteoric careers is that they are all concentrated between the opening of the records in 1546 and the latter
part of the 1550s – during the remaining 40 years of the sixteenth
century there is no sign of this phenomenon occurring at all. This
very rapid social advancement must mainly be attributed to the
cloth industry, and the ending of boom conditions in the trade
during the 1550s brought a great slowing down in the rapidity with
which fortunes were made, and consequently very rapid social and
political advancement was cut off too.

The remainder of this group of oligarchs, those whose families
had been present in the city before their rise to power, consisted
principally of second-generation citizens. The names of the bailiffs
between 1450 and 1520 reveal at the most two oligarchic families
which were still prominent by the middle of the sixteenth century,
so that clearly the turnover of families within the group was very
drastic. Even where the oligarch's father was a citizen, he was
normally in fairly humble circumstances; the wealthy oligarch

father succeeded by an equally wealthy and eminent son was an unusual exception rather than the rule. Thus these members of the dominant ruling group can be split roughly into two fairly equal halves, one marked by coming to the city, making a fortune and joining the oligarchy all in one lifetime, and the other principally composed of the sons of immigrants, usually financially undistinguished, and less commonly the grandsons of such men. So the wealth provided by city business provided an excellent first step up the ladder of social advancement, but there remained the problem of establishing the family in a stable and secure social and economic position.

The only answer to this situation was to move out to the countryside, to become a gentleman. Emigration was nearly as important (although not so frequent) a feature of this urban society as was immigration. This return to the land generally took place in the second or third generations. A good first step was to marry daughters into local gentry families, but although this did take place on a moderate scale, the majority of wealthy citizens' children married within their own social group. A more common first step was to buy land in the surrounding countryside – at first perhaps the odd field near the walls, and then a whole farm further out. This allowed the son to move his activities gradually over from business to a life as a rentier and farmer without any sudden break.

But the number of families which actually achieved this vital social transition was comparatively small compared with the quantity of apparently suitable oligarchic material. One of the most meteoric careers was that of William Mucklowe, the cloth exporter and mercer whose business activities have been described above.[14] His father was a yeoman farmer from Halesowen in the north of the shire, a yeoman farmer who only proved that he was not a villein by claiming illegitimacy; his son William came to Worcester, entered a wealthy career and then the oligarchy, but although he bought a good deal of land he seems to have remained a resident citizen until his death. His son joined the gentry and the family settled near Areley, in the far north of the county, in comparative obscurity.[15]

Another outstanding career was that of Roland Barklay. He was very distantly related to the distinguished Gloucestershire family of Berkeley, but his father was mayor of Hereford in 1545. Roland was the second son, probably coming to Worcester early in the reign of Elizabeth as a clothier's apprentice. In 1583, the year of his father's death, he joined the Twentyfour. His business career was highly successful, and by the early seventeenth century he had moved out to Spechley, some three miles from the city; five of his seven daughters married city men, but of his six sons, two became London merchants, another became a judge and succeeded him as the lord of Spechley, while the remaining three all founded minor gentry families of their own in the villages of the shire. The Barklays continued at Spechley into the present century.[16]

The Wildes were another successful family, and more deeply rooted in the city. A member, probably the first, died as a clothier member of the oligarchy in 1528. His son Thomas was a distinguished clothier and member of the city council, buying the Commandery, a one-time hospital, at the edge of the city. His son Robert converted the building into what was essentially a gentry mansion accidentally within the boundaries of a city, and gave up clothmaking to live on his rents and a little farming like any other country gentleman. He died in 1607. The family lived on here however, suspended between country and town until the later seventeenth century, producing a series of lawyers.[17] This propensity for a legal career is a feature of a number of these city families after their move to the countryside, probably because their financial and social position needed a professional career to strengthen the family fortunes. In any case many of the oligarchs – possibly about half – sent a son to university or the Inns of Court as another sound first step to gentility.

But it remains true that out of these 78 outstandingly successful city families only about a dozen established gentry families in the Worcestershire countryside by the middle of the seventeenth century. Some stayed in the city, especially as the rapidly-gained wealth of the cloth industry diminished and social mobility in the city was consequently reduced; a number of sixteenth-century eminent families may still be identified in the city after the Civil War. Of this dozen *nouveaux riches* families which joined the gentry, only the Barklays and the Wildes, with the possible addition of the Walsgroves of Hallow, could be called in any sense distinguished families on the county scene. The rest were mostly of very minor importance, and some must have rapidly fallen back into the original obscurity of their rural ancestors: the impact of urban families on rural upper class society was very limited. But from the point of

view of the poor immigrant, there remained the real possibility of a
rapid local route to social eminence.

Even if few made the grade and even fewer ever really established
themselves as gentry families, the fact of the existence of such a
movement remains, even if it must be heavily qualified. Perhaps the
failure of the richer citizens to make more impact on rural society
may be partly due to the fact that although the cloth industry produced conspicuous wealth, it was distributed more equally over a
larger group of tradesmen than was the case elsewhere; there was no
great dominant capitalist like Stumpe of Malmesbury, no one
whose wealth and eminence made the transition to rural society a
virtually automatic matter. The Worcester oligarchs were only just
wealthy enough to make the grade, and could not rival in wealth
the great merchants of ports like Bristol or Exeter, so that although
wealthy by Worcester standards, few were rich enough to make a
permanent social success of their country families.

The countryside was not the only goal for the successful city
family. Below the first rank lay others in the city who were ambitious but lacked opportunity. So, just as the frustrated rural immigrants came to Worcester in search of a better life, some citizens set
off for the wider horizons of London. Contacts between the two
cities were frequent, and it was the obvious target for those who felt
that Worcester had little to offer them. It will have been noticed
above that two of Roland Barklay's sons became London merchants,
and the successful London brother or uncle often occurs in Worcester wills. When Richard Badland, a city councillor, died in 1575 his
orphaned second son was sent off to London to be apprenticed.[18] As
with migration to Worcester, many must have gone and few been
really successful.

In a society which was hierarchical and ultimately based its assessment of social gradations on the possession of land, any means by
which social elevation was made possible are important, for this kept
the ruling group open to new talent and thus continuingly able. The
towns provided a main way by which this was achieved, and even
if the process was a long one and few emerged from it, the phenomenon is still an important one. It was much more likely that an
immigrant would make good in the city society without ever reaching the ranks of the gentry, but even in this sense Worcester
provided a fine opportunity for the enterprising, the lucky and the
ruthless to make good.

15

The structure of local government

The medieval government of the city of Worcester is an issue which is of vital importance to an understanding of the later system, which was firmly set on medieval foundations and was in many ways simply a continuation of it. It is however extremely difficult to disentangle the complexities of this medieval apparatus, and in particular the central problem of the inter-related functions of four different bodies, the Merchant Guild, the Trinity Guild, the governing body of the city before its incorporation, and the corporation set up in 1555.

The slow growth of a governing body controlling and representing the citizens can be traced back to 1189 at least, for then the city acquired the right to pay its annual dues to the Crown direct, rather than through the shire authorities. In 1227 these privileges were extended and a merchant guild was formally created; the relationship between this guild embracing the leading citizens and such a governing body as may by then have developed is obscure, but we may presume that by the later middle ages the two organizations, dominated by the same personalities, had fused into one effective institution, for by 1392 the city bailiffs' accounts were heard "in the Guild Merchant".[1]

Rather more relevant to this present study is the relationship developed between this body and the Trinity Guild. This guild was founded before 1372 and by the earlier years of the sixteenth century was responsible for the maintenance of the elementary school,

almshouses for 24 poor people and the repair of the town walls and
the bridge over the Severn. The Guild played an important part in
the social life of the city, and in particular there was a considerable
overlap of personnel between it and the city government. As an
example of this, the Master of the Guild in 1484, Richard Howton,
was high bailiff of the city in 1482 and 1486, and the Master in
1540, John Braughing, had been high bailiff in 1534; it seems to
have been usual for ex-bailiffs to be elected to the post.[2]

Other close connections existed, for new entrants to the Twentyfour, the senior body of the city council, were required to have
already held the post of steward of the Guild; more important was
the fact that the city council was by 1548 electing as an established
custom the principal officials of the Trinity Guild and had assumed
the power to control or advise the Master. We must assume that the
coincidence of personnel in both bodies led to a natural fusion, so
that the Trinity Guild became a social and charitable offshoot of the
city government. The city bye-laws were throughout the sixteenth
century referred to as 'the Acts of the Guild' but this tradition seems
to stem from the original Guild Merchant rather than the Trinity
Guild.[3]

Thus by the middle of the sixteenth century Worcester was ruled
by a body created by a long process of development involving the
coalescence of the early primitive apparatus of government with the
Merchant Guild to form a body which by the fifteenth century we
might call the city council, and the fusion of this body with the principal guild, brought about partly because of the extensive interest of
that guild in activities which were increasingly becoming the pro-
vince of public government rather than private charity.

The result of these fusions was the institution which ruled
Worcester until 1555. Its chief officers were the two bailiffs who
appear in the thirteenth century and were abolished early in the
seventeenth. By the end of the fourteenth century they had been
joined by two aldermen, mentioned in a luckily surviving document
of 1392 which, beside the two bailiffs and two aldermen, lists 31
other names, suggesting that the whole town council appears here.[4]
If Worcester followed the lines of development of other town councils, it would seem likely that already the governing body was
divided into two chambers, possibly of 12 and 24 members. If this
is so, the size of both bodies was doubled at some time in the fifteenth century. Perhaps this happened as the result of some political

truggle concealed from us, but the ordinances drawn up in 1466 nake the then prevailing situation much clearer.[5]

By 1466 the council was made up of two chambers, the Twenty-four and the Fortyeight, sometimes described as the 'great clothing' and the 'commoners' respectively. The traditional two bailiffs and two aldermen had been joined by two chamberlains, financial officers created at some time between 1434 and 1466.[6] Together, the two chambers formed the 'common council', meeting quarterly.[7] The relationship between the Twentyfour and the Fortyeight was a highly co-operative one, although each body was a distinct and separate entity. Each chamber selected one of the chamberlains, an equal number of auditors for the annual hearing of the city accounts, and the Fortyeight had to be present when a grant of city property was under discussion. This system was to be the basis of local government in the sixteenth century.

Some modification took place during the later years of the fifteenth century. Three extra bye-laws were added between 1466 and 1496.[8] The first of them prescribed heavy penalties for the use of aggressive language in the council chamber – "words of occasion or reproof". The second formally relieved members of the council of the obligation to serve in the relatively humble posts of sergeant and constable, apparently because "at some seasons of willfullness" "persons of worship" had been elected as a means of humiliating them. The third act restricted candidates for the office of bailiff to members of the Twentyfour and required that new members of that body should be selected from the Fortyeight.

Taken together, these acts would indicate that some political struggle had been taking place. It would appear that the council was under pressure from elements outside it, presumably townsmen resentful of the dominant and exclusive power of council members. These troubles were reflected in an increasing reluctance to undertake office when elected to it, for the fines for refusal to take office were doubled during this period.[9] Whatever the origin and nature of this conflict, it did not reappear during the sixteenth century, although there was sometimes an eruption of resentment against the council from the many who were excluded from membership. What went on in the later fifteenth century may well have represented the final step in the eradication of popular pressure upon a now self-perpetuating and largely irresponsible council, an exclusive-ness modified only by a strong sense of obligation towards the community as a whole which was maintained until the eighteenth century.

The charters granted to a town by the Crown were the legal basis of its government. Worcester had received a number of important grants in the thirteenth and fourteenth centuries, followed by a series of fifteenth-century confirmations of these grants.[10] But it is unlikely that the city ever received a formal grant of incorporation, that right which endowed the council with the legal fiction of representing, indeed of being, the whole body of the citizens in judicial matters. This was not necessarily crucial, since this right was in practice assumed without challenge, but the lack of such status was potentially an embarrassment, especially when many important towns acquired such charters in the later fourteenth and fifteenth centuries. By the middle of the sixteenth century such backwardness could continue no longer.

In 1551 Worcester received a charter from Edward VI confirming all previous grants, by now a routine arrangement with each new monarch. But in 1553 the city presented some kind of petition to the Privy Council, probably applying for an extended charter, but this fell through with the accession of Mary later in the year. Possibly connected with this was a legal dispute involving the council, which by December 1554 had reached the point where the council's status as a corporate body and its right to exclude the citizens at large from any real participation in city government was at issue. Nothing more of this case is known: it may have been a move to challenge the power of the oligarchy from those outside it, or it may have been a legal manoeuvre to re-open a case in the city courts which had no overt political significance. One of the old charters had been lost, an added complication.[11]

This legal complexity became the pretext for a move to acquire a wholly new governing charter incorporating extended powers and privileges for the city and its council. A committee was set up both to search for evidence to refute the legal doubts thrown on the council's powers and to draw up proposals for a new charter. Originally they planned to apply for the city to be raised to county status, ruled by a mayor and sheriffs, a constitution typical of a number of other important towns at the time, thus giving them complete independence of the county authorities. This was dropped, allegedly for lack of finance, and instead a list of final aims was drawn up, involving a formal grant of incorporation, the confirmation of the whole body of organization and legislation then in force with the addition of any useful new rights which the negotiations could acquire, if they were "commodious and profitable and not chargeable to the said city and the officers thereof".[12]

A major factor in the negotiations for the new charter was the fact that Sir John Bourne, who lived near the city at Battenhall, was Queen Mary's Secretary of State. He had been a member of parliament for the city in 1553 when it was very unusual for a non-citizen to be elected. Without some kind of influential contact at Court it was very difficult for any town to make its opinions felt, so Bourne was carefully contacted by the city's representatives, his wife was given a gift of valuable spices and we may suppose that the city made some kind of implicit or explicit undertaking to him to increase his political influence locally in return for his help. In addition to influence, cash was equally important. By far the largest expense was an endless series of consultations with lawyers spread over the 92 days the city's representatives were in London acquiring the charter; since these delegates were paid a daily sum throughout this period this was another major item. Various sums had to be paid to oil the machinery of the Tudor bureaucracy – charges for finding and copying archives, a payment to one of the Lord Treasurer's clerks "to have his furtherance with his master" and another bribe "to move my Lord Chancellor for to search our book".[13] Charters were essential for any town government but the expense of getting them could be crippling.

This charter, whose detailed provisions are outlined below, solved the immediate legal problem, which was the pretext for acquiring it, but it was still inadequate for the city's needs. Since the projected elevation to county status had been dropped before the real negotiations had begun, the new charter entailed mainly a grant of corporate status which did not in practice extend privileges very far, and the other provisions were of limited importance, the acquisition of custody over orphans' estates being the most significant.

Dissatisfaction with the legal basis of the city's government again becomes apparent in the 1580s. The background to this was a state of continual friction with the shire authorities over a variety of issues, stemming from the political weakness of the city beset by a county administration manned by its social superiors, the local gentry. There were also difficulties over certain legal points in the charter – for instance the city's right to collect and keep the fines imposed on criminals had to be defended in 1583.[14] But the main motive behind a renewed drive for a new chartered basis for city government was undoubtedly a desire to resist more firmly political pressure from the shire.

In 1587 legal advice was taken, ambiguities and faults in the 1555 charter were investigated and an approach was made to Westminster to get a new grant, but all this came to nothing and was abandoned. In 1594 legal advice was again taken, partly because of a flagrant breach of the city's privileges by the shire authorities and partly because the valuable right to levy tolls on the Droitwich salt traffic was in question; both these issues led to legal action. A committee was created to discuss the form of a new charter and the old plan to become a county with a mayorality was raised. Again all this was eventually abandoned without anything being achieved. It was raised again with more determination in 1604. By this time the goal of county status had become the primary objective, and the corporation went as far as to raise £100 to achieve this, but it was obliged firstly to drop the county status element and then the whole question once more. In 1615 yet another attempt failed.[15]

In 1621 success came at last. Corporation members seem to have begun to lose hope, for it was decided to make another effort by only 30 votes to 24 when voting on any issue was unusual and unanimity was normally expected. But by October 1621 the new charter had been obtained and was read to the assembled citizens, although the cost of £200 threw the city treasury into debt. This 1621 charter raised the city to county status, substituted a mayor for the two bailiffs, created six aldermen from the previous two and converted the chamberlains into treasurers, but retained the two chambers of the Twentyfour and the Fortyeight.[16] This seems at last to have satisfied the needs of the corporation, but it had taken at least 70 years of frustrated effort to substitute a more modern constitution for one which was basically medieval.

As has already been stated, the main objective of all this effort seems to have been to escape from the influence of the shire government by achieving complete parity and so absolute independence from it, through county status for the city. This friction must have been the main problem, but the city may also have wished to strengthen its hand against the power of the Council in the Marches, within the pervasive jurisdiction of which it lay. The great difficulty faced by the city in increasing its authority and independence needs some explanation. This difficulty was no new thing, for during the medieval period the city was much more backward constitutionally than its size and wealth would suggest. A clue here is that the Bishop of Worcester wrote to the Earl of Salisbury in 1607 thanking him for frustrating an attempt by the city to secure a charter which infringed his rights.[17]

It is difficult to see how the bishop's rights would be affected, but he may well have resisted any strengthening of the city's power because it would limit his own local influence. The bishop played an important part in the politics of the region, especially through his seat on the Council in the Marches, and he may have been acting in the interest of the cathedral clergy and some of the shire gentry. The dean and chapter of the cathedral, and their predecessors the monks, were probably another conservative party, and at least in the early seventeenth century they were trying to stop a new charter.[18] Their main fear was probably that a more powerful city government would threaten the absorption of the exempt area around the cathedral into the city jurisdiction, although there is no recorded intention to do this on the part of the corporation. Thus the powerful vested interests of the Church may well lie at the root of the considerable delay in getting a sound constitutional basis for city government, as compared with similar towns elsewhere.

Since the 1555 charter was the basis for city government during most of the period under review, it deserves close scrutiny.[19] It confirmed the existing officials, the two bailiffs, aldermen and chamberlains, with a common council composed of the Twentyfour and the Fortyeight. It also approved the other dignitaries, the recorder, town clerk, sergeants-at-mace and constables, with the long-held rights to hold a weekly court of record, markets and fairs. There followed a long list of other privileges, mostly of a legal nature and especially involving independence from the power of the county and royal officials and their administration of justice. The main extensions of the city's rights were the grant of the custody of the persons and goods of orphans and the power for the corporation to buy and hold lands of an annual value of £40. All this placed on a sound legal footing the administrative developments of the later Middle Ages, but rights at this period depended as much on their constant use as on any written grant, and although the charter specifically freed the city from most of the jurisdiction of the county magistrates, this independence had to be claimed and defended repeatedly during the ensuing decades.

The basis of the city government was the council, with its two chambers, the Twentyfour and the Fortyeight. This body was obliged to meet quarterly, normally in March, April to June, September and December. A trend towards extra meetings becomes clear by the later years of Elizabeth's reign when five meetings were normal and six or seven not exceptional. This reflected the increasing weight of business dealt with by local government in general and towns in particular. There were also formal gatherings, at which general business was sometimes conducted, for the annual election of officers at Michaelmas and for the audit of the city accounts every December. An additional annual meeting was held to administer the business of the dissolved Trinity Guild.

All members of both chambers were obliged to attend, and absentees from meetings were regularly fined after the introduction of an ordinance to this effect in 1559. Members were also forced to wear their 'livery gowns' at formal occasions and to attend the funerals of their colleagues. By the 1590s the problem of non-attendance had become so serious that a salutary example was needed, so a member of the Fortyeight seen in the street when he should have been attending the official elections was given the choice of paying a heavy fine of £2 or being dismissed from the corporation.[20]

Admission to both bodies was by election, the Twentyfour selecting their recruits from among the Fortyeight and the Fortyeight from the "most sad and sufficient" of the ordinary citizens: in neither case did anyone outside the corporation have any influence in the choice. New entrants paid an admission fee, thus helping an insolvent corporation and excluding the poorer citizens; throughout the century the Twentyfour paid 16s. 8d. and the Fortyeight half that sum. However, when the corporation was in greater financial difficulties than usual, much higher fees could be charged in individual cases, such as the £6 16s. 8d. paid by a new member of the Twentyfour in 1554.[21]

Refusal to take up office was almost unknown at any level in Tudor Worcester, and only one example, an aletaster, is recorded. This is in marked contrast to some other towns where great difficulty was experienced in finding willing office-holders. This is probably more of a reflection of Worcester's wealth and political stability than any excess of civic loyalty. Another important factor was that its officers were rarely expected to make up any deficiency in their accounts out of their own pockets, as did happen elsewhere. But resignations were another matter, and in 1591 it was decided to punish resignations without the corporation's assent with the astronomical fines of £100 for the Twentyfour and £50 for the Fortyeight. This was an effective deterrent, for the payment of such a fine is never recorded.[22]

The relationship between the two chambers making up the council is an interesting one, especially as bitter political conflict arose on this question in some other towns. Basically, the upper house, the Twentyfour, had a virtual monopoly of power, and the principal function of the lower house, the Fortyeight, was to 'represent' the citizens at large in a formal way, thus giving the Twentyfour a very manageable and usually docile substitute for genuine public participation in city government. By the end of the fifteenth century the Fortyeight had acquired the right to be present when matters affecting city property were under discussion, but their exact role is not clear. They seem always to have chosen two auditors of the accounts and held two of the keys to the archives and treasury, but probably their practical control over the broad range of city business was slight.[23]

At the annual election of city officials, the business seems to have been split into two sections, the 'high election' and the 'low election'. For instance in 1549 the 'high' electors were the Twentyfour and chose the major officials, and the Fortyeight, as the 'low' electors, were only called in to help choose the minor functionaries like aletasters and constables. There were only 24 'low' electors so the Fortyeight must have been halved in number so that they could not outvote their seniors. But in any case the lower chamber's influence was necessarily limited because nearly all the major officials could only be chosen from among the members of the Twentyfour.[24]

The degree of participation of the Fortyeight in the regular meetings of the corporation is equally difficult to define. On the two occasions when voting is recorded, the lower house appears to have voted with the Twentyfour and without restriction of numbers, but in 1559 the Fortyeight were given their own meeting place as if they discussed business as a separate body. At any rate in 1576 some members of the Fortyeight complained that while the charter stated that they formed the common council of the city with the

Twentyfour, they were excluded from some meetings, and while they had the right to elect two of the keepers of the keys to the treasury and so had access to the charters in which they could find their rights specified, the upper house was ignoring this.[25] This protest appears to have been more of a matter of petty irritations than any major revolt against the constitution, for apart from this one incident, harmony seems to have prevailed. In any case, political conflicts within town councils at this period often appear to have their origin in the social or economic structure of the town, and in Worcester there was little conflict in these spheres to reflect itself in the council's affairs.

The bailiffs, as the chief executive officers, were much the most important of the city dignitaries. A high and a low bailiff were elected each year, and the low bailiff was almost invariably elected high bailiff for the second year following his term of office, so that he had a rest of a year between the two posts. The low bailiff acted as a general assistant to his colleague, a kind of practical training for the exacting task of a high bailiff. The latter did not regularly serve more than one term of office; in the first half of the sixteenth century about one in 15 returned to serve a second term but in only one case was a third term served. During the reign of Elizabeth a second term became almost unknown: this seems to have been due to the rarity with which low bailiffs died before they had a chance to take the senior position, since second terms in the earlier period seem mainly due to death removing the only experienced man who had not held high office before.

The duties of the bailiffs were dauntingly extensive. With the aldermen and the recorder they formed the bench of the city magistrates, which involved holding a whole series of different courts. The primary responsibility of the bailiffs was for the maintenance of law and order and the whole administration of justice in the city. With the aldermen they were responsible for the supervision of the markets and the regulation of the economy. Both bailiffs were expected to finance their year of office from the proceeds of their judicial position, fines, tolls, forfeitures and the like. This relieved the city of any obligation to pay them a salary or allowance for what was virtually a full-time position, and at the same time acted as an effective stimulus to their zeal in the execution of their duties.

As general executive officers the bailiffs had wide powers and were free to influence a similarly wide range of the activities of local government. There were few formal limits to their power, although they were forbidden to admit anyone to the freedom of the city on their own initiative, and their emergency measures to deal with the 1597 famine had to receive the formal, if belated, assent of the full council.[26] But the rarity with which the council formally checked the activities of the bailiffs shows the harmony in which the system worked, aided especially by the certainty that any particular bailiff would be only in office for 12 months so that his opportunity to break free from his fellow councillors was very limited. The bailiffs were quite frequently the victims of insult, defiance or even physical assault in the execution of their duties, and in these cases the full weight of the corporation's authority was brought to bear on the offenders.

The two aldermen were principally concerned with economic regulation. They filled the office of clerk of the market – the 1496 ordinances define their role more precisely.[27] They were to supervise the sale of fuel and make daily and weekly inspections of oatmeal, butter and candles, butchers and fishmongers. They were to confiscate food offered for sale at too high a price or in defective quality. They were to hold a court in the Guildhall four times a year to administer fines and generally maintain the elaborate regulations affecting the trade and industry of the city.

The city accounts show that the aldermen were receiving fines from vintners, butchers, tallow chandlers and especially victuallers. The total of fines they collected was not large but increased in the 1550s and 1590s, years of high and erratic food prices when more regulation must have been carried out. In periods less marked by economic difficulty their activities seem to have slackened off, for in 1568 they were threatened with a £10 fine if they did not keep their court at least once a year.[28]

The aldermen also acted as general magistrates with the bailiffs, but their authority was limited, and in 1583 the bailiffs were instructed not to release prisoners committed by the aldermen before the latter had been consulted, and constables were reminded of their obligation to carry out the alderman's orders.[29] The office was normally filled by the previous year's bailiffs, so that they were well qualified to act in an advisory capacity.

The chamberlains were the city's general financial officials, responsible for collecting the regular revenues and for spending them on civic business. This entailed a great deal of supervision of public works and the maintenance of the city's considerable stock of house property. Unlike some towns, Worcester's chamberlains were rarely required to dip into their own pockets to remedy any shortage of money beyond their control. The Twentyfour elected one of their number as high chamberlain and the Fortyeight similarly appointed the low chamberlain, who was then most likely to be elevated to the Twentyfour at the next vacancy. Thus a 'classic' career in office would begin with being low chamberlain, followed by election to the Twentyfour and the high chamberlain's post, then a gap of two or three years followed by a year as low bailiff, the next as alderman, the following one as high bailiff and the last year in office as alderman again. The whole system was designed as a ladder of promotion in which each rung involved observation and training for the next, so that few came to office without some relevant experience. The practices here were all followed consistently without many variations, but it was all entirely customary, without any written or legal justification. An added advantage was that the system reduced political conflict to a minimum, since the candidate for any post was already virtually appointed by the system, reducing electoral tensions to the minimum.

The earliest reference to a town clerk is in 1476. He was the city's legal officer, responsible chiefly for supplying the magistrates with legal advice and for making and keeping the records of the corporation's activities. By 1595 he had a clerk to assist him. He was required to be a citizen if possible, and this always seems to have been so in practice.[30]

Of the town clerks whose names and careers are recorded, John Fleet (1593–9) and William Wiat (1599 onwards) were the sons of prominent citizens who had made their fortunes and sent their sons for legal training. Edward Darnell (1559–80) was admitted to the freedom as an immigrant and also traded as a vintner.[31] Walter Jones (1580–93) was the son of a Welshman who had moved to Witney in Oxfordshire, made a fortune in clothing and married his son Walter to the daughter of a London goldsmith. He was admitted to the freedom of Worcester when he became town clerk in 1580 and was called to the bar in 1584. He prospered, resigned and moved into the countryside, returned to Lincoln's Inn for the furtherance of his legal career, became a Worcestershire J.P. by 1601, received a grant of arms and bought the manor house at

Chastleton in Oxfordshire where he founded a long-lived gentry family.[32]

Jones's was probably the most distinguished career in the office, but its distinction must have rested on his private law practice, which seems to have been normal and probably essential for the incumbent. John Fleet became Queen's Attorney in the Council in the Marches between 1599 and 1609, that is as soon as he resigned his Worcester position, so that for the ambitious the town clerkship was a springboard to a distinguished legal career.[33] Jones served as Member of Parliament for the city on four occasions and Fleet, his successor, twice.

The recordership was more of an opportunity for the city to win the support of a prominent local landed family than a city office as such. There is only one documented instance of a recorder actually even being present in the city, and this was the somewhat unusual occasion in 1539 when he attended a meeting called to discuss allegations of bribery against the town clerk. However the town clerk was formally required to consult the recorder, whose deputy he nominally was, on any intricate points of law which arose in the city courts. Recorders seem always to have been distinguished lawyers and also where possible members of influential local families. Richard Littleton, in office by 1497, was a son of the distinguished local judge Thomas Littleton, and was a county J.P. from 1500–4 and also served on the bench of neighbouring counties. Sir John Packington, in office in 1539 and until 1551, was a distinguished lawyer and the founder of a very powerful county family.[34]

The next three recorders, Sir Robert Townshend (1551–7), Sir John Pollard (1558) and Mr Simons (1558–9), are all rather obscure, and may well have been outsiders forced on the city by outside interests. John Throckmorton (1559–80) was a younger son of that very influential Warwickshire-Worcestershire family, and was also vice-president of the Council in the Marches in the 1560s.[35] George Bromley (1580–7) came from another influential legal family within the shire, while Henry Townshend was from another local but less important family.

There is perhaps a trend from the middle years of the sixteenth century onwards to choose younger sons and less powerful county families – either the county magnates were less interested in the influence the post carried or the city felt itself sufficiently powerful to avoid involving itself with an over-influential, and so demanding, patron. Here there may be a connection with the friction often present during these years between the shire and city governments, a state of affairs which may have discouraged the corporation from becoming too closely attached to powerful shire interests.

The other city officials were surprisingly numerous. There was a hallkeeper to supervise the markets in the Guildhall, and an assistant for the bailiffs and aldermen in their duties in supervising the markets, with his own assistants in turn. There were two officials to superintend the sale of fuel, especially coal at the riverside, a beadle with assistants to control vagrants and a pavier to mend the streets and highways. Each of the gates in the city walls had its keeper, also responsible for the collection of tolls, accompanying the bailiffs when they read royal proclamations, and various other miscellaneous duties. Each of the six wards into which the city was divided had its two constables, elected annually from the "good, honest, sad and discreet" citizens, avoiding those "of simple condition".[36] Their main duty was of course the maintenance of law and order, and they were reinforced in 1597 by a properly organized night watch of eight men, patrolling from 9 p.m. to 5 a.m., partly at the expense of the innkeepers and victuallers.[37] The constables also had a number of other miscellaneous duties, such as helping to collect taxes.

The four sergeants-at-mace were a separate group of officials whose duty it was to aid the magistrates and their courts by serving summonses, empanelling juries, making arrests and the like. This office seems to have been a lucrative one, for in 1584 the Archbishop of Canterbury wrote to recommend a man for a vacancy, and from 1594 both bailiffs were allowed to nominate a sergeant each for their year of office as if this was a valuable right of patronage.[38] Sergeants received a pension or other financial help after their retirement more regularly than any other corporation employee.

16

The functions of local government

Worcester's government operated over a wide range of activities and so came into contact with the citizens' lives at many points. First of all it administered justice. The 1555 charter confirms and defines these duties, which included holding a court of record every Monday before three magistrates drawn from the bailiffs, aldermen and chamberlains; they could deal with a wide range of offences and cases, both criminal and civil (although mostly the latter), and ranging from trespass to debt. The bailiffs, aldermen and recorder were also justices of the peace for the city, and three of them, of whom one bailiff and the town clerk acting for the recorder were essential, could deal in their Quarter Sessions with a wide range of more serious offences including felonies like treason or murder.[1] Since every record of the proceedings of these courts has disappeared, we know very little of how they were conducted or the actual nature of the cases heard.

The only one of the city government's judicial activities which is well documented was the traditional thrice-yearly 'view of frankpledge and sessions of the peace', also known more simply as 'the law day'. This was essentially what in other places would be called a court leet, very similar to the manorial court which was the centre of the administration of unchartered towns and which presumably survived from Worcester's more remote past. The court consisted of two sections, the first concerned with what one would expect, the presentation and punishment of breaches of the law, while the second part produced and amended the local bye-laws. The only surviving complete account of such a court, that of 1553, makes clear its real nature in the heading used for the legislative section of the court's business: "Constitutions and Ordinances made and ordained by the Great Inquest by the general consent of the common council of the City of Worcester at a session of the peace . . .".[2] The great inquest was in fact a jury made up of prominent citizens – naturally the members of the Twentyfour, whose decisions were ratified by the whole corporation.

An originally popular form of government had in this fashion been completely absorbed into the routine judicial functions of city government. The jury in 1553 licensed and punished sellers of ale and food, punished those who profiteered in the supply of food and drink, played unlawful games, filled feather beds in contravention of the regulations, were retained by local gentry, or were "hosts to evil persons": such a miscellaneous collection of minor offences, by tradition dealt with in this way rather than by the magistrates, must have been typical of every meeting of this court.

The jury then went on to formulate the bye-laws, in the past called the 'Acts of the Guild' but now less concerned with the administrative apparatus of government and more with a variety of routine matters; they included the publicizing of measures which the corporation had already decided in private, such as the price maxima for food, drink and candles, much minor management of economic matters and the maintenance of public health and local amenities. Sometimes this body acted as a public watchdog by criticizing the administration of the bailiffs, especially in urging them to enforce neglected pieces of legislation. In 1564, it is suggested, there were two sets of presentments placed before this jury, one set originating with the corporation's officials and another drawn up by the constables, and so presumably in part reflecting public opinion in the wards.[3] Apart from this thrice-yearly review of minor offences and legislation, the bailiffs, aldermen and chamberlains after 1581 met once each week to review generally offences against civic legislation.[4]

The administration of justice in its various forms was probably the most important single duty of the city government, but it was closely followed by the multifarious obligations involved in administering a highly regulated economy. There were markets and fairs to be supervised, satisfactory standards of quality and quantity to be maintained, prices to be controlled, wages to be kept down, general conditions of employment, especially apprenticeship, to be regulated, co-operation with, and occasional supervision of, the individual craft companies to be kept up, while the supply of goods and food had to be ensured in periods of scarcity or high prices. All these branches of economic regulation are dealt with in greater detail above, but it is necessary to point out here how much of the city officials' time and effort was absorbed by it all.

A number of other aspects of the corporation's work are also dealt with elsewhere, such as the provision of relief for the poor, the supression of vagrancy, the upkeep of the city's grammar school, almshouses and charities and a great deal of estate administration, the granting of leases, arranging repairs, collecting rents and super-intending public works. The city administered a number of chari-table bequests, mostly involving help to the destitute but occasionally loan funds to be used to lend money to young men setting up in in trade. But the corporation's responsibilities here were limited, since most charities were superintended by private individuals or the trade companies. What charitable bequests did fall to its administra-tion were usually ones made by people not resident in the city. It also was generally responsible for checking on the administration of a large charitable trust held by the corporation of Gloucester.[5]

The next broad division of local government activity was a wide range of services which may be conveniently grouped together as public amenities of some kind. An ordinance of 1568 urged all council members, innkeepers and "good commoners" to hang lan-terns outside their houses on winter evenings, but this attempt to provide a cheap street lighting system was probably never more than a pious hope.[6] It was the individual citizen's own responsibility to pave the street in front of his house and in 1558, 1568 and 1583 the corporation was obliged to remind all of this fact, but if a sense of duty failed the chamberlains were to pave the offending section and send the householder to prison if he failed to pay them for doing this. A common pavier employed by the private householder for this purpose existed by 1558. In 1594 it was decided to make the pavier a corporation employee but this innovation was quickly cancelled, and instead the pavier was to charge a small standard fee upon the households in front of which he worked, the remainder of his expenses being met by the city.[7] This particular case is a good example of a general trend, local government hesitantly taking on a direct responsibility for what in the past had been the duties of the individual citizen.

The prevention of fire was a constant concern for the Tudor townsman. A number of towns were devastated by very extensive fires, Stratford-upon-Avon probably being the nearest example. Worcester never suffered such a catastrophe, partly by good fortune and partly as a result of good government. In 1466 the use of timber chimneys and thatched roofs was forbidden and the repetition of this prohibition in 1496 and as late as 1584 shows how long it took to eradicate them. But the use of roofing tiles must gradually have become universal, for although fire hooks to drag away blazing thatch were part of the municipal fire precautions in the fifteenth century they are not included in the following century. In 1496 water to fight fires was supplied by the water carriers' carts, but by 1596 bye-laws had established a supply of some 200 leather fire buckets. A major fire risk were the piles of fuel maintained by brewers, bakers, smiths and similar traders. By 1563 no piles of furze and gorse for their furnaces were to be kept within the walls. Probably the presence of a local tile-manufacturing industry did most to avoid the outbreak of a major fire, but certainly the corporation did everything else possible.[8]

The city's water supply was mainly drawn in the sixteenth century from a number of communal wells situated within the walls. Those who lived near them were responsible for keeping them clean and in good repair. The brewers used the river for their industrial supplies, but only from the stretch upstream from the bridge where pollution from refuse and sewage was minimal. Here too women washed their clothes at shallow places. Health regulations banned the disposal of any pollutant above the bridge, but below it the condition of the river was probably serious, for the corporation sank a well on the quayside to supply its storehouse.[9]

By the end of the sixteenth century the state of the water supply was causing concern, either because of population pressure leading to shortage or because of pollution. In 1599 a project for piping water into the city from the open countryside was first mooted. The cathedral-priory had since the fifteenth century received its supply by a pipe over the bridge from the higher ground to the west of the Severn. In 1599 a committee was appointed to draw up plans to bring water to four separate points within the city, and to estimate its cost. Early in 1600 another committee was to see what subscrip-

tions could be raised from private individuals, a task with an un-
encouraging result, for the whole scheme was dropped, presumably
on grounds of cost.[10]

The plans for an improved water supply were revived again in
the summer of 1619 when, at an estimated cost of £200, water was
to be brought from the bridge to cisterns at the Grass Cross and the
Corn Market. This scheme had been completed by 1623, when the
need for larger cisterns was expressed. The source of the water may
have been the cathedral's conduit, since the pipe apparently went no
further than the bridge.[11] This is another example of the problems
raised by the rapid growth of the city's population; again it will be
evident that the pressure became really acute in the early years of the
seventeenth century, and that one result was an increase in the scope
and scale of local government activity.

The corporation was also involved in the promotion of public
health and the prevention of various nuisances. It was well aware of
the connection between bad standards of communal hygiene and
outbreaks of epidemic disease, for in 1579 it ordered the removal of
manure heaps from the streets in order to avoid plague.[12] These
manure heaps were a serious problem to the authorities and frequent
measures were drawn up to diminish the nuisance caused. Eventually
a limited number of areas were earmarked for this use on the outskirts of the city, but the dumping of refuse and manure in the less
frequented lanes like Dolday and Angel Lane continued to be a
source of anxiety. A continual campaign against the keeping of pigs
within the walled area was another feature of these attempts to make
an increasingly crowded city less unpleasant and unhealthy. The
streets continued to be used for the disposal of anything unwanted,
as is shown by prosecutions in the cathedral manorial court for
throwing the contents of chamber pots into the street: this was only
objected to when the offending substance landed on the heads of the
constables. The disposal of industrial waste products by the city's
traders was also controlled, butchers, leather dressers and brewers
being particularly likely to give offence. This material could be
thrown into the Severn as long as this was done below the bridge.[13]
The measures taken to combat outbreaks of plague are outlined
above.

Worcester certainly seems to have been rather less frequently
attacked by epidemics in the second half of the sixteenth century
than were a good many towns, although this may well only have

made the disastrous epidemics of the earlier seventeenth century rather worse because the population had acquired little natural immunity. A vigorous and effective local authority could probably do something to minimize outbreaks of disease, but the battle to keep up reasonable standards of hygiene was a very demanding one, and what evidence we have reflects the authorities' awareness of the problem rather than the extent of their success. A major factor which probably did much to create these difficulties was the continual inflow of migrants from the countryside, for the easy-going habits appropriate to a village of scattered cottages were only slowly eradicated in stiflingly crowded city conditions.

Another minor activity of the corporation was the administration of the orphans' court. The custody of the bodies and goods of the orphaned children of citizens came within the court's jurisdiction under the terms of the 1555 charter.[14] The money inherited by these children was administered by the court, and was mostly lent to any citizen who was reliable and would enter into bonds to return it, while maintaining the children until they came of age, a small proportion of the inheritance being deducted to cover the cost of their upbringing. This provided some Worcester tradesmen with a valuable source of capital, but the corporation did not itself benefit from the institution as a source of cheap loans, as happened at Exeter for instance.[15] The size of the business done by this court was not great, and in the 53 years following its foundation in 1555 only 127 wills were enrolled in its register, and these in ever dwindling numbers.

It will already have emerged how extensive were the activities of the city government, but as yet unlisted are many routine duties – for instance the collection of taxes and provision of armed soldiers on behalf of the central government. Worcester was constantly receiving a flow of proclamations, enquiries and directives from the Privy Council and the Council in the Marches. It is this relationship between the government of the city and the central government and the shire authorities which must next be considered.

The city's contacts with the central government were made principally through the Council in the Marches, although direct contact with the Privy Council was made on special matters as occasion demanded. But the influence of the vigorous Council in the Marches was ever-present, and was probably regarded locally with mixed feelings. Many areas made determined efforts to remove themselves from the Council's jurisdiction – Bristol, Gloucester and Chester in the sixteenth century and the counties of Worcester and Hereford in the seventeenth, but the only attempt to free Worcester came from a private citizen, Robert Wilde, who objected to a legal decision taken against him by the Council. Otherwise the city made no recorded protest against this powerful local agent of the central government.[16]

The Council in the Marches was partly peripatetic and this could be of great advantage to the towns which regularly played host to it, like Ludlow, Shrewsbury or Bewdley, since this brought all the increased trade of an administrative centre, but in Worcester's case the visits were so uncommon that the small commercial stimulus was probably outweighed by the considerable costs of playing host to such a gathering. The first recorded visit was in 1559, when the Council came to meet its new president in Worcester: this cost the city a banquet. It returned for a week in 1561, for which the corporation was required to provide accommodation, 30 feather beds, pasture for 60 horses and every item of domestic equipment for 48 people, even down to 30 candlesticks. Another short visit in the following year cost only a banquet, and more stays took place in 1573, 1578, 1586, 1602 and 1615.[17]

The corporation suffered a continuous bombardment of letters from the Council on almost every issue – the price of food, economic regulation, law and order, musters of soldiers, taxation and a long list of other matters, many of them comparatively trivial. The city authorities acted as the Council's agents in making preliminary enquiries into cases and in sending men wanted for questioning to it. But normally the Council only sent directives on matters of general national or regional policy, leaving the corporation broadly independent in conducting its own affairs, though occasionally it did interefere in local matters when some personal influence was at work, as when it ordered the city to repair the wall of the bishop's palace.[18]

From the city's point of view the main use of the Council was as a superior law court, since to it went cases and disputes which would otherwise have gone to the Privy Council or the courts of Star Chamber, Requests or Chancery in London. The corporation frequently appeared before the Council as either plaintiff or defendant and the private citizen also used it, for instance in appeals against the decisions of the city courts or officials. Far from objecting to the jurisdiction of the Council, the city found itself with a powerful and comprehensive arbiter in legal disputes at a much more convenient distance than the capital, despite the complications presented by the presence of powerful local political figures among the Council's members.

Relations between the government of the city and the authorities in the shire were almost constantly strained. The main area of friction lay naturally in the issues where the city was not fully independent of the county and where a good deal of co-operative working was essential; the most important question here was the mustering and supply of soldiers to make up the total required from the whole county. The county tried to include the city under its jurisdiction in this respect, while the city wished its contribution to be regarded as a distinct one whose size was to be determined by tradition and negotiation rather than the county's convenience. Worcester claimed that the 1555 charter awarded it the right to muster its own citizens, an important privilege since mustering with the county might involve travelling to some distant part of the shire and so the loss of valuable time for many tradesmen. But apart from this the city's precious liberties were at stake, and surrender on this point might have more serious consequences.

In 1539 and 1542 the city apparently received a separate muster commission from the Crown and all was well, but this right was challenged by the county in 1549, provoking the corporation to resolve to continue trying to get separate commissions. In 1554 the city again tried to muster separately but the county insisted that for this purpose it was an integral part of the shire and that the citizens "heretofore have used to serve with the shire, and shall do, as much as in us is".[19] Despite the specific grant of the right to separate musters included in the 1555 charter, trouble continued, for in Tudor England formal written privileges were of little use unless backed by central and local political influence and constantly and insistently exercised.

In 1563 the corporation was forced to appeal to the Privy Council to support its rights, and despite the success which this brought there was a very similar incident in 1569, when again the Privy Council had to be brought in to support the city against its rivals in the county. The shire authorities applied to London themselves in 1573, asking for a commission to force the city to comply with their wishes, but a rival petition from the civic authorities was upheld by the Privy Council.[20]

By the following year the dispute had branched out into a connected field, the proportion of the total number of soldiers required of the whole shire which should be provided by Worcester itself. The city claimed a traditional agreement that it should supply 4 per cent of the total, but in 1574 6 per cent was demanded, and in the same year the county muster commissioners were specifically forbidden to operate within the city boundaries. In 1577 a demand for 10 per cent was only reduced to 8 per cent after a protest, and in 1579 10 per cent was again demanded, although in special circumstances. After this the 4 per cent quota was given up as a lost cause and 6 per cent was the accepted figure during the 1580s. Even now the struggle continued, and in 1590 the Privy Council was still being forced to press the county to respect the city's right not to be mustered outside its own boundaries.[21]

To add to this friction on military matters, there were a number of other issues which divided the two local governments. In 1552 there was a dispute over the jurisdiction of the county court and in 1559 the sheriff of Worcestershire infringed the liberties of the city not only by reading a royal proclamation within the city boundaries, but at the same time and place as the bailiffs did so, thus adding insult to injury. In 1580 the under-sheriff served a writ for the county court on a citizen within the city boundaries, a quite basic contravention of the judicial independence of the city from the county. In 1594 the shire justices arrested a freeman for an offence committed within the city, an even more flagrant breach of the civic privileges.[22] Perhaps such a lengthy history of friction and dispute is to some extent unavoidable when two jurisdictions are so deeply enmeshed as they must be in a county town, especially when a substantial difference in social esteem exists between the two sides. But in Worcester the matter ran rather deeper, towards an open, continuing battle for complete independence on the part of the city, or for practical domination for the shire.

These disputes between the two were reflected in the resentful attitude adopted by the corporation towards the county. In the middle years of the sixteenth century the county courts were held in the castle, beside the city but outside its jurisdiction, but these buildings must have become inadequate, for in 1565 the city allowed the shire magistrates the use of the Guildhall, reserving the right to withdraw this permission with two years' notice and testily reminding the shire officials that the city was quite outside their jurisdiction. But in 1580 the county was given six months to find alternative accommodation, apparently in retaliation for an infringement of the city's rights. Despite a further change of heart in 1585 the bailiffs were instructed by the council not to allow the shire the use of the Guildhall without the permission of the whole council, indicating a suspicion that the bailiffs might be more co-operative than the irate citizens would prefer.[23] This whole chapter of friction and difficulty is the most convincing general explanation of the long struggle to extend the city's privileges and so strengthen its hand against the pressures exerted on it by the county. It is also an example of the extent of those local and regional tensions and political issues about which so little is known, yet such conflicts may well have been more important to the areas concerned than some of the great national issues which are far more familiar to the historian.

But the existence of this long episode of bad feeling did not preclude the possibility of some co-operative measures between city and shire. This was partly imposed from above, for the Council in the Marches organized the fixing of wages and drives against vagrancy, treating county and city as one administrative unit, which the city does not seem to have resented. In emergencies especially, both worked harmoniously together: the famines of 1556–7 and 1597 were dealt with by joint schemes.[24] Much unrecorded practical co-operation must of necessity have existed, and a certain amount of social contact must have gone on between the wealthier members of the city council and the local gentry, but it remains true that political friction widened an already distinct gulf between the differing societies of country and town.

The relationships prevailing between the citizens and the county gentry in spheres apart from this essentially administrative one are difficult to trace with any certainty. The problems of livery and maintenance, and the violence which these institutions bred, continued long into the sixteenth century. In 1496 the civic authorities forbade citizens to take the liveries of county gentlemen, a repetition of the bye-law of 1466 which had also expressed the hope that "peace and rest may be had and continued between gentles of the shire and the city", indicating that some violence had been caused in this area during the disturbed years of the fifteenth century.[25] The charter of 1555 also found it necessary to forbid the practice of retaining and perhaps as a result of this there were two prosecutions in that year. Four weavers were accused of allowing themselves to be retained by "Anthony Kingston, knight", while two other citizens, one a barber, were similarly engaged to "Thomas Folley, knight".[26] The survival of livery and maintenance long after the familiar campaigns of the early Tudors against these dangerous habits is probably a more general phenomenon than is often realized, and was most easily undermined in the towns where the gentry's power was slighter, and also where the risk of violence was most real, for the most likely place for a clash between rival bands of retainers was in the county capital where their masters normally settled their affairs. In the 1580s there were two occasions when violence was caused by rivalry between two bands of retainers or between retainers and townsmen. In another case a battle between two bands of retainers and hangers-on numbering between 400 and 500 was only narrowly averted by Bishop Whitgift.[27]

The relationship between the city government and the great county landed families was not a close one. Sir John Bourne is probably the only local landowner who acted as something like a patron, and even this owed more to his national than his local standing. Sir James Croft, controller of the royal household, received a gift at the 1575 royal visit for his "counsel and friendship", but apart from these two examples it is very difficult to find many traces of the city either being influenced by great families or trying to win their friendship. There was no really outstanding local figure who was also of national standing and so could over-awe the city, as for instance the earls of Leicester and Warwick could do. Even Exeter, much larger and wealthier than Worcester, was much more susceptible to such influence than was Worcester.[28]

The only local figure who was an exception to this rule was the bishop, whose power through his membership of the Council in the Marches and among the shire magistrates was quite considerable, making him the only political figure the city ever regularly tried to influence, or was swayed by. The city's freedom from gentry influence in the choice of the recorders has already been noticed, and the more striking independence shown in the choice of members of parliament will emerge below.

The influence which was brought to bear upon the city came from figures of national rather than local significance. Thomas Cromwell tried in 1537 to force his own nominee as town clerk on the city, an attempt which was politely frustrated.[29] In 1584 the Archbishop of

Canterbury wrote to nominate a man for the office of sergeant-at-mace, and in 1606 Lord Salisbury pressed to have his nominee granted a profitable lease of some city tolls.[30] The paucity of these references, which could be given in great number for many other towns, is a reflection of the independence of the city even from the influence of national figures, but in any case such political influence was expressed much more easily in a local connection than in one where the national force had no local roots.

However there still remained the habitual deference paid by the townsman to his social superiors in the countryside. Sir John Bourne expected "serving men" to take their caps off to him in the street. A townsman accused of telling a member of the Bourne family that "a whore and a pot of ale is metest for thee" was rebuked by the city magistrates and ordered "to use better speeches towards the said Mr Bourne, considering he was a gentleman and of good calling in his country".[31] An extra point of interest here is the use of the phrase "in his country" to describe an area in fact immediately bordering the city, illustrating the sense of two separate communities represented by the city and its surrounding countryside.

The main way in which Worcester could exert some positive influence on national politics was through its members of parliament. The city showed great independence in its choice of representatives, since between 1554 and 1625 it elected solely its own resident citizens. This was quite unusual – for instance during the reign of Elizabeth only three other towns in the country could produce a similar record.[32] From 1441 to 1460 citizens only had been elected, from 1467 to 1477 one citizen and one member of the county gentry, and from this period onwards Worcester departed from its custom of electing only its own citizens on a mere three occasions, in 1553 and 1625–6. The first, in 1553, was when Sir John Bourne was elected, the only local man to achieve great national power at a time when the city was anxious to acquire the maximum assistance from high places to further its application for a new charter. The other occasions were in 1625 when Sir Walter Devereux was elected, a distinguished local magnate who was to be one of the county's few Parliamentarians in the Civil War; his fellow M.P. was Sir Henry Spelman, a Norfolk gentleman whose son was elected for Worcester in 1625–6.[33] The reason for this curious departure from the general rule during these two years is not clear.

So for virtually the whole of that vital century between 1540 and 1640 Worcester remained loyal to its own citizens, while so many towns allowed their seats to be taken by gentry outsiders. Why was this so? Firstly the freedom of the city from the domination of a great local landed family was most important. Worcester also had a substantial class of wealthy citizens to whom it willingly paid regular wages for their stay in London. Many of the leading citizens had close trading connections with London and would have welcomed the opportunity of a subsidized visit to the capital. The corporation's motives may well have been influenced by the importance of the cloth industry, which was more liable than most to regulation and political manoeuvre; the city's M.P.s were defending the cloth interest in Parliament and elsewhere in 1558 and 1572.[34] Close contact with the organs of central government could also be of advantage to the city in a number of other ways – its M.P.s helped to secure the 1555 charter, pressed for a licence allowing the corporation to own more property, promoted a Private Bill to alter the river harbour in 1572 and campaigned against the payment of ship money in 1595.[35] Thus the independence shown by Worcester in the selection of its M.P.s was the result of the lack of dominating local families, the wealth of the leading citizens and the clear advantage to be drawn from the situation by both the city as a whole and the members as individuals.

The way in which parliamentary representatives were chosen varied very much from town to town, and in later fifteenth-century Worcester the regulations were that the election should take place openly and publicly, with all "such as be dwelling within the franchises" eligible to vote.[36] But this seemingly very democratic procedure (which may have been less so in reality) had been eclipsed by the middle of the sixteenth century, as is made clear by an account of a disputed election in 1554.[37] Here the council – Twentyfour and Fortyeight together – selected themselves the two members during a routine meeting. They then came down from the council chamber into the body of the Guildhall and announced to the assembled freemen the council's decision. An objection was raised and a vote taken in which the two parties, totalling about a hundred members, assembled at opposite ends of the hall, joined by members of the council. The issue was whether or not to accept the nomination of the council, so there was still no direct popular election. So by this time not only had the inhabitants as a whole been narrowed down to only the freemen (at most a third of the adult male population) but even they could only accept or reject the official nomination: apparently they normally assented without demur.

The election dispute itself throws light on political conflicts in the city. The two members nominated by the council were challenged by a new candidate who was not a council member and was proposed by a group of other non-members, but they received only about 50 votes from a total cast of about 170. The matter dragged on with petitions, rising tempers leading to brawling, arrests and the intervention of the Council in the Marches. The underlying reason for the dispute, the only one recorded, is never mentioned. There may have been a religious element involved since that year is marked by the Marian reaction against Protestantism, but it seems more likely that this was one of those sporadic outbursts of resentment against the ruling clique which appear at some time in many towns during the period. It appears fairly clear that the traditional mode of election had been quietly subverted by the council, probably partly because of the indifference of the wider electorate. It may be that local politics outside the city boundaries played a part, for closely associated with the account summarized above is recorded a confession by a man that he had been "procured" to oppose the bailiffs before the Council in the Marches by a Mr Compton.[38] The leading figure in the opposition to the council's candidates was fined in the following year for becoming a retainer of a local county gentleman, so there does seem to have been some intermingling with politics in the shire.[39] There is no recorded repetition of this sort of trouble, and the corporation continued, without serious challenge, itself to select its own more distinguished members as the citizens' representatives at Westminster.

17

City government: finance and oligarchic control

One of the basic problems of Worcester's government was the difficulty it experienced in finding finance for its multifarious activities. Rapid inflation soon outstripped a relatively static income so that the last two decades of the sixteenth century were marked by chronic insolvency. During the whole of the period 1540–1600 the civic revenues, although occasionally distorted, maintain a basic level of about £80–90 without any sign of a sustained increase. But expenditure was not only liable to great fluctuation from year to year but also rose on average from about £70–80 yearly early in the reign of Elizabeth to about £120 in the 1590s. Here was the essence of the problem of inflation which faced so many of the corporation's contemporaries, the task of reconciling fixed incomes with rising costs due to higher prices.

City revenue was derived from a number of different sources, but principally from property. The land and houses owned by the city had been acquired in three stages, the oldest, called 'the city lands', a collection of properties slowly acquired over a long period of time in the middle ages and by the middle of the sixteenth century bringing in £21 10s. 0d. per annum. These were the only city estates until the sixteenth century. In 1525 a miscellaneous collection of local properties was acquired from the Crown, the result of a number of forfeitures to it; only the lease of these estates was involved here, and the city had to pay rent itself to the Crown, and since the difference between rents received and rent paid out was only £3, this was only of marginal help to the finances. But in 1548 the corporation bought these lands from the Crown, thus adding £16 10s. 0d. to the annual revenues.[1]

The third group of properties had belonged to the city's two friaries. The decline and eventual dissolution of the Trinity Guild did great damage by removing the financial support for the school and almshouses, walls and bridge. In 1538 a remedy for this was pressed upon Thomas Cromwell by the council in suggesting that a grant of the friars' estates, then forfeited to the Crown, would help to fill the gap left by the Guild's disappearance. The application was successful, at a cost of £541.[2] The annual value of these properties was £16 10s. 0d. and in addition the domestic buildings of the Friaries were used as a quarry for the sale of building materials which realized £350, apart from some held back for public works needs in the future. The net cost of the purchase was recovered out of income in 12 years, leaving the city government with a useful extra source of income.

These three sets of property, situated almost completely within the city boundaries and composed of about a hundred houses and some detached gardens, other odd pieces of land and rents, brought in a total of about £54 10s. 0d. in the middle of the sixteenth century and only £3 more by 1600. Compared with the great rise in expenses and the fall in the value of money, this shows that the estates were failing to provide the necessary financial support for government. This was partly because many of the rents were produced by very long leases which did not fall in for many years, but even when they did expire the chamberlains did not often increase rents, relying instead on cutting the period of new leases down to 21 years wherever possible and increasing drastically the charge made for entering on a new lease (the entry fine). This practice is dealt with below, since it was mainly a means of raising revenue in emergencies.

These estates brought in some 60–70 per cent of the city's regular revenue. The remainder was drawn from a very mixed collection of sources. Fines from the alderman's court with tolls collected from the markets in the Guildhall produced £5–7. Entry dues paid by outsiders who wished to become freemen brought in £10–15 per year. New entrants to the corporation also paid useful fees, but these were sporadic and unpredictable. To these revenues were added a number of other miscellaneous ones, but none were very important and as will have been apparent above, none were subject to the possibility of very much improvement.

The expenditure of local government was both very unpredictable from year to year and subject to an underlying upward movement, at its strongest during the last two decades of the sixteenth century. We may discover how this increase took place by looking at the various heads under which the money was spent. The first was salaries and wages, which rose from around £11 in the 1550s to over £20 after the 1570s. The corporation paid its recorder, retained attorneys in the courts of Exchequer and Common Pleas in the capital and paid its own servants, such as the market supervisors and sergeants-at-mace. It also paid annuities to its retired employees, sometimes to retired members and others in special circumstances, like Sir John Bourne. The increasing bill for these expenses was mainly due to an increasing number of annuitants and the general rise in the number of corporation employees as its activities broadened. Although the worsening financial situation led to a reduction in annuities, professional fees had to be increased and counteracted this. Many officials were paid directly out of the monies they collected, without any record being made in the official accounts at all – the bailiffs, aldermen and chamberlains for example, and for many of the employees whose wages were paid by the city these were only a supplement to an income derived from various traditional dues and tolls which they collected as part of their duties. In this way many officials were paid in a fashion which bypasses the official accounts, and but for this the revenue and expenditure figures would be much larger and the effects of inflation probably more conspicuous.

The second main category of expenditure was on public works. This involved firstly the repair of the buildings making up the city estates, but much more was spent on the maintenance of the bridge, walls, gates and ditch, the river banks and harbour, the Guildhall, toll house and other public buildings. The bridge and quays in particular were liable to flood damage by the Severn. Until the 1570s the corporation spent around £20 per year on public works, but during the last two decades of the century costs spiralled upwards to £38 in 1591–2, £43 in the following year and £41 in 1598–9. These figures exclude the wholly new public works ventures of the 1590s like the new shambles, toll house and water supply scheme.

The third broad category of expenditure was the provision of hospitality. Bishops, assize judges, county magistrates, members of the Council in the Marches, important nobles and anyone with access to influence, especially with the central government – all expected to be received in Worcester in a style matching their importance. At the dearest this could run to a civic banquet or the presentation of two or more oxen; rarely did a visitor receive less than a gift of wine, sugar or cheeses. Expenses here rose more than in any other division, for from well under £20 until the 1570s they reached £35 in 1592–3 and £43 in the previous year. These costs were unavoidable, for those with political influence and social standing considered such a reception their due, and any failure to provide it would have been considered not only as an insult to be avenged but as a direct threat to political power, which often rested on a local standing based on the maintenance of prestige. It was unfortunate that the areas in which expenditure seems to have risen fastest were also those in which price inflation was most pronounced.

These three categories, wages, public works and hospitality together made up some three-quarters of the normal civic expenditure. The other quarter was supplied by a variety of costs: legal expenses were a very frequent drain, there were administrative payments of all sorts, from travelling to London to paper and ink, there were rents and dues to the Crown, and a long list of trivial items. This category, although tending to increase in cost like all the others, remained at about 25 per cent of the total. So the money spent by the corporation rose by about 60 per cent during the half-century under review, and to this normal run of expenses we must add the extraordinary costs which arose from time to time.

The middle of the sixteenth century saw a concentration of these abnormal expenses – £200 to buy the two friaries, at least £100 for the Trinity Guild property, the 1555 charter for £65, the Six Masters' endowment for another £30.[3] In the 1590s, with financial difficulties already serious, £21 was spent on new maces for the sergeants, £42 on building a new butchers' shambles and rather more for a new toll house and water supply scheme.[4] These extraordinary costs, combined with the ever-increasing expense of routine government, led to financial problems in 1560–2 and a state of permanent deficit from 1582/3 until the end of the century, with the solitary exception of 1597/8. These difficulties were not a solely local problem, for very similar crises were occurring in Exeter and Leicester, probably typical of most town governments of the time, faced with a national problem of inflation threatening relatively static incomes.[5] But the ubiquity of the situation made it no less serious for Worcester, which began to look for solutions as soon as the problem became clear.

One expedient was to raise loans specifically earmarked for a particular extraordinary expense, so that many of these transactions do not appear in the city accounts at all. For example loans were raised to buy the Trinity property in 1540, when the individual members of the corporation loaned the city £100.[6] This money was never repaid, and this was true of the majority of cases and was probably obvious to the lenders: calling a gift or even a tax a 'loan' was a familiar ploy of the state's tax collectors at the time. A number of other expenses, such as the frequent cost of supplying and arming soldiers for the Crown, the wages of members of parliament and emergency costs for famine and plague were all normally met without drawing on the municipal revenues proper; instead the normal routine was for members of the corporation to pay half out of their own pockets, while the citizens in general found the other half, by what was in fact a scheme of local taxation. But the legal grounds for imposing frequent general levies on all the inhabitants for the general expense of local government were extremely hazardous, so that a rating system could only be applied where allowed by parliamentary statute, and then only for specific ends, the most common being poor relief. A scheme to impose a small annual tax on all the freemen in 1598 was abandoned, probably because legal advice had pointed out that it had no justification in law.[7]

It is worthwhile here to point out that members of the corporation made large contributions of their own money to the general expenses of city government. This was quite common in some other towns too, and members could obtain some financial advantage from the corporation without raising any question of corruption, but it remains true that the councillors made a very real financial contribution when there were revenue difficulties. In this situation the oligarchy is seen at its best, taking a paternal responsibility for the welfare of the citizens and making some sacrifice for the general good. However there was a limit to the extent to which this practice could be taken, and it remained tolerable only when used in unusual circumstances.

Sometimes genuine loans, with a real intention to repay, were raised. The cost of the 1555 charter was met by the corporation members and the citizens, and this loan was rapidly repaid. The loss of the Trinity Guild revenues placed a grave financial strain on the city government, so that in 1545 it was obliged to raise a loan from the parish authorities within the city to pay for the repair of the walls and gates. Another loan from the parish churchwardens in 1564 was paid back by the middle of the 1570s, while £35 was again provided from this source in 1579.[8] But the impoverishment of the parish churches after the Reformation reduced this to a source of emergency finance of very marginal importance.

The financial difficulties of the mid-sixteenth century were caused by a series of unusual expenses, often incurred in creating new sources of revenue, so that emergency loans very largely solved a temporary, although serious, situation. The problems of the last two decades of the century could not be solved so easily. Since little reduction of spending was possible, income expansion was the only device possible. The first measure tried was to build up a reserve which could then be drawn on in emergencies, but this was not possible until the annual audit revealed a consistent surplus in the 1560s, and the small sum accumulated was very rapidly swallowed up in the difficult 1580s. From this point on, the previous year's deficit had to be made up before any other measures were taken, so that it became progressively more difficult to catch up with solvency. To make matters worse it became more difficult to collect what revenue was available because rents and freemen's admission fines slid ever more into arrears.

The only course left open was to increase the revenue from the corporation estates. General surveys of both the state of city property and the leases on which it was let out were a regular feature of the chamberlains' administration, and as the crisis situation of the 1580s became clear, a further survey was ordered. All leases with less than 12 years left to run were examined, and reversionary leases of these properties were to be sold to the highest bidder. In 1591 a new survey was organized to raise entry fines and rents where possible.[9] But this policy of maximizing property revenues was not really centred on rents. In many cases they were allowed to remain static, or at best were raised very slightly. Instead, all revenue-raising efforts were concentrated on entry fines, which could be used to bring in large sums almost immediately; in order to impose these heavy burdens on tenants without serious opposition, annual rents were left unchanged at their traditional, uneconomic levels.

These campaigns raised considerable sums: £86 in 1581/2, £92 ten years later and similar sums in four other years, so that during the last two decades of the century at least £390 was raised by this expedient: this was the only means by which a real threat of bankruptcy was staved off. The raised entry fines which produced all this extra revenue usually varied between 20 and 40 times the amount of the annual rent of the lease, so that the fine was often greater than the total rent for the duration of the lease. Since the middle years of the sixteenth century leases had normally been confined to 21-year terms, although occasionally 41-year ones were granted in order to impose an even greater entry fine. In this way the urgent need for ready cash was met, but at the considerable price of sacrificing a regularly expanded revenue in the future. But at least the term of leases had been drastically cut, unlike those granted by the cathedral, which did not reduce its normal 60-year term to 40 years until the 1590s.[10] Another aspect of the city's policy is that it reflects the great demand for property leases in the later years of the sixteenth century, presumably the result of the growth of the city's size and consequent shortage of housing and land.

But even the entry fines could not act as a permanent solution to the financial crisis, and in 1594 a vain attempt was made to acquire a licence from the Crown to buy and hold land to the value of £100 per annum.[11] Due to the loss of the early-seventeenth-century account books it is not possible to be certain how the corporation solved its financial problems, but the whole subject is a good illustration of the impact of the inflation of the time on bodies with relatively fixed incomes derived from property; the innovation and development achieved by local government against this background is evidence of the compelling force of those circumstances which obliged municipalities to expand the scope of their activities in spite of their financial problems.

The oligarchy

The men who ruled the city, dominated its society and economy, and placed their stamp upon most aspects of its life are found most significantly and conveniently gathered together in the membership of the corporation. It is by now a commonplace of urban history that at least by the high middle ages a small ruling class had developed, its power based largely on wealth. Despite the familiarity of this trend, it still seems worth while to look closely at the structure and behaviour of this most important of urban institutions. Much the best way of demonstrating the plutocratic nature of the oligarchy is to analyse taxation records. This gives a stratified picture of the richer classes in the city, and by comparing the membership of the corporation with those who are highly taxed, we may see to what extent the corporation was monopolized by the wealthy. For this purpose the subsidy assessments of 1555–6 and 1585 have been used.[12]

This analysis shows that the upper body of the corporation, the Twentyfour, was virtually co-extensive with the richest men in the city. In the earlier subsidy, 13 of the 15 most heavily taxed citizens are members of the Twentyfour, while 20 members appear in the richest 31 in the tax list. In 1585 a similar situation is revealed, with the Twentyfour supplying 12 of the richest 18, and 19 of the top 28. The Fortyeight represented a much wider group, for although the Twentyfour absorbed about three-quarters of its income group, the Fortyeight only covered about a quarter of its own financial stratum, a group distinct from that of the upper house and comprising most of the self-employed tradesmen. But since the upper house enjoyed much more power than the lower, it is clear that the corporation was almost exclusively drawn from the richest citizens; taking both bodies together, the earlier subsidy confirms that 49 of the 71 richest citizens were members of the corporation.

Thus Worcester was ruled by a small group of wealthy men. Their inventories at probate show that most of them left personal goods and assets worth between £100 and £300. These were much slighter fortunes than in the first rank of provincial towns, especially those with access to sea-borne trade: in Exeter a citizen was not considered really rich with less than £1,000 while in Norwich the peak at the end of the sixteenth century surpassed £20,000.[13] In

Worcester only a handful of the wealthiest citizens could have realized more than £1,000. But despite this, wealth was probably made more quickly and in greater quantity than in many inland provincial centres below the rank of the great regional capitals and seaports, mainly because of the cloth industry.

The existence of this wealthy oligarchy needs little explanation. In urban society wealth and social status were virtually synonymous, while generally social eminence and political power marched together. In Worcester everyone was *nouveau riche* – there were very few old-established families whose inherited prestige could counteract the influence which money rapidly attracted. In any case, a substantial income was essential to any member of the corporation, since such a substantial proportion of its spending came from its members' own pockets.

The personnel of city government, as a result of being supplied by the wealthiest citizens, was necessarily unrepresentative of the bulk of the inhabitants. The trades of the members of the Twentyfour show this clearly: of the 78 members between 1540 and 1600 the trades of 59 are recorded in some way. These show that the members of the council were naturally drawn from the wealthiest trades, so that many other branches of the economy were ignored. Of these 59 men, 33 (or 56 per cent) were connected with the cloth industry, and many of the other traders were dabbling in cloth as a sideline. The wealthy distributive trades, mercers and drapers mainly, were the most over-represented of all, providing 24 per cent of the corporation members although they supplied during this period probably under 10 per cent of the traders. The food and drink trades also suffered distortion with five brewers, one baker and no butchers at all. With the addition of a lawyer, two tanners, one shoemaker and two innkeepers this completes the total number of trades represented.

It can be readily seen that many of the city's important, but not particularly wealthy, trades were either grossly under-represented or not represented at all. The membership of the Fortyeight seems to have redressed the balance only partially. But the crucial importance of the cloth industry to the city was reflected in an intensified form in its council, and this distortion of the true numerical proportion of tradesmen within the community was an inevitable corollary of the domination of local government by the very wealthy.

The oligarchy was a small and tightly knit group. The incidence of inter-marriage between its constituent families was very high, and the ramifications of these family links meant that ties of blood connected a high proportion of its members. Friendship joined many others, and the evidence of wills shows that it was probable that members would act as executors and overseers of each other's estates, and receive small bequests as tokens of friendship. These links are difficult to illustrate in a brief and effective fashion but as an example, Roland Barklay who joined the Twentyfour in 1582–3 was married into an oligarch's family, and of his seven daughters four married into the families of fellow-members of the Twentyfour.

But the oligarchy was constantly subject to the infusion of new families and the loss of old ones. Only 11 sons followed in their fathers' footsteps into the ranks of the council, while only three sets of brothers or cousins served. Thus despite the small size and apparent exclusiveness of the group, the families which made it up were always changing, and there is little sign of the small and stable clique of families which dominated the government of a city like Exeter.

Thus Worcester was ruled by a small group of pre-eminently rich men, closely knit, but open to fresh blood. Although grossly unrepresentative of the town as a whole, either financially or economically, it was too fluid to harden into a caste, too bound up with the everyday life of the city to become remote and too deeply imbued with a paternalistic sense of obligation, of responsibility to the community as a whole, to drift into petty self-interest. In the prevailing tough conditions of business life, real ability was essential even for those who inherited capital, so that the oligarchy was in fact a fairly pure 'meritocracy'. It seems to have been rather less self-interested, more efficient and less exclusive than many such oligarchies in other towns and at other times, although perhaps partly because it could afford to be so.

18

Religion

The history of religion and the church in Worcester during this period is naturally dominated by the Reformation and the issues to which that movement gave rise. These topics also enable us to examine the routine organization of religious life, the social and economic standing of the clergy and the relationships prevailing between the ecclesiastical authorities and the citizens. But first of all we must look at the pre-Reformation religious institutions and their dissolution, for this destruction constituted one of the most striking changes in a community otherwise little affected by the transition from medieval to modern times.

The most important of the city's religious houses was the cathedral-priory, but since it continued in existence under a dean and chapter without very drastic change, it is dealt with below. Next came the two friaries. The Black Friars was founded in 1347 on a site just inside the northern walls of the city; it never became a large or wealthy house and at the Reformation had a prior and about five friars, supported by an income of about £7 yearly from its estate of "rotten houses".[1] The Grey Friars was founded early in the thirteenth century and stood between Friar Street and the eastern walls of the city.[2] It had enjoyed the patronage of the Beauchamp family and was rather more important than the other friary, with perhaps ten friars at its end and an income from lands of about £10 yearly.

Both sets of friars, apart from their preaching, seem to have made their main impact on the citizens as sources of funeral services, for many contemporary wills contain bequests to the friars in return for their attendance at the testator's funeral, and sometimes the grave is to be in the friars' churchyard rather than in the cathedral cemetery which was the only general burial place available. This may be one indication that the friars were popular in the city and made an appreciated contribution to its life. Both houses were dissolved in 1538 and their fabrics and estates were bought by the city in the following year. The Black Friars was completely demolished and its site used for gardens, but large sections of the Grey Friars were bought from the city by the Streetes, a wealthy clothier family, and converted into an opulent town house. What may have been the refectory of the Friary still stands today.

The priory of Whistones, which belonged to the Cistercian nuns, stood at the city boundary on the road to the north. Founded before 1255, it had later a prioress and seven nuns, although there were probably fewer by the sixteenth century.[3] Although it always had financial problems its revenues at the Dissolution exceeded £56 annually.[4] It is rarely mentioned in contemporary wills and its role in the life of the city must have been small: in or about 1536 it was dissolved and its buildings partly demolished. Beside this priory stood St Oswalds, a hospital to care for the poor and sick. It had a history of medieval poverty and at the Reformation enjoyed an income of less than £15 yearly.[5] Although it lost its estates then, the hospital continued to function, and in the seventeenth century the city clothier family which had bought its lands, the Cowchers, returned them, and with some other gifts the revenues in 1665 amounted to £98, supporting ten elderly people in almshouses. This foundation, re-endowed and re-built, still exists.

The city's other hospital, St Wulstans in Sidbury, was founded just outside the walls in about 1085, and by the later Middle Ages functioned both as a small monastic establishment and as a hospital for the poor and sick. In view of its commitments, its income of nearly £80 was rather inadequate; Wolsey intended to dissolve it in 1524 but it survived until 1539, when it was granted to a courtier, Richard Morrison; he seems to have made some attempt to prolong its life as a hospital, but in 1544 the estates went to support Christ Church College, Oxford, as Wolsey had intended.[6] The hospital building itself, also called the Commandery, was bought by the Wildes, another rich clothier family, and converted into an impressive dwelling house.

Thus the fate of the city's religious houses was either demolition or conversion to rich town houses; all of the foundations were impoverished and their usefulness to the citizens, for this reason alone, must have been small. It is unlikely that many local people were unduly upset at their destruction, and only the friars seem to have won some regard: enough evidence of scurrilous behaviour by the friars was publicized at the Dissolution to destroy this favourable local standing.[7] Thus, since also the cathedral-priory lived on under a different administration, the immediate impact of the Reformation on Worcester was not as great as might have been expected.

The reign of Edward VI saw the completion of the destructive side of the reform movement, primarily the dissolution of the guilds and chantries. The main local target here was the Holy Trinity Guild, which beside maintaining at least one chantry priest, kept up the city's school, walls and bridge, and all on an annual income declared to be under £13.[8] The close relationship between this body and the city government has already been indicated, but its social function must have been very significant, as indicated by a number of bequests to it by wealthy citizens. The chantries in the cathedral and parish churches followed suit – a list of clerical personnel in the city in 1532 indicates that the ten parish churches had eleven chantry priests between them.[9] We may suspect that the Edwardian Reformation destroyed institutions which meant a great deal more to the citizens than the monastic bodies attacked by Henry VIII.

The whole progress of the Reformation involved the re-distribution of a good deal of property in the city. The fact that most of the priory lands were used to endow the cathedral preserved some hundreds of tenants in the city from a disturbing change of landlord, but for the rest a period of uncertainty was unavoidable. The lands of both friaries went to the corporation, and those of Whistones Priory, including a good deal of urban property, to a wealthy clothier, Richard Callowhill.[10] St Wulstans passed soon after its sale to a rich city family while the lands of St Oswalds, after a similar initial passage of ownership by an outsider, were acquired by another wealthy citizen. So the property of the monastic bodies went almost entirely to local institutions and individuals. The holdings within the city of other local monasteries – Tewkesbury, Pershore, Evesham and Malvern principally – were also bought by rich citizens: Richard Sheldon purchased Tewkesbury Abbey's Worcester city property.[11]

In this way the wealthier townsmen and the community as a whole enriched themselves from the Dissolution; outsiders, whether county landowners or courtiers, played no very significant part. This may be partly due to the unattractiveness to outsiders of the scattered, run-down property concerned and also to the wealth of leading citizens. It also shows how little local opposition could be expected to the destruction of bodies which had outlived both their usefulness and their resources and which also offered the opportunity of enrichment to the local wealthy classes.

However, the destination of the chantry lands redistributed under Edward VI reveals a rather different pattern. Of about one hundred houses and some gardens and small fields, the disposition of which is recorded, a citizen appears only once, as the partner of a Gloucestershire gentleman in buying for £1,300 a block of property including 37 Worcester houses.[12] All the rest of this large amount of property went to courtiers, landowners in distant parts of the country, London merchants, a local gentleman and the newly-founded grammar school at Stourbridge.[13] Thus taking into account all the dissolved lands of the religious bodies, outsiders seem to have acquired the lion's share, despite unusually substantial investment by local people. We do not know how much of the property acquired by outsiders later filtered down into citizens' hands, but there is little record of it. Thus the Reformation did provide some chance for local people to enrich themselves, while it did not involve any great disturbance of landlord for many people.

The cathedral-priory was a most important factor in the life of the city. Its property holdings were very extensive, those in the city being valued at nearly £100 at the time of the Reformation; in 1649 a survey found that it owned 189 houses in Worcester, a figure probably very close to the sixteenth-century one.[14] This means that the cathedral owned between 10 per cent and 20 per cent of the houses in the city, beside large areas of meadow, wood and pasture in the immediate vicinity. The presence of the monastic community must have been a commercial advantage to the local traders, quite apart from the stream of visitors to the cathedral. The shrine of the Virgin there was a focus of pilgrimage: the seventeenth-century Catholic historian Habington tells us that at the time of the autumn fairs a great pilgrimage was made, when the devout would fall to their knees at their first sight of the cathedral steeples. This was again inevitably a source of wealth for the townsmen, for when the image of the Virgin (said to be ten feet tall and like a giant) was removed in 1537 a townsman created a disturbance by protesting that the city would be impoverished by the resultant cessation of the flow of pilgrims.[15] It is perhaps significant that this financial consideration was the reason for the only recorded local protest against all the upheaval and destruction of the Reformation. But the refounded dean and chapter still provided a group of wealthy consumers dependent on the city shops, and the flow of people to the centre of diocesan administration continued unabated.

Probably the economic shock to the city from the transition from prior and monks to dean and chapter was minimized by the decline of the monastic community towards the end of its life, for it seems to have come to supply many of its needs from its own properties and employees, while at least by the sixteenth century the prior lived out on his own estates like any other gentleman, rarely seen in the city at all.[16] The monks had fallen in numbers to little over 30 by the Reformation. Judging by their religious names, which appear to have been based on their birthplaces, most of them were drawn from within the city's region and very few from villages more than 20 miles from Worcester.[17]

The cathedral-priory also played an important part in the life of the community through its possession of the parish of St Michael around the precincts as a privileged area, exempt from the municipal administration. Through the manorial court which governed this area under the cathedral officials' direction, the Church controlled part of the lives of a group of townsmen otherwise indistinguishable from the remainder of the citizens. The grammar school (as opposed to the elementary school run by the city authorities) was also administered by the cathedral. Some considerable social contact between the wealthier citizens and cathedral dignitaries is indicated by references and bequests in wills.

Thus the cathedral and its dignitaries, prior or dean, monk or prebendary, played an important role in Worcester's life, and the Reformation had a very limited influence. The estates of the priory were passed to the cathedral without very much alteration as far as the urban property was concerned, and the economic role of the Church was not drastically reduced. Possibly the main change, apart from the ending of overt pilgrimages, was that there were fewer local men at the cathedral, as the monks from the surrounding region were replaced by officials drawn from all over the country. But this change took place slowly, since many of the monks continued in office for some years under new titles, although the trend may have contributed to worsening relations between city and cathedral.

But friction between these two closely neighbouring bodies was no new thing. The fact that the sanctuary of the cathedral precincts acted as a refuge for criminals, who could thus escape the jurisdiction of the city officials by crossing a street, was the subject of strife in the middle ages. In 1460 some offenders living in the sanctuary were forcibly removed from it, and despite the city's acknowledgment in the following year that no official held any authority within the precincts, another such incident probably took place in 1494. In 1516 some minor disputes over property and jurisdiction between the priory and the city were settled, and it was agreed that the monks should enjoy all the legal privileges and immunities of regular resident citizens, a considerable concession on the city's part.[18]

The remainder of the sixteenth century saw no real recurrence of this friction between the two jurisdictions and relations seem to have been quite close. No differences over doctrinal emphasis divided them, while the cathedral aided the city in the provision of poor relief – much more than the monks had given – and the city gave £20 towards a new organ in 1612. The corporation sat in state in the cathedral on Sundays, supplying its own tiered seating.[19] But although the old vexed question of jurisdiction was not actively revived, there remained the problem that the tradesmen living within the precincts could evade the city's careful regulations while enjoying all the advantages of the market (the area contained a large number of shopkeepers concerned with food and drink, butchers especially).

Although normally freemen of the city were obliged to live within the municipal boundaries, those living in the sanctuary were exempt from this requirement if they paid all the dues asked of them.[20] This was perhaps an attempt to encourage these traders to take up the freedom and so bring themselves at least partially within the city's control. There were some signs of slight friction – in 1558 the sanctuary butchers were forbidden to operate within the city proper, but this seems to have been a temporary prohibition.[21] Informal arrangements must have been made, and in any case the sanctuary traders were not numerous enough to undermine the planned economy of the city to any drastic extent, although their independence was irritating.

This generally harmonious relationship between city and cathedral was brought to an end in the early seventeenth century. Doctrinal differences appear to be at the bottom of this rift, for the tone of the citizens' religious attitudes was becoming increasingly Puritan while the cathedral establishment moved towards a more Laudian position. All came to a head in 1637. The bishop had his own dispute with the cathedral authorities and supported the citizens when they protested at the opposition of the dean and chapter to the traditional sermons delivered in the cathedral by the preacher paid by the citizens under corporation sponsorship. The dean accused the citizens of not attending cathedral services and stated that the preacher, chosen by shopkeepers, had called the cathedral dignitaries "altar mongers".[22]

The government at Westminster tried to smooth matters over and ordered the corporation to attend cathedral services. But in 1639 trouble revived, and the corporation, with the bishop's support, asked for a permanent preaching place in the cathedral while the dean complained that the citizens ignored the services and that their leaders sat in greater state in the cathedral than they did in their own Guildhall. The dispute flared up again in 1641 when the corporation accused the dean and chapter of a wide range of Laudian practices.[23] The outcome of all this is not clear, but the very poor state of relations is all too obvious. Either as part cause or part result of this situation the issue of the privileged precincts was raised again, being used as an explanation of the city's poverty in 1622: it is suggested that if the sanctuary were to be included in the city then the money to meet taxation demands would be more easily found.[24]

We have already seen how the ecclesiastical authorities tried to foil all attempts by the city to increase its chartered powers, and this may reflect a long-standing tacit intention of the city to absorb the sanctuary within its own boundaries. In any case this aim emerged during the Civil War, for in 1649 the corporation agreed to support a petition, originating among the citizens at large, for the incorporation of the whole privileged area within the city.[25] Thus the religious crisis of the seventeenth century revived the medieval friction between church and city, and probably a deeper and more serious gulf opened between them than had ever existed between monk and townsman. The episode is also a significant indication of the local conflicts which, joined with national issues, could lead to civil war.

By looking at the probate records of the cathedral dignitaries we can glean some impression of their position within the urban community. The first dean was Philip Balarde or Haford, who died in 1557, having been the last abbot of Evesham. His manor house at Elmley Lovet was large and well furnished, and at another at Crowle he had sheep and oxen.[26] His lodgings at Worcester were quite humble by comparison, but the inventory totalled £260. Clearly his life was still very much that of the country gentleman with occasional city business, as that of Prior More of Worcester had been. The changes of the Reformation took some time to work, especially when there was an overlap of personnel between the two régimes. John Pedder, dean from 1559 to 1571, held much property on lease from the cathedral, and his wife was a member of a prominent city family.[27] Francis Willis (1586–96) was also farming on quite a large scale – he bequeathed his wife £50 worth of cattle – and his total bequests amounted to over £150. He lived in some state, with a cook, a horseman and other men and maidservants. The four friends he named as overseers of his will indicate the range of his social contacts – two of the most important county magnates, the most distinguished clothier in the city and the president of an Oxford college.[28]

The members of the chapter had very varied social and economic positions. The early dignitaries were of very ordinary financial standing, with inventories rarely worth more than £40. This was mainly made up by household goods and some small debts, without any landed property. But during the reign of Elizabeth their wealth grew greatly: Richard Hall's inventory of 1575 was worth £172 and he owed money to Worcester mercers and other tradesmen for the supply of luxury textiles and the like.[29] Arthur Purefoy (1590) was worth £120 and in 1598 Gilbert Backhouse left an inventory worth £586; his rooms in the cathedral close were richly furnished with pictures, maps and expensive hangings, he had a small farm in the country, personal clothing worth over £20 and debts and cash worth £354.[30] He must have been operating a substantial money-lending business, and there is evidence that some of his colleagues were doing the same, for they sometimes have recorded among their property the small items left by their debtors as security for loans.

Many of the later, richer members of the chapter held extensive leases of the cathedral lands, both tithes and actual property. Even the earlier, poorer dignitaries kept a manservant and later ones had a series of domestic servants. Books were usually an inconspicuous part of their worldly goods but Gilbert Backhouse owned £20 worth, and specifically bequeathed works by Luther, Calvin's *Institutions*, the Geneva English Bible and Hooker's *Ecclesiastical Government*. Thomas Leonards had a much larger library, worth at least £30 and extending to over 400 volumes, mostly commentaries on particular theological subjects, but with a pronounced Calvinist trend since he owned most of Calvin's works and attacks on Anglican apologiae but no defence of the Anglican position.[31] But apart from these two cases the other members of the chapter do not appear to have been particularly bookish.

It will already be clear that the economic and social position of the members of the cathedral chapter improved very strikingly during the period under review. This may well have been exaggerated by the presence of elderly ex-monks during the early years, but access to cathedral property, on what must have been favourable terms, elevated their successors to the economic standing of the richer citizens, and their social status was naturally higher. The cathedral community was, as one would expect, a separate and closely knit one; the wills of its members mention principally other cathedral clerics, although some appreciable degree of social contact with the wealthier citizens is revealed.

Relations between the city and the Bishop of Worcester have already received some treatment. The bishop was a rather remote figure, based at his castle at Hartlebury and visiting the city only irregularly on official occasions. His power was very considerable, not only because of his ecclesiastical position but also as a county magistrate and an important figure on the Council in the Marches. This made him a distant, primarily political figure, a force for the city to beware of rather than any very positive element in its life.

For the individual citizen the religious life of the community revolved around one of the ten parish churches among which the city was divided. The economic and social status of the urban clergy was not high, and contrasts painfully with that of the cathedral chapter described above. The average inventory totalled about £20, not very striking by Worcester standards, and since this figure remained static as time went on, inflation was steadily eroding their economic position. The incumbents of St Martin's, however, were unusually wealthy with an inventory worth £129, and those of St Peter's enjoyed a rather better income than most with inventories valued at £30 to £40:[32] in both these parishes there was some agricultural land which provided both glebe and tithes for the living, while in the purely urban parishes where both these sources of income were negligible there was a large group of clergy with inventories reaching only £4–6, and some with assets valued at only £1. Domestic arrangements were always very simple; houses rarely had more than four rooms and often only one, while personal clothing, furniture and other household goods were more sparse even than those of other citizens at the same very modest level.

As the century drew on the ownership of books dwindled; their quantity was directly related to the wealth of the incumbent concerned. The vicar of St Nicholas' owned in 1547 books on grammar, medicine and astronomy beside divinity, and a "round board astrology". The breadth of this library was exceptional, and normally the parish priest owned only theological works. Another in 1556 had 126 books valued at over £4 but libraries like this became rarer with the passage of time, although most incumbents owned at least a few books.[33]

The income of the priests in the various parishes varied: before the Reformation the average was just over £12 per year, but this conceals inequalities ranging from the £20 of rich St Helen's to the £5 of the small parishes of St Alban and St Clement.[34] What alteration the Reformation made is not clear, but the anomalies in the situation remained until some rationalization, through amalgamating smaller parishes, was attempted during the Interregnum.[35] Social contact between incumbents and their parishioners does not seem to have been particularly close judging by bequests in wills; only the wealthier ones appear in the wills of the laity, presumably because the poor majority were the associates of citizens too poor to make a will: as usual, financial and social status were very closely linked.

Little information is available on the general standards maintained by the city clergy in their work. The vicar of St Andrew's from 1582–99 admitted that he had no degree and did not preach.[36] The visitation of 1593 revealed no complaints at all against the clergy and only one case where the church fabric needed attention.[37] Similarly the 1613–17 visitation revealed no complaints about the clergy, so that we must presume that apart from the poverty which afflicted most of them, the general level of their work was not low enough to invite specific censure.[38]

The churchwardens and parochial officials in general had less responsibility than those in the countryside because the city government took care of most of their civil duties. The accounts of the St Andrew's churchwardens show that they were mainly concerned with the upkeep of the church fabric; poor relief activities were very slight indeed and confined to years when the problem was especially acute. The parochial income, derived from a very small amount of property, offerings, seat money and bellringing fees rarely came to more than £2 per year.[39] St Swithin's had more property – in 1536 it owned 19 houses and its income was over £19, and even by 1557 this had only been reduced to £14.[40] By contrast, the accounts of the wardens of St Michael's, in the cathedral precincts and so outside the jurisdiction of the city government, show what the parochial authorities would have had to do if that government had not existed.[41] Income normally reached some £5 to £6 yearly, from which the church fabric had to be maintained and a good deal of poor relief work financed, entailing not only large donations from parochial funds but also a formal rating of the whole parish in 1599 and 1601.[42] The administration of all the parishes was often chaotic and always amateur, but the work of at least those within the city proper was sufficiently limited to reduce the significance of this.

One of the most interesting aspects of the religious history of any local community is the specifically doctrinal impact of the Reformation and its aftermath, the issues of residual Catholicism and incipient Puritanism. From a national point of view Catholicism in the western areas was a much greater threat than Puritanism, and Worcestershire was, even more than the other border counties, one of the most persistent centres of militant Catholicism. Despite this background, the city of Worcester was not a Catholic stronghold. The parochial clergy were either sympathetic or amenable to Protestantism, for while there were three deprivations of clergy during the reign of Mary there was no similar upheaval on Elizabeth's accession.[43] The bishop's report to the Privy Council in 1564 revealed that on the corporation one bailiff and one alderman were Protestant and one of each and the town clerk Catholic. This situation was similar to that in the county, where sympathies were about equally divided. However, the city was much more Protestant than neighbouring Hereford where 21 members of the council were pro-Catholic, 10 were neutral and none was Protestant, or Warwick in which there were seven confirmed Catholics and only one firm Protestant.[44]

This residual Catholicism in the city council soon disappeared, and the old faith became essentially a feature of the Worcestershire countryside, and not of its towns. Only seven recusants are recorded in the city in 1592–3, of whom only one, Anne the wife of John Steyner, was a member of the wealthier classes; her husband was suffering for his faith in 1610.[45] A Worcester doctor was reported in the latter years of Elizabeth's reign to be "a great seducer of others"; at the same time there were 82 convictions of country people at the shire assizes for not attending church, of whom 38 were women and about 15 gentlemen, mostly "of no great credit of countenance".[46] Compared with this, very few citizens could have been prosecuted, for the visitation of 1593 detected only four people from all the city parishes not attending church. By contrast, the gravity of the recusant problem in the shire was reported to the central government in 1594 and 1596.[47] Catholic priests were sure of a welcome in many a manor house, the local gentry were deeply implicated in the Gunpowder Plot and in the Civil War the landowners of the shire were largely Royalist in sympathy. This deeply conservative stance of the local magnates contrasted very strongly with Worcester's inclinations, as will appear from an examination of the Protestant and Puritan trends in the city.

Protestantism was an early and solid growth here: Lollardy was present in the area early in the sixteenth century and in the 1520s the images on the city's high cross was defaced by early Lutherans. It was no accident that the Protestant propagandist printer Oswen chose Worcester as the site of his press to cover Wales and the Marches.[48] This is not to say that Worcester was blatantly Protestant since it must have been at least tactfully conformist to win its charter from Mary and the favour of the Catholic Sir John Bourne. The city would probably have been conformable to any orthodoxy imposed tactfully from above up to the middle years of Elizabeth's reign, but from this point onwards there appears a Puritan trend in the city's religious inclinations.

The corporation decided to appoint a city preacher in 1589, paid

£10 per year by a tax on all the freemen. He was also guaranteed the living of All Saints, and the council sent a present of six cheeses to the Archbishop of Canterbury to encourage his assent to the scheme.[49] The appointment of municipal preachers was not in itself unique, although the date here is quite early, for many towns took this step during the same period. What was more significant was the doctrinal outlook of the men appointed to these positions, and in Worcester men of unorthodox views seem to have been appointed, like the first to hold office, Robert Abbot. By 1628 these preachers were receiving a stipend of £40, probably considerably more than any of the parish clergy. The position of the city preacher and the clear preference of the citizens for his sermons rather than the cathedral services was one of the reasons for the quarrel between city and cathedral under Charles I.[50]

This clash between Laudian clergy and Puritan citizens was not purely doctrinal in nature, for its economic implications were considerable. Whereas the 1593 visitation by the ecclesiastical authorities punished offences which were almost completely sexual in nature, that of 1613–17 shows a great emphasis on the punishment of work on Sundays and holy days, concerning trades as diverse as barbers, butchers, clothiers and boat-owners.[51] This change of attitude could only increase the irritation caused to the citizens by the clergy. Radical Protestant opinion seems to have had a popular basis, for the only two trade companies to contribute to a collection for the assistance of Geneva in 1583 were the weavers and tailors, representing the poor self-employed citizens.[52] But the religious radicalism of Worcester is probably more conspicuous than widespread, for hostility to Puritanism at the outbreak of the Civil War in the city was marked, and of course it was a Royalist stronghold; probably there was considerable religious conflict in the city in the years leading up to the Civil War and the outcome of this struggle and the bitterness it engendered may well help to explain its surprising orthodoxy later. The undoubtedly radical indications just outlined may well only reflect the opinions of a minority which provoked a much more significant conformist reaction.

19

Charity, education and culture

Charity

Charity is an important factor in the study of early modern urban society for two reasons: firstly because it provided vital services which augmented the welfare efforts of local government, and secondly because it provides the historian with a guide to trends in the mental climate of the times through changes in the direction and amount of charitable bequests. Variations in priorities serve as an indication of changes in religious and social ideas and attitudes. It has been suggested that between 1540 and 1640 there was a great increase in the total amount of money given to charity and a drastic diversion of gifts from religious ends to social and secular ones, from the church to poor relief, a trend especially marked among the merchants of large towns.[1] How does Worcester fit into this thesis?

An examination of the total amounts given to charity in Worcester over the period 1520–1620 shows there was no very striking increase (see table 11). The amounts given in the middle years of the sixteenth century were roughly equal to those of the years 1600–20, while the last three decades of the sixteenth century were markedly below even this level. This depression may be partly due to the stagnation in the cloth industry for those years, but the economic difficulties could not have been on such a scale as completely to explain this feature.

Amounts of money bequeathed to charity in all surviving wills

	1529– 1549	1550– 1559	1560– 1569	1570– 1579	1580– 1589	1590– 1599	1600– 1609	1610– 1619
Religion	£160	11	11	5	3	6	27	12
Poor relief	140	192	376	59	60	53	202	183
Roads and public works	22	53	20	–	–	–	31	40
Education	–	22	100	–	7	12	–	–
Loan Funds	–	–	–	30	–	–	72	20
Guilds and companies	2	½	7	–	–	–	–	4
Total bequeathed	324	278	514	94	71	71	332	259
Total value of inventories	£1767	4866	2145	4836	3896	4739	7231	9464
Proportion bequeathed to charity	18%	6%	24%	1.9%	1.8%	1.5%	4.5%	2.7%

Table 11 Analysis of charitable bequests

	1529– 1549	1550– 1559	1560– 1569	1570– 1579	1580– 1589	1590– 1599	1600– 1609	1610– 1619
Religion	50	4	2	5	4	7	8	5
Poor relief	43	69	73	63	85	75	61	71
Roads and public works	6½	19	4	–	–	–	9	15
Education	–	8	20	–	10	17	–	–
Loan Funds	–	–	–	32	–	–	22	8
Guilds and companies	½	–	1	–	–	–	–	1

Table 12 Proportion of total charitable bequests distributed to various ends (percentages)

The basic problem here lies in the method by which the figures are compiled, since they ignore a number of important extraneous factors. The effect of inflation, which makes money progressively less valuable, the condition of prosperity or slump which controls the quantity of money available to be bequeathed, variations in the size of the population and death rate and so the number of testators available to make bequests – all these are major factors, so far ignored, which can distort the picture. A far more significant approach is to compare the total given with the total available to be given at any one time, thus avoiding all the distortions listed above. The most practical way of doing this is to compare the total bequests to charity in a period with the total values of inventories preserved for that period. The resultant figures are not an expression of the average proportion of personal wealth given to charity, since for this we should need every inventory for the wills containing bequests, but if we compare the ratio between total bequests and total inventory values we get an artificial figure which is significant by comparison with the other figures in the series in revealing a trend.

The results of such an analysis do not support the conclusions so far advanced for the nation as a whole: Worcester testators gave to charity in the decades 1550–69 substantially greater sums than in the first two decades of the seventeenth century, although the national pattern would suggest that they should have been giving up to four times as much by the 1620s. The very low level of charitable giving in the last three decades of the sixteenth century is followed by an improvement after the turn of the century, but although substantial, this rise is still much less than the accepted pattern. This evidence would suggest that the citizens of Worcester were never so generous as in the middle decades of the sixteenth century, and although there was an improvement in the early years of the next century, the overall trend is a declining one.

Why should Worcester be so different from the accepted picture? It is a single city, and so may be a little eccentric, although hardly to this degree. But the main reason seems to be that a different (and probably more valid) method of compiling and analysing the facts reveals a rather different situation. In particular this study has been concerned with a wider social class than was the national one, confined as it was to the 'leaders of society'; even if these leaders did become much more generous, they do not appear to have acted as true social leaders, for their followers in the middle ranks of provincial urban society seem to have been few in number.

The Worcester material compiled in this new fashion does tell us a good deal about the temper of Worcester society and its changes. The most striking change is the collapse in bequests to the church – half of the total in the pre-Reformation period, but down to 4–8 per cent in the following decades. This is a national trend, as is a slight recovery in the years after 1590. Similarly the proportion bequeathed to the poor rises from 40 to 70 per cent of the total. But compared with the national situation, Worcester again emerges as rather eccentric, for the fall in religious bequests is more drastic than elsewhere and the proportion given to the poor is always much larger than anywhere else studied: even in London only half as much is given to poor relief as in Worcester. Bequests for road building and improvement are unusually high in Worcester, especially early in the seventeenth century, while gifts for educational foundations are much smaller here.

The pronounced preference for the relief of poverty rather than religious benefaction shows something of the attitude of the local wealthy classes, more secular and more aware of their social obligations than in many other areas. Alternatively, perhaps, the church was less in need of money in Worcester and the poor more so, but little evidence could be produced in support of this. A great interest in the repair of roads shows the experience of a class frequently travelling in the course of business. Education received less because the city's schools were generally well endowed and what bequests were made were quite adequate. A significant feature of these bequests is that, quite unlike London, Worcester citizens were never interested in making bequests to communities outside their city, while in London many left some benefaction to the parish of their birth if they were immigrants, as many were; Worcester had a high proportion of recent immigrants but they seem to have retained very little sentimental attachment to the place of their birth, perhaps an indication that provincial towns absorbed immigrants more completely into their social fabric than ever London could.

So the charitable bequests of the citizens of Worcester reveal something of their outlook, in particular a greater secularism, evident before the Reformation and after it growing strongly. This may well reflect the extremely businesslike, affluent and above all practical outlook of the inhabitants of such a highly industrialized and urbanized provincial city. This pronounced characteristic must be explained in economic and purely local terms as much as social ones. The citizens, hard headed and tight-fisted to the last, showed little inclination to increase the proportion of their wealth which they left to charity, a contrast with the national pattern which may be due to the distorted nature of our view of that pattern or to the particular characteristics of this individual urban community.

Education

One of the major characteristics of the early modern period was a great expansion in the number of educational foundations and the use that was made of them, and in this respect Worcester was typical of a national trend. By the middle of the sixteenth century it possessed two schools, an elementary one run by the civic authorities and a secondary grammar school administered by the cathedral. The city school was an ancient foundation, becoming attached to the Trinity Guild in the later fourteenth century. By 1548 it was held in the Trinity guildhall and its schoolmaster was paid partly from guild funds and partly from the donations of members.[2] For the previous five years it had been suspended due to lack of finance, but in 1547 a new master had been found and the school had re-opened with about a hundred pupils.

The school survived the dissolution of the guild, the last guild schoolmaster being retained on a Crown pension of £6 yearly, but in 1550–1 the city council bought the Trinity Hall and assumed partial responsibility for the school. After a prolonged wrangle because the master left the city in 1553 but insisted on continuing to draw his pension, the school was again closed down until 1559 when a new master was appointed, paid £6 a year by the council and supplied with a new schoolhouse, rented and repaired. This state of affairs was continued during the following year, with the addition of an under-master.[3]

This arrangement seems generally to have been less than satisfactory, for leading citizens began to bequeath property to the corporation for the endowment of the school; the first was a wealthy clothier, Thomas Wilde, who in 1558 left land for a free school to teach "A.B.C., mattins, evensong" and other educational pursuits, basically as a preparation for the more advanced studies available at the cathedral grammar school. A further endowment appeared in 1560 with the death of another rich cloth manufacturer, Robert Youle, and in the following year a royal charter re-founding the school was obtained. This charter clearly states that the object of the institution was to prepare pupils for the cathedral grammar school, probably a formal demotion in status since it is reasonable to suppose that the city school did have some more advanced pupils in the past.[4]

This re-foundation combined the Trinity Almshouses with the school as a single institution governed by a corporation of six members, the Six Masters: these were to be drawn from the personnel of the city corporation's senior body. Queen Elizabeth provided annuities for both the school and the almshouses, so that with the endowments already mentioned and a few more which trickled in during the rest of the century, the Six Masters disposed of an annual income of between £40 and £50 during the remainder of Elizabeth's reign.[5]

This money was spent in salaries for the schoolmaster and his assistant, and on occasional repairs to the fabric of the schoolhouse, but increasingly the major part of the revenues was spent on aid to the poor, leaving the school to run itself. No stationery, writing equipment or books were bought by the authorities, so the pupils had to supply these for themselves. This accounts for the presence of school books in the local shops: a haberdasher has "accidence" books, a mercer two dozen primers (worth 5s.), three service books (4s. 6d.). 11 "accidence" (2s.), and five dozen "a.b.c." (1s. 8d.), while another mercer has primers and Latin books.[6] Very little else is known of the 'Free School' or 'Queen's School' for the remainder of the period, so we must presume that its routine, adequate performance continued without controversy or disturbance.

The cathedral grammar school was in effect a post-Reformation foundation, for although the monks had attempted to set up a school for their choristers at the end of the fifteenth century, the bishop, patron of the city school, had quickly crushed it.[7] But as part of the re-foundation of the cathedral after the dissolution of the priory a grammar school was included as an integral part of the new dispensation, under the dean and chapter's authority. Forty poor boys, the King's Scholars, were to be educated for four or five years; they were to be accepted only if aged between nine and 15 and in possession of certain basic skills like reading and writing. The master and under-master were to divide the teaching of some five or six classes between them. The school day was to begin at 6 a.m. and end at 5 p.m. and the curriculum was devoted, as was usual at the time, to teaching Latin: no Greek was specified although the master was required to be proficient in it. The pupils were forbidden to use any language but Latin, even when at play.[8]

It is difficult to reconstruct the routine life of the school since few of its records survive, but certainly the masters were not at a financial disadvantage – the chief master's salary was set at over £15 in 1542, raised to £20 two years later. The school quickly gained a good reputation, especially under its distinguished headmaster Henry Bright (1589–1627); he was a Worcester man, as the assistant master almost invariably was, and his epitaph in the cathedral describes him as the "famous schoolmaster" who taught Latin, Greek and Hebrew to great effect. Another schoolmaster, Roger Golborne, who died in 1559 and was then described as "sometime" schoolmaster as if he had retired, was of very modest means, for his inventory was valued at only £14, with £1 6s. 8d. in books.[9]

However, when the schoolmaster Thomas Bradshawe died in 1586 he held extensive leases of cathedral property and could afford to leave his daughters £100 each in cash. The famous Bright also left landed property.[10] Thus access to the leases of cathedral estates, presumably granted at very easy terms, was a great source of profit to the schoolmasters as it was to the other cathedral officials in this period. No probate records survive for the masters of the city's school, but we may presume that they lived in poverty compared with their fortunate fellows at the cathedral grammar school.

Who attended these schools? The city school had about one hundred pupils before its re-foundation and its seems likely that this figure would have increased rather than diminished during the rest of the century. No early estimate exists for the cathedral school but it is probable that from the beginning the 40 scholarship boys were joined by many others: in 1637 the school was said to have two hundred pupils.[11] But we should not presume that all, or even a majority of these schoolboys came from the city itself. Possibly a high proportion of those in the elementary school were locally born but even here the foundation charter was acquired not only at the request of the citizens but also of "many other of our subjects within our county of Worcester".[12] Many country boys must have prepared to go on to the grammar school.

As far as the cathedral school itself was concerned, the names of the King's Scholars probably give a fair indication of the origins of the total membership. During the periods 1547–53 and 1591–1640 these pupils were predominantly drawn from the countryside, for only about one in ten bear recognizable city names. Thus the schools helped to extend Worcester's role as the supplier of specialized services to the people of the countryside, encouraging the inflow of visitors and so the city's function as a regional centre. As far as the citizens were concerned, educational opportunity had been provided over the full range and at a good standard; the two schools probably supplied as much education and to as many city boys as was required.

We are left with the task of probing the problem of what the attitude of these townspeople was to the whole subject of education. We can gain some clues from the instructions recorded in wills detailing the fashion in which the testators' children were to be brought up. Wills made in the first half of the sixteenth century tend to emphasize the moral content of education by the use of such injunctions as "bring up my children in the love and fear of God", "see them virtuously brought up in the fear of God" or a general request that they should be "virtuously brought up".[13] During the course of the century there tends to be a gradual growth of a more practical and vocational outlook, although the moral note remains significant: "bring my children up in virtue and learning and to some other godly exercise whereby they may be able hereafter to get their living in the way of truth that God may be pleased therewith" (1557); "in the fear of God, in learning and in good manners" (1560); "in learning and in other godly exercises to the intent that he may be able to get him an honest living" (1549). Children are to be brought up until they can be apprenticed or until they can read and write (1573) or to be "brought up at school and to be taught to write and read and his duty first to serve God and then to man" (1609).[14]

The attitude revealed by many of these quotations is an essentially practical one: the vocational skills of reading and writing were what Worcester parents wished their children to acquire, mixed with a moral and religious discipline. The ability to read, write and perform simple calculations was necessary for even the most humble self-employed tradesman. Many inventories mention the 'shop book' in which debts were recorded, seemingly a basic feature of most businesses, for credit was essential in an economy rooted in the seasonal nature of the agricultural year, so that the incomes of rural debtors arrived in irregular instalments, and it lacked the banking facilities to smooth out such a pattern.

This need for elementary education extended to employees too, for while their employer was away buying raw materials, settling debts or selling cloth they would be expected to take charge of the routine administration of the enterprise, and this became a permanent feature when widows continued to run their late husband's business. Few women seem to have been able even to sign their own names, and women's education receives only one mention, in a significantly wealthy family in 1602, when the daughters were to be brought up "according to their calling" with "good education".[15] This vocational bias applies even to the rich families who sent their sons to the universities and the Inns of Court, for the object in most cases was to produce a professional lawyer, a natural intermediate stage in the passage from successful tradesman to country gentleman. All these factors would tend to suggest that the educational establishment to which the citizens owed most was their own elementary school which provided them with those basic skills which they required for their work.

The sixteenth century has been seen as an era of educational revolution, and certainly the opportunities open to Worcester citizens were greatly expanded during this period. What impact did this have upon the attainments of the townspeople? One convenient test of this is literacy, as reflected by the proportion of the population able to sign their own names. One collection of signatures is contained in the bonds entered into by those taking custody of orphans' goods between 1561 and 1580.[16] Those able to sign their own names rose from 60 per cent of the total in 1561–3 to 69 per cent in 1563–72 and 77 per cent in 1573–80. This indicates that as far as this group of people are concerned the proportion of illiteracy is almost halved over a 20-year period following the re-foundation of the city elementary school. Despite the fact that only the wealthier tradesmen are probably represented here and that it is possible that the social group concerned may have become more exclusive during the two decades concerned, thus intensifying the trend, the fact remains that this is striking evidence of rapidly spreading literacy.

Another collection of signatures and marks appears in the masses of bonds concerned in the granting of probate and marriage licences by the diocesan authorities. The proportion of men able to sign their names rises from 60 per cent in 1588–94, to 64 per cent in 1594–9 and 65 per cent in 1600–20. The social groups represented here are a much wider sample than those covered by the orphans' bonds, although the lower classes are still under-represented. It tends to confirm the previous evidence that the Elizabethan period was marked by a rapid rise in the proportion of the population able to write (and so presumably to read) and also suggests that this rise was levelling off by the turn of the century. By that time as much as perhaps half of the city's male population could sign their own names and so had received some kind of education. This significant spread of literacy is a most important feature of the period, in the political as well as the more obvious cultural and religious spheres.

Cultural life

The cultural and intellectual activities of a city like Worcester in this period are difficult to reconstruct since much has left no written record. Like most towns at this time Worcester saw its drama trans-formed from medieval mystery play to a performance recognizably modern, produced by travelling rather than local actors. The mystery play, or the 'pageants' as it was always called in Worcester, originated in the medieval past: its date of origin and the text used are lost. Towards the end of the fifteenth century it appears that there were five distinct episodes in the play, put on by as many craft guilds, three on Corpus Christi Day (11 days after Whitsunday) and two more on the following Sunday.[17] Even by this date there seems to have been some reluctance on the part of the guilds to shoulder the expense involved in the production.

The decision to mount the play came to be made annually, and is recorded in 1555, 1559, 1565 and 1566, but after this last date there is no further mention of its existence. The exact date of the last performance must remain in doubt, but certainly all was finished by 1584 when building in the Corn Market in which the wheeled stages were stored was stated to be vacant and was re-used for other purposes. The costumes for the players must have been numerous and elaborate, for in 1556 they are listed as part of the household goods of a draper, as if he were storing them: they were valued at the considerable sum of £30.[18]

Despite the demise of the pageants, the city's dramatic tradition had other facets. A number of small groups of players existed in the city, attached to the various parish churches. The Journal of Prior More records the patronage of a number of these during the period 1518–37: the young men of St Helen's, for example, put on "Robin Hood". These groups were small and very informal, and we find no record of them after the Reformation, although they may well have lingered on in some form for a number of years. The cathedral had its own miracle players, for the costumes were still extant in 1578, when they included enough for two or three actors and "the devil's apparel".[19]

The travelling players made a slow start in Worcester, and did not become really popular until the 1590s. The first visits were very spasmodic, being recorded in 1563, 1568 and 1573, but performances in 1587 and 1588 were followed by annual visits from 1590–2 and five between 1596 and 1600. The corporation normally sponsored these performances, and in 1585 it was resolved that players could only give their show before the bailiffs, and all plays in the Guildhall at night were banned.[20] The city itself produced a modest group of itinerant players, for in 1630 a labourer from the cathedral precincts was indicted for presenting at Upton-on-Severn, under a forged licence from the Master of the Revels, "motion with diverse stories in it as also tumbling, vaulting, sleight of hand and other such like feats".[21]

The fact already outlined that the proportion of the population able to read increased substantially during the Elizabethan period renders very important a consideration of the literary culture of the citizens – what did they read? Wills and inventories provide evidence of ownership of books and an analysis of the proportion of households recorded as containing books reveals that in the period 1550–89 about 4 per cent of the inventories reveal the presence of books in the homes of laymen. But in the 1590s this modest figure suddenly increases to 16 per cent, and this state of affairs is maintained during the first decades of the seventeenth century. These figures, which exclude the professional collections of clergymen and lawyers, would indicate a striking proliferation of book-ownership in the late Elizabethan period which would parallel the increasing literacy rate already suggested: unfortunately it is impossible to tell how much these books were read.

An important qualification of this surge in book-ownership was that the range of subjects and tastes covered was very narrow. Most people owned only bibles or prayer books and those whose books were more numerous than this still confined their reading to devotional works – for instance the rich clothier who died in 1611 leaving, among others, three volumes of collected sermons and *The Pensive Man's Practice, The Direction to Die Well* and *The Silver Watch Bell*.[22] Some inventories do not list books by title so that it is possible that some secular works have slipped by unrecorded, but the overwhelming predominance of works of piety remains. The clerical libraries contained only a minute number of non-theological treatises and these are largely of a geographical nature: thus one large clerical library of some 400 volumes included only one recognizable secular work, "a geographical description".[23] Other clerics owned chronicles and books on astrology and medicine, but they were rare. So this evidence would suggest that the book-buying public was almost exclusively concerned with religious or practical matters, and that its coverage of subjects for entertainment or general interest was negligible.

No professional bookseller is recorded in the city, although the local mercers stocked school textbooks and the stationer Alexander Kidson seems to have imported books to order for the bishop.[24] Most books were probably bought in London or from travelling salesmen. But Worcester did for a short time have its own printing press. John Oswen, an Ipswich printer, was licensed in 1549 to print religious works with a monopoly in Wales and the Marches.[25] In 1553 he was admitted to the freedom of the city, but he had printed his first work there in 1549 and until the accession of Mary ended his strongly Protestant activities he produced a total of 20 different devotional works. No printing press replaced this one until early in the eighteenth century, but the episode does show that the area provided a good market for this kind of work and the most convenient distributive centre for Wales and its borders.

The citizens of Worcester were in fact far more musical than they were literary in their tastes. Prior More patronized many groups of singers and musicians, many of them again on a parochial basis, but these seem to have died out after the Reformation. The town waits were in existence by 1568 but by 1585 there was some difficulty in staffing them. These civic musicians may well have died out altogether, for in 1599 at the bishop's request what appears to have been a group of church musicians was made into the city waits, with the possibility of some reward from civic funds at the end of the year. This group appears to have survived until suppressed by Puritans in 1642. The chequered and unimpressive career of this body contrasts with the successful and highly professional musical bodies in other cities, prominently Norwich.[26] The probate records survive of either a music teacher or a member of the waits. Harry Smith leaves to his "boys" "all my instruments both viols and recorders and their books" – the total value of instruments and books was £6 which, coupled with £2 worth of "players' gear", suggests a considerable collection.[27]

Musical instruments were quite common in Worcester households. A total number of 25 instances are recorded: a few were virginals, valued at 10s. and upwards and found only in wealthy homes where they perhaps represented a status symbol rather than a genuine enthusiasm. However the majority of instruments are stringed ones which one would expect to be used to accompany the human voice – normally the lute, occasionally the cythern and even the harp in two cases. These instruments were clearly there because they were used, and one suspects frequently; for pleasure and relaxation the townspeople were much more likely to turn to a musical instrument than to a book.

Taste in the visual arts is equally difficult to reconstruct. The number of houses containing pictures shows a striking increase in the 1590s and the early seventeenth century, but the subject of them is rarely given except in a few cases of portraits of the reigning monarch. Maps were frequently used as wall decoration in the wealthiest town houses: Robert Wilde for instance had hanging in his main parlour one large map of the world and another small one of "certain countries".[28] The main form of decoration in most town houses was painted fabric hangings covering most of the wall surface; these were general, even in quite poor homes. The house of a butcher held "the story of the prodigal child" and another "the history of the tower of Babylon".[29] Probably these biblical subjects were typical of those which did not consist of simple areas of plain colour. A painter worked in the city, but he seems to have been mainly concerned with architectural decoration rather than with pictures, although he may have executed some of the wall hangings.[30] In pre-Reformation times a few houses contained images or other pieces of devotional art, mainly the alabaster figurines produced in the Nottingham area.

Worcester boasted one identifiable monumental mason. Most of the monuments in the cathedral and parish churches must have been made in London or one of the competent regional schools; only the rich could afford them and so their artistic and technical quality was normally adequate. However in Worcester Anthony Tolly, the carpenter son of a brewer, set up in business as a mason. Only two of his tombs can be identified with certainty, but both are important commissions, the monuments of bishops in the cathedral. Both are bad. Inept in design and clumsy in execution, they are a product of artistic provincialism at its worst; the importance of the commissions would suggest a lack of awareness of the poor quality of Tolly's work.[31]

Thus the intellectual and cultural life of Worcester is a mixture of lively participation and awakening in some ways and narrow, incompetent provincialism in others. It is difficult to abstract any element and label it distinctly 'urban', although if anything were, perhaps the drama would be the most amenable to such treatment; in most respects the culture of Worcester was a diluted and imitative form of the prevailing taste in the manor houses of the shire.

Conclusion

This survey would be incomplete without a glance at what happened to Worcester after the conclusion of the period covered. As has been seen, its prosperity in the sixteenth century depended very largely on the broadcloth manufacture. This traditional product continued to remain the staple, with no clear attempt to emulate the newer textiles introduced by other regional industries. The traditional market dwindled slowly and comparatively steadily without any sudden commercial catastrophe, but by the earlier years of the eighteenth century the cloth industry was clearly only a shadow of its former self and by the end of that century it had almost completely vanished. Unlike many towns which were greatly dependent on cloth, Worcester did not cling to its last remnants or sink into obscurity. The predominance of the industry while it lasted had tended to obscure the basically healthy regional role of the city, a social and market centre which sustained it until the rise of two distinctive specialities which were to replace cloth – the making of gloves and porcelain.

The manufacture of gloves was not at all an important feature of the Tudor city's economy, but by the middle of the eighteenth century it had grown to such size and importance that it almost rivalled the lost cloth industry in the numbers employed, although not in terms of the wealth produced. The manufacture of fine china and porcelain was introduced in the middle of the eighteenth century and developed quickly. Behind this industrial renaissance lay the economic factors which had always aided the city – its geographical position, communications and importance as a regional centre for a wide area whose prosperity increased greatly during the early years of the Industrial Revolution. The navigable Severn remained of great importance, and when at the beginning of the nineteenth century Worcester was joined to Birmingham by canal, the presence of the water link with the sea took on even greater significance; engineering and other branches of heavy industry were soon established.

Worcester's importance as a regional centre is shown by the development there in the eighteenth century of some of the refinements of a provincial capital: flourishing theatres, early and proliferating newspapers, a lively social and cultural life in general, and the presence for a season of many of the gentry and aristocracy of the region.[1]

Some explanation of Worcester's role in the Civil War seems necessary, for its stubborn defence of the king's cause between 1642 and 1646 and the Battle of Worcester in 1651, which represented the final crushing of that cause, were the city's chief intrusion into national history. Why should such a city, with its highly enterprising, independent, mercantile outlook become a Royalist stronghold? Many large cities, and clothmaking districts in particular, were notorious for their opposition to Charles's government. Indeed there is ample evidence from Worcester itself that there existed before the war a powerful Puritan and Parliamentary element.[2] What probably happened was that Worcester was swamped by its region: the local landowners were strongly Royalist and automatically centred their activities on the county town. The citizens had always shown a high degree of deference to their social superiors in the countryside and were easily pushed into a loyalist stance; events then hardened this original standpoint and made its reversal ever more difficult. Worcester lay too near the Highland Zone, too far from the sophisticated and highly urbanized south and east to escape such a fate. But much of this is supposition and the explanation of Worcester's stubborn Royalism still awaits its historian.

The Civil War and its two sieges caused considerable physical damage, especially in the suburbs where both sides indulged in extensive demolition. The city also suffered from disruption of its trade and heavy fines imposed by the republican government. Worcester's own administration continued to be based on the 1621 charter throughout the rest of the seventeenth and the eighteenth centuries, and under the corporation's leadership a thorough programme of rebuilding and improvement was carried out during the eighteenth century, beginning with the rebuilding of the centre of local government, the Guildhall, in 1721-3, and terminating in an ambitious project centred on a rebuilt Severn Bridge opened in 1781. Thus the regional role and general prosperity and importance of the sixteenth-century city have been preserved, although a heavy price for this has been paid in the destruction of most of the Tudor buildings which once graced it.

In conclusion, perhaps the main points of this study may be briefly re-emphasized. The most important single feature of Worcester's history in the early modern period was expansion, and especially in terms of population; the side-effects of this movement raised many problems of growth and shortage of resources for the citizens. Next in importance was the economic predominance of the cloth industry, the wealth which it created and the impact of that wealth on urban society, a feature of the city's economy so conspicuous that it tends to obscure the basic function of Worcester as an important regional centre, living by supplying the needs of country folk.

Of lesser significance, but of very considerable interest, was the perfection of the city's constitutional independence from the shire and the final development of a system of government of medieval origin but destined to support the city for centuries to come. The period saw a major expansion in the participation of local government in the life of the community. Perhaps the historian's natural interest in change and development tends in this study to obscure the basic continuity of the theme, the combination of commercial and industrial enterprise with a large measure of administrative and social conservatism. Many important changes took place, and they have been probed in the previous pages, but much of the environment, physical, mental, social or economic of the citizen of Worcester continued in an already familiar and traditional pattern throughout the sixteenth century.

This study has attempted to show how the demographic, political, social, religious, economic and cultural histories of an English provincial city may be brought together to express the essential unity of a vigorous, powerful, homogeneous urban community, sharing many of the characteristics of its contemporaries, yet in its own way, unique.

Abbreviations

Accounts	Worcester Corporation Archives, Account Book 1540–1600
A.P.C.	*Acts of the Privy Council*
B'ham Ref. Lib.	Birmingham Reference Library
Bloom, *Charters*	*Original Charters relating to the City of Worcester*, ed. J. H. Bloom (W.H.S., 1909)
Buchanan	K. McP. Buchanan, 'Studies in the Localization of Seventeenth Century Worcestershire Industries', *T.W.A.S.*, N.S. XVIII–XIX (1940–2)
Cal. Pat. R.	*Calendar of the Patent Rolls*
Camden	W. Camden, *Britannia*, trans. R. Gough (2nd edn, 1806)
Ch.O. I	Worcester Corporation Archives, Chamber Order Book vol. I, 1540–1601
Ch.O. II	Extracts from Worcester Chamber Order Books, 1540–1669, transcribed by V. Collett (typescript, 1943, B'ham Ref. Lib. 574621), vol. II
C.R.O.	County Record Office, Worcester
Fiennes	*The Journeys of Celia Fiennes*, ed. C. Morris (1947)
Follett	F. V. Follett, *A History of Worcester Royal Grammar School* (1951)
Green	V. Green, *The History and Antiquities of the City and Suburbs of Worcester* (1796), 2 vols
Habington	T. Habington, *A Survey of Worcestershire*, ed. J. Amphlett (W.H.S., 1895–9)
H.M.C.	Historical Manuscripts Commission
Hoskins	W. G. Hoskins, *Provincial England* (1963)
Humphries	J. Humphries, 'The Elizabethan Estate Book of Grafton Manor', T.B.A.S., XLIV (1918)

Leach	A. H. Leach, *Early Education in Worcester* (W.H.S., 1913)
Leland	*The Itinerary of John Leland*, ed. L. Toulmin Smith (1908)
Letters and Papers	*Letters and Papers Foreign and Domestic of the Reign of Henry VIII*
MacCaffrey	W. T. MacCaffrey, *Exeter 1540–1640* (1958)
More	*The Journal of Prior William More*, ed. E. S. Fegan (W.H.S., 1914)
Noake, *Monastery and Cathedral*	J. Noake, *The Monastery and Cathedral of Worcester* (1866)
Noake, *Worcester*	J. Noake, *Worcester in Olden Times* (1849)
Orphans Wills	Worcester Corporation Archives, Orphans Court Will Register
Orphans Recognizances	Worcester Corporation Archives, Orphans Court Recognizance Register
P.H.W.	W. R. Williams, *The Parliamentary History of The County of Worcester* (1897)
P.C.C.	Prerogative Court of Canterbury, Will Register, Somerset House, London
Prob.	Probate Records, Worcester C.R.O.
P.R.O.	Public Record Office
Q.S.P.	*Calendar of the Quarter Session Papers*, ed. J. W. Willis-Bund (W.H.S., 1900)
Register	R. Flenley, *A Calendar of the Register of the Queen's Majesty's Council in the Dominion and Principality of Wales and the Marches of the same 1569–1591* (Cymmrodorion Record Soc., 1916)
Smith	Toulmin Smith, *English Gilds* (Early English Text Society, Original Series No. 40, 1870)
S.P.D.	State Papers, Domestic Series
Talbot Farm Accounts, Household Accounts	Photostat copies of Farm and Household Accounts of the Talbot Family of Grafton Manor, B'ham Ref. Lib. 603707
T.B.A.S.	*Trans. Birmingham Archaeological Society*
T.W.A.S.	*Trans. Worcestershire Archaeological Society*
Valor Ecclesiasticus	*Valor Ecclesiasticus temp. Henr. VIII*, ed. J. Caley, vol. III (1817)
V.C.H.	*Victoria County History*
V.F.P. I, II	Worcester Corporation Archives, View of Frankpledge vols I, II
Warwick	A. D. Dyer, 'The Corporation of Warwick 1545–1588'; Univ. B'ham Lib., B.A. Dissertation, 1963
W.H.S.	Worcestershire Historical Society

Bibliography
of major sources

Primary sources

WORCESTER CORPORATION ARCHIVES, THE GUILDHALL, WORCESTER
Account Book 1540–1600; Chamber Order Book vol. I 1540–1601; View
of Frankpledge vols. I and II; Orphans Court, Will Register and Recog-
nizance Register; Liber Recordum for 1522, 1564/5, 1575/6, 1582/3;
Town Clerk's Notebook; Royal Charters 1555, 1621; Ordinance for the
Better Regulation of the Bailiffs and the rendering of their Accounts,
1392; Star Chamber Decree 1504.

WORCESTERSHIRE COUNTY RECORDS OFFICE, SHIRE HALL AND ST HELEN'S,
WORCESTER
Diocesan Probate Records 1500–1620; Consistory Court Deposition Books
vols. 1–4; Visitation Act Books 1597, 1613–17; Treasurers' Accounts of
Six Masters Charity; Parish records and registers of All Saints', St
Martin's, St Nicholas', St Swithin's and St Andrew's, Worcester.

PRINCIPAL PROBATE REGISTRY, SOMERSET HOUSE, LONDON
Will Registers of the Prerogative Court of Canterbury 1500–1620.

PUBLIC RECORD OFFICE
Exchequer King's Remembrancer, Subsidy Rolls E.179, Port Books E.190.

BIRMINGHAM REFERENCE LIBRARY
The Areley Hall Collections.
Household and Farm Accounts of the Talbot Family of Grafton Manor.

WORCESTER CATHEDRAL LIBRARY
Court Rolls of the manor of Guestenhall.
Registers of the Priory and Dean and Chapter.

MAJOR PRINTED SOURCES

T. Blount, *Boscobel* (1660)

Calendar of the Quarter Session Papers, ed. J. W. Willis-Bund (W.H.S., 1899–1900).

W. Camden, *Britannia*, trans. R. Gough (2nd edn, 1806).

Churchwardens' Accounts of St Michael in Bedwardine, Worcester, 1539–1603, ed. J. Amphlett (W.H.S., 1896).

The Diary of Henry Townshend of Elmley Lovett 1640–63, ed. J. W. Willis-Bund (W.H.S., 1915–20).

Early Education in Worcester, ed. A. H. Leach (W.H.S., 1913).

V. Green, *The History and Antiquities of the City and Suburbs of Worcester*, 2 vols. (1796).

T. Habington, *A Survey of Worcestershire*, ed. J. Amphlett (W.H.S., 1895–9).

The Itinerary of John Leland, ed. L. Toulmin Smith (1908).

The Journal of Prior William More, ed. E. S. Fegan (W.H.S., 1913–14).

The Journeys of Celia Fiennes, ed. C. Morris (1947).

Original Charters Relating to the City of Worcester, ed. J. H. Bloom (W.H.S., 1909).

The Parish Book of St. Helen's Church in Worcester, ed. J. B. Wilson (1900).

The Parish Registers of St Michael-in-Bedwardine, Worcester 1546–1812 (Worcestershire Parish Registers, 2nd series, vol. II, 1954).

The Parliamentary Survey of the Lands and Possessions of the Dean and Chapter of Worcester, ed. T. Cave and R. A. Wilson (W.H.S., 1924).

Toulmin Smith, *English Gilds* (Early English Text Society, Original Series No. 40, 1870).

Valor Ecclesiasticus, ed. J. Caley (1810–34).

Major secondary sources

A Bibliography of Worcestershire, ed. J. R. Burton (W.H.S., 1903).

E. O. Browne and J. R. Burton, *Worthies of Worcestershire* (1916).

K. McP. Buchanan, 'Studies in the Localization of Seventeenth Century Worcestershire Industries', *T.W.A.S.* N.S. XVII–XIX (1940–2).

A Calendar of the Wills and Administrations proved in the Consistory Court of the Bishop of Worcester 1451–1652, ed. E. A. Fry (W.H.S., 1904–10).

F. V. Follett, *A History of Worcester Royal Grammar School* (1951).

T. R. Nash, *Collections for the History of Worcestershire* (2nd edn, 1799).

O. M. Lloyd, 'Family Records from the Areley Hall Collection', *T.W.A.S.*, N.S. XVIII (1941).

A. MacDonald, 'Anthony Tolly and the Tomb of Edmund Freake, Bishop of Worcester (1584–91) in Worcester Cathedral', *T.W.A.S.*, n.s. xix (1942).

J. Noake, *Worcester in Olden Times* (1849); *The Monastery and Cathedral of Worcester* (1866).

Victoria County History of Worcestershire, vols I (1901), II (1906), III (1913), IV (1924).

"W.R.", *A Concise History of the City and Suburbs of Worcester* (1816).

W. R. Williams, *The Parliamentary History of the County of Worcester* (1897).

J. W. Willis-Bund, *The Civil War in Worcestershire* (1905).

R. Woof, *Catalogue of the Manuscript Records and Printed Books in the Library of the Corporation of Worcester* (1874).

Notes

Chapter 1

1. F. M. Stenton, *Anglo-Saxon England* (2nd edn, 1947), 43–4.
2. *V.C.H. Worcs.* vol. IV (1924), 381–2.
3. W. G. Hoskins, *Local History in England* (1959), 176–7.
4. Especially Doharty (1741), Young (1779) and Green (1796).
5. Printed as the frontispiece to T. Blount, *Boscobel*, 1660; based on a MS. plan drawn about 1650 (British Museum, Add. Mss. 11, 564:1).
6. Leland, vol. II, 90.
7. *V.C.H. Worcs.*, vol. IV, 376, 379, 384.
8. Leland, vol. II, 89–92, Camden, 519–20; J. Speed, *Theatre of the empire of Great Britaine* (1611), vol I, 51; Fiennes, 232.

Chapter 2

1. Parish registers of All Saints' (begins 1561, C.R.O.), St Helen's (begins 1538, *The Parish Book of St Helen's Church in Worcester*, ed. J. B. Wilson, 1900), St Martin's (begins *c.*1542, C.R.O.), St Michael's (*The Parish Registers of St Michael-in-Bedwardine, Worcester, 1546–1812*, Worcestershire Parish Registers, 2nd series, vol. II, 1954), St Nicholas' (C.R.O., begins 1564) and St Swithin's (begins 1538, in custody of the incumbent).
2. T. R. Nash, *Collections for the History of Worcestershire* (2nd edn, 1799), vol. II, Appendix, cxvii.
3. *The Diary of Henry Townshend of Elmley Lovett 1640–63*, ed. J. W. Willis-Bund, vol. I (W.H.S., 1920), 104–5.
4. W. G. Hoskins, *Provincial England* (1963), 70, 72, 87.
5. The parish registers involved are those of Alvechurch (B'ham Ref. Lib. Photostat 536738), Aston (*The Registers of the Parish Church*

of Aston-juxta-Birmingham, vol. I, ed. W. F. Carter, 1900),
Birmingham St Martin's (*Transcript of the first Register Book of
the Parish Church of St Martin, Birmingham, 1554–1653*, ed.
J. Hill and W. B. Bickley, 1889), Handsworth (MS. transcript in
Notebooks of John Hill, vols 23–6, 36, B'ham Ref. Lib. 661029,
661042), Harborne (B'ham Ref. Lib. Photostat 465140), Kings
Norton (in custody of incumbent), Northfield (B'ham Ref. Lib.
Photostat 465134), Solihull (*The Register of Solihill*, Parish
Register Society, vol. LIII, 1904) and Yardley (B'ham Ref. Lib.
Photostat 450347).

6. *The Registers of Bushley in the Deanery of Upton 1538 to 1812*
(Worcestershire Parish Register Society, 1913); *A Transcript of the
Register of the Parish Church, Bretforton*, ed. W. H. Shawcross
(1908).

Chapter 3

1. S. Thrupp, *The Merchant Class of Medieval London 1300–1500*
   (1948), 194–5; J. C. Russell, *British Medieval Population* (1948),
   194–7.
2. Noake, *Worcester*, 166.
3. Ch.O. I, 1540–1601, f.93; V.F.P. I, f.136v; *Register*, 171–2; *A.P.C.*
   1581–2, 44.
4. Ch.O. I, fos. 187v–8, 189; Ch.O. II, 14–17, 23, 60, 83.
5. V.F.P. II, f.bv.
6. *Q.S.P.*, vol. I, cliv; *Early Chronicles of Shrewsbury 1372–1603*, ed.
   W. A. Leighton (1880), 88; T. Atkinson, *Elizabethan Winchester*
   (1963), 215–16; Ch.O. I, f.148v.
7. See Chapter 13.
8. C. Creighton, *A History of Epidemics in Britain* (2nd edn, 1965).
9. Philip Tinker, *Elegiac Verses on the Plague of Pestilence* (n.d.,
   printed in Worcester *c*.1780).

Chapter 4

1. Major sources for price and wage levels: Corporation Archives,
   Accounts, vol. I, Orphans Recognizances; C.R.O., Six Masters
   Treasurer's Accounts, St Andrew's Churchwardens' Accounts;
   B'ham Ref. Lib., Areley Hall Collections, especially Jeayes 29 and
   Z. Lloyd 50/12; *More; Churchwardens' Accounts of St Michael in
   Bedwardine Worcester 1539–1603*, ed. J. Amphlett (W.H.S., 1896).
2. W. Beveridge *et al.*, *Prices and Wages in England*, vol. I (1939);

E. H. Phelps Brown and S. V. Hopkins, *Economica*, N.S.
XXIV–VI (1957–9).
3. Beveridge, *op. cit.* 89, 144, 201.
4. V.F.P., 2 vols.
5. J. E. Thorold Rogers, *A History of Agriculture and Prices in England*, vol. III (1882), 639–42.
6. V.F.P. I, fos. 106v–7, 126v–7v.
7. V.F.P. I, fos. 295, 296, 309, 315, 151, II f.4v.
8. Leland, vol. II, 94.
9. V. Green, *The History and Antiquities of the City and Suburbs of Worcester*, vol. II (1796), Appendix, lxiii–iv.
10. V.F.P. I, f.148v, 151v. II, f.12.
11. Ch.O. I, f.96; V.F.P. II, f.70.
12. V.F.P. II, fos. 6, kv; I, f.268; II, ff.6v, ev; Ch.O. I, f.25v; *Statutes of the Realm*, 1 Eliz. ch. 15.
13. Habington, vol. II, 469.
14. Ch.O. I, ff.95v, 98, 103; Accounts, 1565/6, 1566/7, 1567/8, 1573/4.
15. *V.C.H. Shropshire*, vol. I (1908), 454.
16. C.R.O., Diocesan Probate Collection, 1567:97, 1575:98, vol. VI, f.307.
17. Prob., 1588:157; V.F.P. II, f.kv.
18. *Ibid.*, 1592:23, 1602:60a, 1605:30, 1595:9b, 1604:119.
19. *V.C.H. Shropshire*, vol. I, 454.
20. Prob., 1579:82, 1586:50.
21. *Ibid.*, 1590:37.

Chapter 5

1. The Gough map: E. J. S. Parsons, *The Map of Great Britain* (1958).
2. Habington, vol. II, 418; Q.S.P., 212.
3. Prob., 1559:II:297.
4. *Ibid.*, 1581:27, 1605:167g; 1613:203c.
5. Leland, vol. II, 88.
6. P.R.O., Exchequer K.R., Port Books, E.190.
7. *Ibid.*, 1133/6.
8. E.g. in 1566 and 1576, *ibid.* 1130/9, 1129/18.
9. *Ibid.*, 1129/18.
10. *Ibid.*, 1133/6.
11. *Ibid.*, 1135/1.
12. V.F.P. II, fos. 40, 62, 149, 152v.
13. *Ibid.*, f.pv, Ch.O. I, f.177v, 78v.
14. Mrs Baldwyn-Childe, 'The Building of the Manor House of Kyre Park, Worcestershire', *The Antiquary*, XXI (1890), 204–5.
15. *Ibid.*, XXII (1890), 52.

16. Will Registers of the Prerogative Court of Canterbury, Somerset House, 2 Bakon.
17. Prob., 1586:50.
18. *Ibid*., 1604:119.
19. *Ibid*., 1579:82.
20. See Chapter 8.
21. C.R.O., Consistory Court Records, Deposition Books, vol. I, f.417.
22. Prob., 1586:50, 1579:82.
23. T. S. Willan, *River Navigation in England 1600–1750* (1936), 103.
24. Fiennes, 232.
25. C.R.O., Visitation Act Book 1613–17, f.384v.
26. Toulmin Smith, *English Gilds* (Early English Text Society, Original Series, vol. 40, 1870), 397.
27. Ch.O. I, f.113v; Simonds D'Ewes, *The Journal of all the Parliaments during the Reign of Queen Elizabeth . . .* (1682), 213, 219, 221; Ch.O. I, f.139v, Accounts 1568/69; £20 was as much as the usual total expenditure on public works.
28. *Statutes of the Realm*, 9 Henry VI ch. 5, 19 Henry VII ch. 18, 23 Henry VIII ch. 12.
29. Corporation Archives, Star Chamber Decree 1504.
30. Green, vol. II, Appendix, lxvi; V.F.P. I, f.39–39v, 98, 132v–133.
31. Ch.O. I, f.152v, 154v, V.F.P. II, f.148–148v.
32. Ch.O. I, f.177v.
33. 'Extracts from Worcester Chamber Order Books 1540–1669', transcribed by V. Collett (typescript, 1943, B'ham Ref. Lib. 574621), vol. II, 120, 146.
34. *Cal. Pat. R. Henry VII*, vol. II, 461–2.
35. Corporation Archives, Orphans Recognizances, loose MS. (statement of accounts of executors of Thomas Bromley).

Chapter 6

1. Habington, vol. II, 426.
2. Talbot Farm Accounts 1573–5 (B'ham Ref. Lib. 603797), 21–33; J. Humphries, 'The Elizabethan Estate Book of Grafton Manor', *T.B.A.S.*, XLIV (1918), 1–124.
3. Worcester's market region was found to be very similar in shape and size when surveyed after the last war: J. Glaisyer *et al.*, *County Town* (1946), 11.
4. C.R.O., Consistory Court Deposition Books, vol. I, fos. 59v–68.
5. *Elizabethan England by William Harrison*, ed. F. J. Furnival (1876), 140.
6. Figure 13 is based on a list in V.F.P. II, fos. 47–47v.

7. Noake, *Worcester*, 200–1.
8. Green, vol. II, Appendix, lxvi.
9. Ibid., lxv; Ch.O. I, fos. 77v, 150v, 174, 179v, 191v; V.F.P. I, f.270v.
10. *Cal. Pat. R. Philip and Mary, 1554–5*, 83–4; Ch.O. I, f.110.
11. Ch.O. I, f.189; V.F.P. I, f,132v–3, II, fos. 10, 96, 139v, 150v–151v, 153, 159, 210v, 215, 236v. The tenants of estates held by the Crown in 1066, 'ancient demesne', enjoyed freedom from most tolls throughout the country.
12. *Cal. Pat. R. Philip and Mary, 1554–5*, 83; Habington, vol. II, 426.
13. V.F.P. I, fos. 79v–82, 346–8v.
14. *Ibid*. fos. 1–5.
15. Figure 14 is based on V.F.P. I, fos. 79v–82, 346–8v.
16. Figure 15 is based on V.F.P. I, fos. 1–5.
17. Figure 16 is based on V.F.P. I, fos. 15v–18v, 28–30v.
18. Ch.O. I, fos. 84–5, 88.
19. *Ibid*., fos. 83, 271.
20. *Letters and Papers*, vol. IX, 21–2, vol. XI, 534–5.

Chapter 7

1. Hoskins, 78–80; J. F. Pound, 'The Elizabethan Corporation of Norwich', University of Birmingham Library, M.A. thesis, 125.
2. Hoskins, 108.
3. *Ibid*., 80, 108; W. T. MacCaffrey, *Exeter 1540–1640* (1958), 163.
4. P.R.O., Exchequer K.R., Subsidy Rolls, E.179 200/27.
5. Orphans Wills, f.71; Prob. 1552:104; 1559:II:1; 1566:65; 1583:104a.
6. Prob. 1567:72.
7. *Ibid*., 1583:104a; 1558:125.
8. *Ibid*., 1552:104.
9. *Ibid*., 1556:120; 1573:69d.
10. *Ibid*., 1580:6a; 1583:104a.
11. *Ibid*., 1559:II:1; 1604:11; 1558:41.
12. *Ibid*., vol. VI f.336v; 1558:298; P.C.C. 10 Maynwaryng.
13. Prob. 1573:69v.
14. J. Humphries, 'The Elizabethan Estate Book of Grafton Manor', *T.B.A.S.* xliv (1918), 56, 63, 80.
15. Prob. 1559:II:269.
16. *Ibid*.
17. *A Calendar of the Wills and Administrations proved in the Consistory Court of the Bishop of Worcester 1451–1652*, ed. E. A. Fry (W.H.S., 1904–10).
18. Prob. 1575:107.
19. *Ibid*., 1614:191.

20. *Ibid.*, 1594:45.
21. Orphans Recognizances, executors' accounts, loose MS.
22. *More*, e.g. 235; Talbot Household Accounts 1576–7, 56.
23. Ch.O. I, f.45; *Cal. Pat. R. Henry VII*, vol. I, 330; Prob. 1596:15.
24. P.C.C. 9 Tirwhite.

Chapter 8

1. *Calendar of State Papers, Domestic Series, 1547–80*, 516.
2. Smith, 383.
3. Leland, vol. II, 91; Camden, vol. II, 470; Habington, vol. II, 426–7.
4. H. Heaton, *The Yorkshire Woollen and Worsted Industries* (1920), 85. The absolute figures from aulnage returns are rather notional but comparative levels from different areas are probably more significant.
5. G. D. Ramsey, 'The Distribution of the Cloth Industry in 1561–2', *English Historical Review*, LVII (1942), 361–9.
6. V.F.P. I, fos. 234v–5; P. J. Bowden, *The Wool Trade in Tudor and Stuart England* (1962), 29–30.
7. Prob. 1612:100; 1588:157.
8. *Ibid.*, 1557: 189.
9. Talbot Farm Accounts 1573–6.
10. Smith, 384; V.F.P. I, fos. 149v, 169.
11. Account Books; Smith, 384; a tod usually weighed 28lb.
12. Prob. 1618:38; 1611:48a.
13. *Ibid.*, 1555:26.
14. Smith, 383–4.
15. P.C.C. 23 Babington.
16. *Ibid.*, 1599:80f; 1612:100; P.C.C. 65 Capell; 117 Weldon.
17. Ch.O. I, f.74v.
18. Prob. 1556:45c.
19. P.C.C. 14 Populwell; Prob. 1545:25.
20. Prob. 1578:30.
21. *Ibid.*, 1585:84b.
22. *Ibid.*, 1576:94; 1611:169; 1588:124; 1588:157; 1611:169; P.C.C. 5 Spencer, 117 Weldon, 12 Bolfelde, 29 Loftes.
23. Prob. 1612:100.
24. *Ibid.*, 1611:169; 1610:63.
25. Ch.O. I, fos. 59v, 78.
26. *V.C.H. Worcs.*, vol. III, 385; P.C.C. 117 Weldon; Visitation Act Book 1613–17, ff.386, 390v, 400v, 417.
27. Prob. 1554:84; 1577:58; 1579:82.
28. *Ibid.*, 1593:80b; 1612:100.

29. *Ibid.*, 1602:111; 1605:127c; 1611:125d.
30. *Ibid.*, 1541:61; 1556:37; 1601:91.
31. *Ibid.*, 1556:37.
32. *Ibid.*, 1551:72; 1605:127c; 1611:125d; 1541:61; 1601:91; P.C.C. 34 Bodfelde.
33. Prob. 1551:76; 1551:86a; 1551:117a; 1554:80; 1558:280; 1560:25; 1561:24; 1578:100a; 1616:181.
34. MacCaffrey, 161; G. D. Ramsey, *The Wiltshire Woollen Industry in the Sixteenth and Seventeenth Centuries* (1943).

Chapter 9

1. Prob. 1559:II:297.
2. P.C.C. 29 Bolein.
3. Prob. 1588:124; Orphans Wills f.42v.
4. Ch.O. I, fos. 94, 94v, 98v.
5. B'ham Ref. Lib. Zachery Lloyd Collection, 51/1.
6. E. M. Carus-Wilson, *Medieval Merchant Venturers* (1954), chart facing p. xviii.
7. B'ham Ref. Lib., Areley Hall Collections, Jeyes 29.
8. *Letters and Papers*, vol. IV pt ii, 1956.
9. Prob. vol. II, f.66v; P.C.C. 15 and 29 Fetiplace.
10. V.F.P. I, fos. 234v-5. See Chapter 13.
11. *V.C.H. Worcs.*, vol. II, 290; Noake, *Worcester*, 175.
12. *S.P.D. James I 1619-23*, 391; *V.C.H., Worcs.*, vol. II, 292.
13. Smith, 383.
14. *Statutes of the Realm* 25 Henry VIII ch. 18.
15. 5 and 6 Edward VI ch. 6.
16. V.F.P. I, fos. 234v-5; V.C.H. II, 289; Accounts 1555/6, 56/7, 57/8; 4 and 5 Philip and Mary ch. 5.
17. Ch.O. I, fos. 67v-8, 74; V.F.P. I, f.274v; Ch.O. I, f.77, 83v, 87v, 92v.
18. Ch.O. I, f.83v; *Original Charters relating to the City of Worcester*, ed. J. H. Bloom (W.H.S., 1909), 13.
19. *V.C.H. Worcs.*, vol. II, 290; Green, vol. II, Appendix, lxxi-v.
20. Clothiers Company, Weavers Apprenticeship Book.
21. *V.C.H. Worcs.*, vol. II, 291; Weavers Apprenticeship Book, f.225.
22. Historical Manuscripts Commission, *Salisbury MSS*, pt 17 (1938), 180; *V.C.H. Worcs.*, vol. II, 289.
23. Weavers Apprenticeship Book, fos. 228-30.
24. Smith, 383; Ch.O. I, f.74v.
25. V.F.P. II, fos. 76v-77v.
26. *V.C.H. Worcs.*, vol. II, 289.
27. Buchanan, *T.W.A.S.*, n.s. XVIII (1941), 34-7.

28. Prob. 1598:72c.
29. *Ibid*. 1575:59b; V.F.P. II, f.190v; Prob. 1586:63a.
30. Green, vol. II, App. lxiv; Buchanan, N.S. XIX (1942), 46.

Chapter 10

1. Prob. vol. VI, fos. 296–8; P.C.C. 39 Daughtry.
2. Prob. 1576:14; 1602:65f; 1605:105.
3. *Ibid*., 1556:152.
4. *Ibid*., 1608:135a; vol. V f.2.
5. *Ibid*., 1580:72.
6. Buchanan, *T.W.A.S.*, N.S. XVII (1940) 42–5.
7. Prob. 1611:43.
8. *Ibid*., 1574:74g.
9. *Ibid*., 1559:II:13; 1560:232; 1577:13a; 1616:181.
10. *Ibid*., 1610:162a.
11. V.F.P. I, f.9v.
12. Prob. 1557:10; 1558:280.
13. 1545:30.
14. 5 Elizabeth ch. 8; Ch.O. I, f.153.
15. V.F.P. II, f.269v.
16. V.F.P. I, f.8v.
17. Ch.O. I, f.77v, 88v; as a general rule, a citizen was required to be a party to all market transactions, and bargains solely between foreigners were prohibited.
18. V.F.P. I, f.8v, II fos. 67v, 269v.
19. Ch.O. I, f.111; V.F.P. II, f.65v.
20. Prob. 1560:284.
21. *Ibid*., 1564:29.
22. Ch.O. I, f.100.
23. Prob. 1572:70; 1613:157.
24. *Ibid*., 1602:60a.
25. *V.C.H. Worcs.*, vol. II, 267–9; Buchanan, *T.W.A.S.*, N.S. XIX (1942), 52.
26. Prob. 1569:70.
27. *Ibid*., 1541:64.
28. *Ibid*., 1569:70.
29. *Ibid*., 1571:101b.
30. *Ibid*., 1596:82.
31. *Ibid*., 1587:150b; 1551:116.
32. *Ibid*., 1562:3.
33. *Ibid*., 1591:64.
34. *Ibid*., 1587:125; 1591:64.

35. Prob. 1573:87.
36. *Ibid.*, 1598:19.
37. *Ibid.*, 1573:23a.
38. *Ibid.*, 1554:80.
39. V.F.P. I, f.146v, II, f.tv.
40. Prob. 1615:67a.
41. Reddle is a red dye used for marking sheep.
42. J. F. Ede, *A History of Wednesbury* (1962), 138–9.
43. Verjuice is a kind of vinegar.
44. Prob. 1577:58; 1579:82.
45. *Ibid.*, 1560:25; 1611:169; 1545:179; 1558:164.
46. *Ibid.*, 1560:126; 1607:82.
47. R. H. Hilton, 'Building Accounts of Elmley Castle, Worcestershire, 1345-6', *University of Birmingham Historical Journal*, x (1965), 80; Humphries, 17, 38; *The Old Order Book of Hartlebury Grammar School 1556–1752*, ed. D. Robertson (W.H.S., 1904), 14–15.

Chapter 11

1. Warwick, 27–9; *V.C.H. Leicestershire*, vol. IV, 99–104.
2. Prob. 1615:70; 1558:298; 1541:64.
3. Prob. 1545:25; 1567:72.
4. *Ibid.*, 1568:42; 1551:119; 1557:187.
5. V.F.P. I, f.150v, II, f.4v; Ch.O. I, f.87v, 131v, 142v.
6. Ch.O. I, f.1v.
7. Prob. 1572:81; 1618:57.
8. Hoskins, 108.
9. Prob. 1576:73.
10. Prob. 1602:85.
11. *Ibid.*, 1558:860; 1602:85; 1605:47.
12. *Ibid.*, 1570:46; 1566:64.
13. *Ibid.*, 1609:171q.
14. P.C.C. 26 Bodfelde, Prob. 1535:157.
15. Prob. 1587:62; 1578:100a.
16. Grafton Manor Estate Book, 58; *More*, 358.
17. Prob. 1552:25.
18. Orphans Wills, f.68; Prob. 1560:25; 1607:165d; 1608:60c.
19. Prob. 1608:60c.
20. *Ibid.*
21. Prob. 1551:118; 1593:1; 1608:60c.
22. *Ibid.*, 1608:60c.
23. *Ibid.*, 1582:50.

24. Green, vol. II, Appendix, lxiii.
25. Orphans Wills, f.84; Ch.O. I, fos. 165v, 163.
26. Prob. 1611:181e.
27. V.F.P. II, fos. 6v, vv.
28. Green, vol. II, Appendix, lxv; Ch.O. I, fos. 204, 191v.
29. Ch.O. I, fos. 12, 93v, 111, 129v.
30. *Ibid.*, f.61v.
31. V.F.P. I, fos. 267–267v.
32. *Ibid.*, fos. 147, 297v; Green, vol. II, Appendix, lxiii.
33. Ch.O. I, f.156v.
34. V.F.P. II, f.rv; Ch.O. II, p.25; Ch.O. I, fos. 118, 120v.
35. Ch.O. I, f.37.
36. *Ibid.*, f.61.
37. P.C.C. 10 Bolein; Prob. 1585:89b.
38. Ch.O. I, f.78v.
39. Prob. 1567:97; 1585:89b; 1590:37.
40. *Ibid.*, 1585:89b.
41. *Ibid.*
42. V.F.P. I, fos. 266v–267.
43. V.F.P. II, f.189; *Register*, 171.
44. V.F.P. I, f.271.
45. V.F.P. II, f.2.
46. *V.C.H. Worcs.*, vol. IV, 386.
47. Prob. 1561:24; 1599:115c.
48. E .O. Browne and J. R. Burton, *Worthies of Worcestershire* (1916).
49. Prob. vol. VI, f.362; vol. VII, f.118.
50. P.C.C. 45 Bakon.
51. Prob. 1618:154.
52. *Ibid.*, 1605:82a.
53. See Chapter 15.
54. Grafton Manor Estate Book, 101.
55. Prob. vol. VI, f.250v; vol. VII, f.296; vol. VI, f.289v.
56. *Ibid.*, vols. VI, f.250v, VII, f.296.
57. Consistory Court Deposition Books, vol. II, f.380v; C.R.O., Photocopy of Lambeth Palace MS, B.A.2553.
58. Prob. vol. VI, f.290v.
59. *Ibid.*, 1573:69v; P.C.C. 22 Bodfelde.
60. Prob. 1592:152.
61. *Ibid.*, 1613:171.
62. *Ibid.*, 1594:60v; 1575:97.
63. P.C.C. 57 Soame; Talbot Household Accounts, 51.

Chapter 12

1. V.F.P. II, f.107.
2. *V.C.H. Worcs.*, vol. IV, 386.
3. *Ibid.*
4. Green, vol. II, Appendix, lxxi–v.
5. Ch.O. I, f.111, 108.
6. P.C.C. 12 Bodfelde.
7. P.C.C. 12 Weldon.
8. V.F.P. II, f.143v.
9. V.F.P. I, f.272v; Ch.O. I, f.122v.
10. V.F.P. II, f.10/.
11. Prob. 1606:f.133kk.
12. *Ibid.*, 1607:30.
13. *Ibid.*, 1555:70.
14. Green, vol. II, Appendix, lii–iii.
15. H.M.C. *Salisbury MSS*, pt 17 (1938), 180; *V.C.H. Worcs.*, vol. II, 292.
16. Smith, 390.
17. Ch.O. I, f.86.
18. V.F.P. I, f.335v.
19. V.F.P. I, fos. 151v, 328v, II fq.
20. Cathedral Library, Manor of Guestenhall Court Rolls, Oct. 41 Eliz., March 44 Eliz.
21. Consistory Court Deposition Books, vol. IV, f.409v.

Chapter 13

1. Price indices from E. H. Phelps Brown and S. V. Hopkins, 'Wage Rates and Prices: Evidence for Population Pressure in the Sixteenth Century', *Economica*, xxiv (1957), 306.
2. See Chapter 4.
3. See Chapter 3.
4. Bloom, *Charters*, containing the Priory leases, quite exceptionally includes no properties here; blocks of houses are referred to in P.C.C. 22 Bodfelde, 101 Parker; Prob. vol. VI, f.336v, 1567:75.
5. P.C.C. 22 Bodfelde, 34 Bodfelde; Cathedral Library, Priory Registers, A. VI vol. II, f.86.
6. Prob. vol. VI, f.296, 1579:82; 1582:48.
7. P.C.C., 90 Dorset, 24 Lawe.
8. Ch.O. II, 15.
9. Ch.O. I, fos. 87, 157, 157v, 168v, 175, 178, 209.

10. V.F.P. II, f.28v; 3 Henry VIII ch. 18.
11. Ch.O. I, fos. 98, 117, 118; V.F.P. I, fos. 149, 152v, 309, 313v, 320v; II, f.cv.
12. Hoskins, 131–48.
13. Manor of Guestenhall Court Rolls, April 42 Eliz., April 43 Eliz., Oct. 43 Eliz.
14. V.F.P. I, fos. 116v–123; at about the same date some 101 people in Exeter were similarly placed, about the same proportion of the population (MacCaffrey, 113).
15. V.F.P. II, fos. 221v–222.
16. V.F.P. I, fos. 50–54v.
17. *Ibid.*, fos. 234v–5.
18. Ch.O. I, fos. 187v, 188v, 189; II, 3–5, 14–15, 17.
19. Accounts 1555/6, 56/7; Ch.O. I, f.66v.
20. V.F.P. II, fos. 221v–222. Similar schemes were adopted in a number of towns in this year.
21. V.F.P. I, fos. 43–46v.
22. *Ibid.*, fos. 116v–123.
23. *Ibid.*, f.198.
24. V.F.P. II, f.10.
25. Ch.O. I, fos. 133v, 137, 138.
26. *Cal. Pat. R. Eliz.*, vol. II, 215.
27. C.R.O. Six Masters Treasurers' Accounts.
28. *Ibid.*, fos. 42v–48v, 50, 50v, 54–5.
29. *Letters and Papers*, vol. XX, pt i, 570; V.F.P. II, f.175v.
30. C.R.O. St Andrew's Churchwardens' Accounts.
31. See Chapter 19.
32. V.F.P. II, f.o.
33. E.g. V.F.P. I, fos. 71–3.
34. Ch.O. I, f.62v; V.F.P. I, fos. 334, 148v, 168v.
35. Ch.O. I, f.58v, 88v; V.F.P. II, f.9v; Ch.O. II, 15.
36. Manor of Guestenhall Court Rolls, 43 Eliz., April 43 Eliz., Oct. 10 James.
37. Ch.O. I, f.139; Accounts 1596/7, 1598/9; Ch.O. I, fos. 199v, 201.
38. Ch.O. II, 24, 27; Prob. 1620:209b.

Chapter 14

1. Based on P.R.O., Exchequer K.R., Subsidy Rolls, E.179, 200/131.
2. The Bishop's Survey of 1563, T.R. Nash, *Collections for the History of Worcestershire* (2nd edn, 1799), vol. II, Appendix, cxvii.
3. The lists in the Account Book rarely record more than five per year.
4. V.F.P. I, fos. 43–6v, 50–4v, 116v–123.

5. Consistory Court Deposition Books.
6. *Ibid.*, vol. II, f.418.
7. Green, vol. II, Appendix, lvi; Accounts.
8. Corporation Archives, Liber Recordum.
9. MacCaffrey, 164–5.
10. V.F.P. II, f.o.
11. *Calendar of the Bristol Apprentice Book 1532–65*, pt I 1532–42, ed. D. Hollis (Bristol Record Society, xiv, 1949).
12. *The Shrewsbury Burgess Roll*, ed. H. E. Forrest (1924).
13. *Lay Subsidy Roll for the County of Worcester circa 1280*, ed. J. W. Willis-Bund and J. Amphlett (W.H.S., 1893), 1–6; *Lay Subsidy Roll for the County of Worcester 1 Edward III*, ed. F. J. Eld (W.H.S., 1895), 35–6.
14. See Chapter 9.
15. B'ham Ref. Lib., Areley Hall Collections; O. M. Lloyd, 'Family Records from the Areley Hall Collection', *T.W.A.S.*, n.s. xviii (1941), 18–30.
16. P.C.C. 36 Porch; W. R. Williams, *The Parliamentary History of the County of Worcester* (1897), 93.
17. P.C.C. 36 Porch, Prob. 1607:145.
18. Orphans Recognizances, executors' accounts, loose MS.

Chapter 15

1. *V.C.H. Worcs.*, vol. IV, 380–1; Corporation Archives, Ordinance for the better regulation of the Bailiffs and the rendering of their accounts 1392.
2. *V.C.H.* IV 478; *Early Education in Worcester*, ed. A. H. Leach, W.H.S., 1913, 172–8. Names of guild masters from Prob. vol. I, f.55, Accounts 1540/1, Leach 176.
3. Accounts 1542/3; Ch.O. I, ff.32, 26.
4. Worcester Corporation Archives, Ordinance for the better regulation of the Bailiffs and the rendering of their accounts 1392.
5. Smith, 370–409.
6. They appear in the 1466 Ordinances but not in an official grant to the Priory of 1434 (Bloom, *Charters*, 162).
7. A very common arrangement. Some towns either halved the size of each body or had only one chamber of 12 or 24 members.
8. Smith, 408–9; Green, vol. II, Appendix, xlix–l.
9. Smith, 386; Green, vol. II, Appendix, l–li.
10. M. Weinbaum, *British Borough Charters 1307–1660*, (1924), 124; *V.C.H. Worcs.*, vol. IV, 380–2.

11. Accounts 1550/1; H.M.C. *Hatfield House MSS*, pt 1 1883, 120; Ch.O. I, f.53v; V.F.P. I, fos. 225, 226.
12. V.F.P. 1, fos. 38, 278, 226–226v; *Cal. Pat. R. Philip and Mary 1554–5*, 81.
13. V.F.P. I, fos. 277–9v.
14. Ch.O. I, f.155v.
15. *Ibid.*, fos. 165v, 189, 189v; Accounts 1594/5; Ch.O. II, 5–9, 28, 31.
16. Ch.O. II, 46, 48; *V.C.H. Worcs.*, vol. IV, 388.
17. *S.P.D. James I 1603–10*, 392.
18. Noake, *Monastery and Cathedral*, 548–9.
19. *Cal. Pat. R. Philip and Mary 1554–5*, 80–86: original in Worcester Corporation Archives.
20. Ch.O. I, f.77, 26v, 184v.
21. Green, vol. II, Appendix, li; V.F.P. I, f.12.
22. Ch.O. I, f.54, 177–177v.
23. Green, vol. II, Appendix, li, l, xlix.
24. Ch.O. I, fos. 34v–35v.
25. *Ibid.*, fos. 85, 79v; II, 46, I, fos. 132v–133.
26. V.F.P. I, f.272v; Ch.O. I, fos. 158v, 197.
27. Green, vol. II, Appendix, liv–lv.
28. Accounts 1553/4, 1557/8; V.F.P. 1, fos. 149v, 169.
29. V.F.P. II, f.n.
30. V.F.P. I, f.179; II, f. vv; Green, vol. II, Appendix, li.
31. Accounts 1545/6; Prob. 1594:45.
32. Chastleton House MSS, at Shakespeare Institute, Stratford-upon-Avon, *MSS.* 6, 33, 35; Accounts 1580/1; W. R. Williams, *The Parliamentary History of the County of Worcester* (1897).
33. *Register*, 333.
34. Ch.O. I, f.1; Green, vol. II, Appendix, li; History of Parliament, *Biographies of the Members of the House of Commons 1439–1509*, ed. J. C. Wedgwood (1936), 547; *Worthies of Worcestershire*, ed. E. O. Browne and J. R. Burton (1916), 123–4.
35. *Register*, xiv.
36. Green, vol. II, Appendix, lviii.
37. Ch.O. I, f.200v.
38. *Ibid.*, fos. 160v, 190.

Chapter 16

1. *Cal. Pat. R. Philip and Mary 1554–5*, 83–5.
2. V.F.P. I, fos. 266v–272v.
3. *Ibid.*, f.324v.
4. *Ibid.*, II, f.269.

5. Ch.O. I, f.21Av.
6. V.F.P. I, f.150.
7. Ibid., f.147, II, f.n.; Ch.O. I, fos. 73v, 108, 188v, 190v, 194v.
8. *V.C.H. Warwickshire*, vol. III, 223; Smith, 382, 385–6; Green, vol. II, Appendix, lxiii; V.F.P. II, f.ov; Ch.O. I, fos. 83v, 90v, 194v.
9. Consistory Court Deposition Books, vol. I, fos. 59v–68; Ch.O. I, f.101v.
10. Ch.O. I, f.205v, 206v.
11. Ch.O. II, 41, 53.
12. V.F.P., 11, f.bv.
13. Green, vol. II Appendix, lxvi–ii.
14. The court's rules are set out in Orphans Wills, ff.1–4.
15. MacCaffrey, 62–3.
16. *Register*, 197–202; *S.P.D. James I 1603–10*, 398; *Acts of the Privy Council 1571–5*, 337–8; Ch.O. I, f.110; V.F.P. II, fos. 76v–77v.
17. V.F.P. I, f.97; Accounts 1561/2; Ch.O. I, f.138; V.F.P. II, fos. 107–8; *S.P.D. 1581–90*, 337; V.F.P. II, f.256; Ch.O. II, 30.
18. V.F.P. I, f.136.
19. *Letters and Papers*, vol. XIV, pt i, 303, vol. XVII, 510; Ch.O. I, fos. 33v, 204v–05v.
20. V.F.P. I, fos. 130–2; II, f.jv; Ch.O. I, f.91; *S.P.D. 1547–80*, 460; V.F.P. II, fos. 41v, 42v–43v.
21. V.F.P. II, 67v–8, *A.P.C. 1571–5*; 263; V.F.P. II, f.94v; Ch.O. I, f.134; Accounts 1587/8.
22. V.F.P. I, fos.182v, 48; Ch.O. I, fos.146, 189.
23. Ch.O. I, f.96v; V.F.P. I, fos. 182v, 146v; Ch.O. I, f.158v.
24. See Chapter 13.
25. Smith, 385; Green, vol. II, Appendix, lv.
26. V.F.P. I, f.268v.
27. *S.P.D. 1581–90*, 186; *A.P.C. 1580–1*, 36; Green, vol. I, 268.
28. Noake, *Worcester*, 181; Warwick, 58–61; MacCaffrey, 203–21.
29. *Letters and Papers*, vol. XII, pt ii, 249, 431.
30. Ch.O. I, f.160v; *H.M.C. Salisbury MSS*, pt 18, 415
31. Noake, *Monastery and Cathedral*, 535; Consistory Court Deposition Books, vol. II, f.159.
32. J. Neale, *The Elizabethan House of Commons* (1949), 156.
33. *Parliamentary History of Worcestershire*, 38–9, 95.
34. Accounts 1557/8; V.F.P. II, f.132v.
35. V.F.P. I, f.276v, II, f.216; Ch.O. I, 113v–114, 175v.
36. Green, vol. II, Appendix, lx–lxi.
37. Ch.O. I, fos. 48–51.
38. V.F.P. I, f.217.
39. *Ibid.*, f.268v.

Chapter 17

1. *Letters and Papers*, vol. IV pt i, 689; Ch.O. I, f.26. Much of the background and detail of this chapter rest on the Corporation Account Book vol. I, 1540–1600.
2. *Letters and Papers*, vol. XIII pt ii, 211; vol. XIV pt i, 140, 298.
3. Ch.O. I, f.6; Accounts 1560/1.
4. Accounts 1598/9, 1599/1600.
5. MacCaffrey, 55–7; Hoskins, 99.
6. Ch.O. I, f.6.
7. *Ibid.*, f.203.
8. *Ibid.*, fos. 55, 12v; V.F.P. I, f.70v; Ch.O. I, fos. 117v, 144, 155v.
9. Ch.O. I, fos. 12v, 62v, 76v, 129v, 141v, 150v, 179, 180.
10. Cathedral Library, Registers A VII, vols 1–6.
11. Ch.O. I, f.189.
12. V.F.P. I, fos. 87–9, II, fos. 160v–162.
13. MacCaffrey, 252, 263–4; Pound, 62–121.

Chapter 18

1. *V.C.H. Worcs.*, vol. II, 167–8.
2. *Ibid.*, 169–72.
3. *Ibid.*, 154–6.
4. *Valor Ecclesiasticus*, vol. III, 229.
5. *V.C.H. Worcs.*, vol. II, 177–9; *Valor Ecclesiasticus*, vol. III, 229.
6. *V.C.H. Worcs.*, vol. II, 175–7; *Valor Ecclesiasticus*, vol. III, 228–9.
7. *Letters and Papers*, vol. IX, 380–1.
8. *V.C.H. Worcs.*, vol. IV, 578–9.
9. C.R.O., Bishop Bell's Visitation Book, f.33.
10. *Letters and Papers*, vol. XVIII, pt i, 534.
11. *Ibid.*, vol. XIX, pt ii, 186–7.
12. *Cal. Pat. R. Edward VI*, vol. II, 185–7.
13. *Ibid.*, vol. I, 273–4, 361; II, 53–5, 378; III, 27, 375; V, 159.
14. *Valor Ecclesiasticus*. vol. III, 220; *The Parliamentary Survey of the Lands and Possessions of the Dean and Chapter of Worcester*, ed. T. Cave and A. A. Wilson (W.H.S., 1927), 169–220.
15. Habington, vol. II, 426; Noake, *Monastery and Cathedral*, 532–4; *Letters and Papers*, vol. XIV, pt i, 155; vol. XII, pt ii, 218.
16. D. Knowles, *The Religious Orders in England*, vol. III (1961), 108–126.
17. Noake, *Monastery and Cathedral*, 209.

18. Bloom, *Charters*, items 1648, 1063-4, 1576; Cathedral Library, Registers, A XII, fos. 65-6, 62v-64v.
19. See Chapter 13; Ch.O. II, 23; Accounts 1588/9, 1595/6.
20. Green, vol. II, Appendix, lvi.
21. Ch.O. I, f.74v.
22. *S.P.D. Charles I 1636-7*, 359, 390, 495.
23. *Ibid., 1639-40*, 79, 106-7; Ch.O. II, 151; Noake, *Monastery and Cathedral*, 558-60.
24. *S.P.D. James I 1619-23*, 391.
25. Ch.O. II, 216.
26. Prob. 1558:805d.
27. P.C.C. 30 Holnay.
28. *Ibid.*, 77 Drake.
29. Prob. vol. VI, f.289v.
30. *Ibid.*, vol. VIII, f.93, 1598:56.
31. *Ibid.*, 1598:56.
32. *Ibid.*, 1612:52.
33. *Ibid.*, vol. V, f.207, 1556:95.
34. *Valor Ecclesiasticus*, vol. III, 231-4.
35. W. R. Buchanan-Dunlop, 'Seventeenth Century Puritans in Worcester', *T.W.A.S.*, N.S., XXIII.
36. *Ibid.*
37. C.R.O., Visitation Act Book 1593, fos. 3-15v.
38. C.R.O., Visitation Act Book 1613-17.
39. C.R.O., St Andrew's Churchwardens' Accounts.
40. C.R.O., St Swithin's Parish Records, parcel 18.
41. *The Churchwardens' Accounts of St Michael in Bedwardine, Worcester, 1539-1603*, ed. J. Amphlett (W.H.S. 1896).
42. *Ibid.*, 137, 140-1, 151-2.
43. C.R.O., Canon Davenport's Lists and Indexes, 'Presentations to Benefices,' items 211-13, 'Presentations Etc 1526-1602', 35, 38, 39.
44. 'A Collection of Original Letters from the Bishops to the Privy Council 1564', ed. M. Bateson, *Camden Miscellany*, vol. IX (1895), 4-7, 14-15, 7-8.
45. *Recusant Roll No. 1, 1592-3*, Catholic Record Society, vol. 18. (1916), 361, 367; *S.P.D. James I 1603-10*, 593.
46. C.R.O., photocopy of Lambeth Palace MS. B.A. 2553, 1, 10.
47. C.R.O., Visitation Act Book 1593, fos. 7, 11, 11v, 13; H.M.C. *Hatfield MSS*, vol. IV, 497, vol. VI, 265-7.
48. Noake, *Monastery and Cathedral*, 210-11, 215; T. R. Nash, *Collections for the History of Worcestershire* (2nd edn 1799), vol. II, Appendix, xcvii; see Chapter 19.
49. Ch.O. I, f.185; Accounts 1588/9.

50. Ch.O. II, 76.
51. C.R.O., Visitation Act Books 1593, fos. 3–15v, 1613–17, fos. 371v–417.
52. V.F.P. II, f.143v.

Chapter 19

1. W. K. Jordan, *Philanthropy in England, 1480–1660* (1959), *The Charities of London 1480–1660* (1960).
2. F. V. Follett, *A History of Worcester Royal Grammar School* (1951), 2–9; Leach, 176–7.
3. Leach, 179–80; Accounts 1550/1, 51/2, 58/9, 59/60; Follett. 22–9.
4. Orphans Wills ff.6, 19; Leach, 203–13.
5. C.R.O., Six Masters Treasurer's Accounts.
6. Prob. 1544:69, 1583:104a, 1580:6a.
7. *V.C.H. Worcs.*, vol. IV, 489–91.
8. Leach, 123–5, 130–3.
9. *Ibid.*, 149; *V.C.H. Worcs.*, vol. IV, 484–5; Leach, 244; Prob. 1559:II:328a; Noake, *Monastery and Cathedral*, 457.
10. P.C.C. 55 Spencer; Noake, *Monastery and Cathedral*, 457.
11. Leach, 176–7; *S.P.D. Charles I 1636–7*, 359.
12. Leach, 203.
13. Prob. vol. V, f.336, 1552:24, 1559:II:313.
14. *Ibid.*, 1557:185, 1560:76; P.C.C. 5 Coode, 27 Peter; Orphans Wills, f.75.
15. P.C.C. 74 Harte.
16. Orphans Recognizances.
17. Green, vol. II, Appendix, liii.
18. V.F.P. I, fos. 272v, 292v, 334v, 338; Ch.O. I, fos. 156, 157v; Accounts 1583/4; Prob. 1556:152.
19. *More*, 293; Noake, *Monastery and Cathedral*, 546.
20. Ch.O. I, f.104; Accounts; V.F.P. II, f.q.
21. *Q.S.P.*, 470.
22. Prob. 1611:169.
23. *Ibid.*, 1610:112.
24. *Ibid.*, 1575:107.
25. *Cal. Pat. R. Edward VI*, vol. I, 269; Accounts 1552/3; *A Bibliography of Worcestershire*, ed. J. R. Burton (W.H.S. pt ii, 1903), 1–3.
26. Ch.O. I, fos. 104v, 161v; Accounts 1599/1600; Ch.O. II, 156.
27. Prob. 1575:97.
28. *Ibid.*, 1607:145.
29. *Ibid.*, 1558:805v, 1605:93a.

30. *Ibid.*, 1620:116; Grafton Manor Estate Book, 37, 38.
31. A. Macdonald, 'Anthony Tolly and the Tomb of Edmund Freake, Bishop of Worcester (1584–91) in Worcester Cathedral', *T.W.A.S.* N.S. XIX (1942), 1–9.

Conclusion

1. F. M. Martin, 'Cultural and Social Life in Worcester in the second half of the Eighteenth Century 1740–1800', University of Birmingham Library, B.A. Dissertation (1962).
2. W. R. Buchanan-Dunlop, 'Seventeenth Century Puritans in Worcester', *T.W.A.S.*, N.S. XXIII (1946), 33–7.

Index